The Never-never Land...

Wilson Barrett

THE NEVER-NEVER LAND

Selected Fiction

THE SIGN OF THE CROSS
By Wilson Barrett
Illustrated. $1.50

OLIVE LATHAM
By E. L. Voynich
$1.50

THE ISSUE
By George Morgan
Illustrated. $1.50

AN ANGEL BY BREVET
By Helen Pitkin
Frontispiece. $1.50

POKETOWN PEOPLE
By Ella Middleton Tybout
Illustrated in colors. $1.50

HEART OF LYNN
By Mary Stewart Cutting
Illustrated. $1.25

PIGS IN CLOVER
By Frank Danby
$1.50

A SEQUENCE IN HEARTS
By Mary Moss
$1.50

KITTY OF THE ROSES
By Ralph Henry Barbour
Illustrated in colors. $2.00

THE
NEVER-NEVER LAND

BY

WILSON BARRETT
Author of "The Sign of the Cross," etc.

PHILADELPHIA AND LONDON
J. B. LIPPINCOTT COMPANY
1904

Published September, 1904

Electrotyped and Printed by
J. B. Lippincott Company, Philadelphia, U.S.A.

CONTENTS

CONTENTS

THE NEVER-NEVER LAND

CHAPTER I

THE GREAT DROUGHT

At Woolloogolonga Gully, in the Never-Never Land of
Queensland, Australia, it was one hundred and twenty in
the shade. The sun pierced down through the red gum-
trees unchecked, the very leaves fearing to oppose more
than their edges to its rays. Not a drop of water had
fallen for many months. A little north of Woolloogolonga there were children seven years of age who had
never seen rain. The earth was baked to cracking-point.
The water-holes were dried up. The beds of the streams
were mud or sand, into which cattle and sheep had
staggered, in a vain attempt to quench the raging thirst
that was devouring them, only to fall and die. Their
skeletons and rotting carcasses were everywhere. The
sky by day was molten brass, by night burnished copper.
The reflection of the bush-fires coloured it from dome to
horizon-line, and through the smoke the moon and stars
gleamed a glowing blood-red. The birds dropped dead
from the scorched boughs. Thirst-maddened wallabies
hopped painfully about in the futile search for a drop of
water or a blade of green grass. Distracted squatters and
selectors had torn down trees and stripped them of their
leaves to feed their starving sheep.

And the flies! Everywhere the flies! The hateful,
poisonous, ubiquitous, persevering flies—Egypt's plague,
perennial, pestilential. Mingled with their buzzing could

be heard the clear ping-g-g of the mosquito, while overhead the wur-r-r-r of the locusts rang like thousands of electric rattles, never ceasing, never pausing.

Outside the wooden, bark-roofed hut known as Jack Landon's homestead sat Bill, one of his chums. Bill had another name, but, in the usual happy-go-lucky way of the " back-blocker," his patronymic appellation was probably unknown, certainly unused. Bill was long and loose of limb, unshaven and unwashed. The precious water was too scarce to waste in cleansing the exterior man; there was barely enough to moisten the interior. Bill was lazily pulling at a wooden pipe, looking longingly every now and then at the flabby and nearly empty water-bag, which hung with its dipper from the bough of the barked and ringed gum-tree against which he was leaning. The gaunt, spectral, dead and dying trunks, some half cremated, all fatally stricken and hideously ugly, stood out everywhere as far as the eye could reach, making the land look like a huge, weird cemetery. Acres and acres of stumps of the eucalypti, from which the superstructure had been lopped, met the gaze in every direction. It was Thompson's selection, half cleared for grazing, on which Jack Landon had been allowed to build a home for himself, his wife, and child.

" Coo-ee!" rang out some five hundred yards away into Bill's bush-trained, quick ears.

" My word! Dan Murphy!" said Bill, brushing away, mechanically and lazily, the flies from his nose and eyelids.

" Coo-ee!" rang out Dan Murphy a second time, and " Coo-ee!" echoed Bill, too hot, too lazy, too spiritless to move, as he watched the broad, squat figure of Dan Murphy trudging, scorched and footsore, towards him.

Dan was a red-bearded man of fifty, who carried on his back the usual bundle, known by bushmen as a " swag." Taking off his ragged felt hat, he mopped his head with an old coloured handkerchief, and gaspingly muttered—

" Blue blazes! but it's hot."

" My word !"

" Fur the love o' sin, gimme a dhrink."

" No fear !"

" Bill, yer manners is as illigant as yer face is beautiful. It's wather I'm wantin'—not whisky. Give us a dhrink."

" No fear, I tell you. We haven't a quart left." Bill looked anxiously at the water-bag.

" Me playful Bill, I'll trade wid yez; two mouthfuls o' whisky for iv'ry wan o' wather." Dan held up his flask.

" My word !" Bill slowly rose and put the dipper into the water-bag. " Where's the whisky ?"

" Where's the wather ?"

The exchange was made, and both men drank eagerly. Bill gasped for breath, and ejaculated, " My word !" Dan licked his lips and said, " Be gob !"

Drinking again, Bill gasped, " My word !"

" Houd there ! Yez had yez whack," growled Dan, reaching for the flask.

" Two mouthfuls ! That my whack ? No fear !"

" What mouthfuls ! Be gob, Bill, me jule, Nature intended ye for a perambulatin' post-offus, and that gully in the face uv yez ye miscalls yez mouth is the shlit intinded for noosepapers and parcels. Shtop, yez son uv a horse-leech ! Yez'll suck it dhry and swally the bottle."

" What's yer givin' me ? Vitriol ?" asked the gasping Bill.

" Bill, me son, yez palate's out uv taste. It's Dunville's best."

Bill mopped his eyes with the back of his hand, and queried—

" What's brought yer here ?"

" Shank's mare, me dacent felly, and a letthur for Jack."

" Jack Mowbray ?"

Dan seated himself painfully and carefully beside Bill, and slowly and contemplatively licked the empty water-dipper as he replied—

" No; Jack Landon."

"My word! A letter for him?"

"That same. The second twin. It's hard to tell t'other from which when they're apart. Is he here?"

"No fear."

"Is his missus?"

"Yus."

"Sober?"

"You bet! Jack Mowbray has cut off her booze."

"Be gob! Sal's a beauty! I've known her for years. She's a daisy! She's a pache!"

"What he married her fur gits me." Bill thoughtfully scratched his leg.

"He didn't. She married *him*. He'd been dhrunk three weeks. She picked him up in Sydney streets, kept him dhrunk until she'd tied him to her, and when he sobered up he—er—er——"

Dan stopped, looking at the hut, at the door of which was now standing a handsome, dissipated, buxom woman of thirty-two. She was roughly and slatternly dressed in cotton print, and wore a sun-bonnet, dirty and out of shape. This was Landon's wife, known as Sal Landon, and invariably addressed as Sal. Looking sourly at Dan, she asked the wholly unnecessary question—

"That you, Dan Murphy?"

"That same—wid a thurst on 'im loike a little purgatory. It's a thirsty country, ma'am," grumbled Dan.

"Curse the country!" snarled Sal.

"It's done, ma'am—cursed from 'ere to blue blazes. The bush is afire fur fifty miles. Noah's flood 'ud hardly put it out."

Sal eyed Dan with an ill-tempered scowl, at once wrathful and distrustful.

The woman must, at one time, have been very beautiful, in a florid, common way. Even now she was strikingly handsome. Her form, though full, was still superb. Her face was of the Saxon type, her eyes a clear china blue. Her auburn hair was bunched up in great coils round her large, well-shaped head. Her bare brown arms would have delighted the heart of a sculptor. Her thin cotton gown, wet with perspiration, revealed the lines of her figure, which it fitted like a second skin. Untidy and unkempt as she was, she was yet strangely attractive. Vice and drink had blurred the picture—they had not destroyed it. Naturally graceful, she fell insensibly into attitudes that were full of unstudied picturesqueness. A very dangerous, selfish, and merciless woman, blessed with health and strength that no dissipation or indulgence seemed able to kill; a creature born to enslave and degrade men through their grosser passions; as destitute of moral principles as an iceberg is of verdure; selfish, sensual, and idle. Yet, by cunning and scheming, she had become the wife of John Landon, a gentleman by birth and instinct.

"Flood!" she sneered. "No fear, in this God-forgotten hole! Who's givin' our water away? You, Bill?" she queried, as she saw the dipper in Dan's hand.

"No fear," grunted Bill.

"No, ma'am; the playful Bill gives nothing away. It was a trade we did—whisky fur wather."

At the word "whisky," Sal's eyes glinted eagerly.

"Who's got whisky?" she asked quickly.

"Meself, ma'am."

"Ask me to drink."

"If I thought you wouldn't be afther taking me at me word, I would ax yez."

"Here; a glass of water for a nip of whisky. Is it a go?"

"It's a go. Put the wather in this." Dan held out his water-bottle. "Divil a wan o' me ever thought to trade whisky for wather."

"Give us the stuff," Sal pleaded hungrily.

As Dan passed the flask to her a man came quietly forward and took it, saying as he did so—

"No, you don't, Dan; whisky is tabooed here. You ought to know that."

"Give that to me!" screamed Sal.

" No, Mrs. Landon; I think not. It would not agree with you," was the quiet answer.

" I'm in pain. I will have it!"

" You're in no pain, and you won't have it."

" What is it to do with you? You're not my husband, anyway."

" No; and it is a matter for mutual congratulation that I am not."

" You're a meddlesome, interfering swagger, that's what you are!"

" And you're——" Here he paused for a second, and then continued quietly, " my chum's wife. That's what you are."

The speaker was John Mowbray—a fine specimen of healthy manhood, above the middle height, broad-chested, muscular, hard as the proverbial nails, and tanned to a deep, rich, olive-brown by the southern sun. He wore a wavy, dark chestnut beard; his eyes were hazel, his features clear-cut, yet full of strength and latent force. Roughly dressed as he was, in moleskin trousers tucked into old riding boots, a deep red shirt, open at the neck, without button or tie, and a turned-down, limp, grey wide-awake felt hat, he was as unmistakably a gentleman as the woman he was addressing was not a lady. One of the many thousands who are sent, or drift into the colonies— bred, educated, and trained as gentlemen—to work like common navvies or farm hands for a living, until they " strike something rich," or die in the bush, to be buried in unmarked graves, even their names forgotten.

Jack eyed the vulgar creature with contemptuous in-difference for a second, and then turned with a kindly smile to Dan.

" What's the trouble, Dan?"

" I was afther being down at Larimer's post-offus and they asked me to bring along this letter fur Jack Landon, if I was coming this way."

" And were you coming this way?"

" We'll not discuss that. I've bringed the letthur."

"A letter for my husband! I'll take that." Sal stretched out her hand for the missive.

"Excuse me, Mrs. Landon; I'll take it. Landon and I are partners, you know," interposed Jack.

"How do you know that this is business?"

"How do you know that it isn't?"

"P'raps it's money come from home. Let me open it."

"No, madam; your husband shall do that himself."

"Look here! I'll give my husband a bit of my mind about you."

"Ah! He's often given me a bit of his mind about you."

"You're a pretty pair!" sneered Sal.

"Um. So-so. Externally, we are not a bad match. Otherwise, Landon's worth a dozen of me."

"What's he ever done?"

"Put up with you for years, for one thing. I should have broken your neck long ago," coolly answered Jack with a smile which made it difficult to judge whether he was joking or in earnest.

"I do believe you would," chuckled the woman, with a leer of admiration at Jack, which he declined to notice.

"Your belief is well founded, Mrs. Landon."

"You're a man, you are! You'd have suited me better than Landon."

"That doesn't flatter me, nor get you the whisky, Mrs. Landon."

"Oh, drop your Mrs. Landon!"

"I do, willingly."

"I'm full up on it. Call me Sal."

Jack looked at the landscape.

"Give us just a nip, Jack!" pleaded Sal, with an insinuating and coaxing touch on his arm.

"No, ma'am; not the thousandth part of the thousandth part of a 'nip.' Dan, pocket that," said Jack, giving the flask to Dan.

"Don't drink it this weather. Hold your bottle." Here Jack slipped a small water-bag from his broad shoulders.

"Great Jordan! Where did yez pump this from?" asked Dan, amazed.

"Little Wallerby Creek."

"Fifteen miles, be gob! Did yez hump it all the way yezself?"

"Every blessed, burning, blazing, bush-bound, dusty, earth-parched, stony, shadeless, fly-blown inch, my thirsty chum," replied Jack, as he poured the water into Dan's bottle.

"And yez give this ter me?" Dan's honest Irish face twitched with emotion.

"Umm-umm," Jack assented lightly.

"Jack, you're a—a—a— No, I won't say phwat yez are."

"And, Dan, for humping it ten weary miles with this letter for Landon, you're a—a—a— No, I won't say phwat you are. Now, Mrs. Landon, have a sip of this. It's sweeter by a lot than that mud-congested pint of dregs in your bag there." And he offered Sal the dipper half filled with water.

"Plain water?" asked Sal, with a grimace.

"Umce. Plain water. Worth its weight in gold-dust, and almost as scarce. Where's Smudgee?"

"How should I know?" snapped out Sal, readjusting the bosom of her dress, which had burst open, and was exposing a little more of her person than was quite seemly.

"True. She is your child. How should you know where she is?"

"Put a drop of whisky in this, Dan, if you love me," entreated Sal, holding out the dipper.

"Not a drop, Dan, if you want to live," growled Jack.

Sal glared at him. He turned coolly from her, and, looking round, asked—

"Where's Smudgee?"

"Somewheres about," Sal muttered sulkily, pinning up the gaping opening in her dress.

"Wherever she is, she'll be thirsty." Putting his

hand to the side of his mouth, Jack called, " Coo-ee! Smudgee!"

There was a moment's pause, and then, from the bush some few hundred yards away, came the answering call in a girlish voice—

" Coo-ee! Jack-ie!"

Jack's eyes lit up with kindliness as he looked at the queer little figure that came eagerly towards him. It was Sal's daughter, Lucy, better known as " Smudgee," a nickname Jack had playfully given her when she came to him one day more than usually grimy, from a somewhat too close encounter with the cooking grate. Smudgee was a child of about twelve. Her figure was, like that of many Australian-born girls, wonderfully developed for her age, and there was little to conceal it. She had on but one garment, a frayed, torn, and dust-stained old cotton print frock, which barely reached to her knees. Her breasts showed firm and round under the too tight dress. Her bare legs and arms were brown and muscular. Her hips were more like a young woman's than a child's. Her face was handsome like her mother's, but without its vulgarity and selfishness. Smudgee's eyes were brown and fearless. They had a habit of looking straight into the eyes of others, and seeing through them to the mind beyond. Thoughtful eyes they were, too, in spite of their strange quickness. Her light brown hair, tousled and fussy, stuck out aggressively through the interstices of her ragged straw hat. It was an odd, pretty, lovable little person who turned up a smiling, pleased face to Jack, as she said—

" What ho! Knight of the empty pocket."

Jack took off his hat and made her an elaborate bow, which she answered with an equally ceremonious curtsey. It was part of an innocent little comedy they enacted at times, in which the delighted Smudgee played a princess and Jack her faithful and devoted knight.

" Well, Princess, how goes it?"

Smudgee replied, moistening her lips—

"Fusty, Jack—fusty as—'ell and Tom——"

Jack hurriedly interrupted her, and nipped in the bud the coming flower of rhetoric, saying—

"Pass, Smudgee; pass. Comparisons are odious."

Poor Smudgee had no companions but the men on Thompson's selection and her father's chums. She seldom saw a child or even a woman, save her mother, who was utterly indifferent to her. Her language was that of the shearing-shed and the boundary-riders, with whom she was accustomed to bandy chaff, seldom coming off second-best. These men encouraged her to the greatest impertinences: roared with laughter at her rudest sallies. Not the best of training for a girl, it must be admitted. Jack corrected her faults affectionately; her father carelessly, occasionally; her mother bullyingly, always. Bred in the gutters of Sydney herself, she cared little to give her daughter a better chance than had been her own. Smudgee's father took but scant notice of her. What love and affection she got came solely from Jack, who showed such brotherly interest in her doings and wishes that he had captured her faithful little heart and endeared himself to her since she was a tiny dot of six. When her father and mother failed to move her with scoldings and thumpings, a word from Jack, or even a look, would bring instant obedience and submission.

"Thirsty, are you? Then put your lips to this, my Princess." And Jack handed Smudgee some water.

Smudgee seized the dipper eagerly, and raised it to her parched lips; but, suddenly pausing, peered over the rim of it, sharply asking—

"Had any yerself?"

"Going to, Princess; going to."

"S'elp yer die?" This was uttered with great solemnity.

"So help me die!"

"I know yer! Jist like yer, ter give it all away and go firsty yerself. 'Ere; 'ave 'alf o' this." And Smudgee held out the dipper.

Jack pretended to drink, saying, "There you are."

"You didn't take a blooming drop. I know yer!"

Jack, with mock fierceness, raised his hand and roared—

"Drink, or I'll kill you, Smudgee!"

Smudgee, quietly sceptical, remarked, "Garn! Take a mouf-ful fust."

"There! I've nearly swallowed the lot," lied Jack, after taking a sip.

"Ha, ha! I know yer!" Now she drank greedily. "O—h! O—h! O—h! Ain't it good! It's like that champagernee you brought us from Sydney, after you'd been in——"

Jack interrupted her.

"Hold on, Smudgee! Don't get reminiscent. Memory is a poor plaster for aching consciences."

"Can't forget some fings. Wish I could," answered Smudgee thoughtfully.

"Ah! you're not the only one who wishes he could forget, and can't. Have a sup, Bill?" asked Jack, as he handed the dipper to Bill.

"My word! I just will. Dan's whisky has burnt the linings out of my shirt-front," answered Bill; and he drained the dipper dry.

Dan had risen, and was looking towards the bush.

"Be gob! that looks like a big blaze over to Thompson's way."

Jack watched the direction in which Dan had pointed and answered—

"If the wind rises, there'll be a big blaze every way. The earth's tinder, the sun fire, and there's not enough water between here and Wallerby Creek to drown a fly in. All I got, on the tramp to Craig's yesterday, was a soak of my handkerchief in the mud of a horse's hoof-print; and I sucked and lingered over it as if it had been nectar, or Smudgee's champag-ne."

"I heard the Craigs was missing. Did yez find 'em?" queried Dan.

"After two days' search, we did. The whole family

were in a muddy water-hole, with blankets over them to keep off the sparks and burning embers. 'What are you doing there?' we shouted. 'Come out of that!' Craig shouted back, 'Come and lead us out. We're blind.' And it was true. They fought the infernal fire till it blinded them, and then groped their way to the mud-hole, to avoid walking into the flames. They had been standing there for sixteen mortal, agonizing hours when we found them, not daring to move. We sent them down to Sydney, to the hospital. Every stick of their farm was gone. House, barns, crop, stock, horses—even the very fences were wiped completely out. Where yesterday stood a prosperous holding, there is to-day nothing but cinders. And that's the end of ten years of hard and honest work. Oh! but it's a lovely place, this ' Never-Never Land.' There's only one other as beautiful, and that's h——"

Smudgee, who had been listening with deep interest, gave a warning cough, and Jack continued, " Umm— that's down under."

" You was jist goin' to say 'ell. *I* know yer!" said Smudgee reprovingly.

"Right, Princess! *You* know me." And Jack gave her an affectionate little hug.

" How's the claim doin'?" asked Dan.

" Can we wash for gold in a sun-dried gully? If we haven't water to drink, what can we do with our lovely claim? For two broiling, brick-baking months, we haven't found enough gold to gild the hind leg of a mosquito."

Smudgee looked at her knight with grave interest as she sat down on the dried leaves, crossed her bare, shapely legs, and twisted the toes of one foot through those of the other. Jack, though outwardly seldom sad or depressed, had a little trick of dropping occasionally into a minor key in speaking, very suggestive of unsatisfied longings and hope deferred. He was a singularly reticent man, as most bushmen are, and said little or nothing of himself at any time; but Smudgee's quick, divining little spirit felt his moods, and was always in deep sympathy with them. She gave a small sigh as she saw the fleeting cloud on his face, and, drawing a piece of string from the bosom of her dress, she said, looking up at Jack—

"Lend us yer knife, Knight."

"What for, Princess?"

"To cut this string. I want ter mend me 'at." And Smudgee began to tie up the separated plaits of her old hat, with full sense of the merit of her extreme tidiness and neatness.

"Come 'ere and be in attendance, Knight," commanded the royal Smudgee. Jack obediently sat beside her. "Jist cut that string up inter six little bits, while I tie up these cracks. There; that's it. I suppose yer never was a knight to a princess afore me, was yer, Jack?" asked Smudgee; a tinge of anxious trepidation was in her voice.

"Never such a princess as you, Smudgee."

"Was there ever any princess at all—afore me?"

"No; I don't think there was. But why do you ask?"

"Well, yer see, Knight, it ain't much fun to be one of a crowd, is it? If I'm yer only princess, I got yer all ter myself. If there's been a lot of 'em—well, there yer are, yer know!" And Smudgee gave a sweeping but some- what vague wave of the old hat, which apparently took in the whole landscape.

"Well, you're the only princess I've served up to now. I say, Smudgee, that hat will do you credit yet."

"Yus. I suppose a real princess wouldn't mend her old hat with strings, would she?"

"No; not if she could afford to buy a new one."

"Now tell us a story of a real princess, and suppose all the time I'm 'er. I'll keep the flies off yer."

"Right, Smudgee. So here goes." And the good- hearted fellow, lying flat on his back, with his hands under his head and his hat tilted over his nose, told her in his own fashion the story of Lancelot and Elaine—artfully weaving in a happy dénouement by bringing Elaine back to life and marrying her to Lancelot. Tears gathered in Smudgee's eyes and stole down her grimy cheeks; her bosom rose and fell in sympathy with the story, and when the tale was told, she said,—

"Knight, was I Elaine all through that?"

"Yes, Princess."

"Well, then you was, a' coorse, Sir Lancelot. Ah! *I like that story.*"

CHAPTER II

THE TWO JACKS

DAN and Bill had lazily smoked and listened to Jack. Sal was asleep and placidly snoring. The sun had gone down with true antipodean alacrity, and all was dark, save for the light from the sky-reflected bush fires. As the moon rose and the stars appeared, they gleamed red and sombre through the rolling clouds of smoke. Faint sounds of crackling branches came at intervals from a distance. The pungent smell of burning eucalyptus-trees filled the nostrils, and the smoke-tinged air made the eyes smart and run with water.

The heat was intense. The lungs were scorched with air that came like a hot blast from a mighty furnace. Jack's voice was tired with his recital; the others had no desire to speak—it was enough to lie still and gasp for breath. Jack rose, and, going into the cabin, brought out a bush lamp—a tin saucer filled with mutton fat, with a wick stuck in the centre. This he lit and placed on a stump a few yards away. Quickly, it was a focus for a swarm of flies, moths, and mosquitoes, that fell, with little hisses of burning wings and bodies, into the devouring flames. Everything, everywhere, was scorched or burning.

" Be gob! it's hell bruck loose," grunted Dan.

" Thank God, there's no wind," Jack murmured.

" Coo-ee!" came a call from the scrub.

" Landon, for a guinea!" and Jack gave an answering cry.

It was Landon. As Jack moved forward to meet him, the effect was startling. It was, in that dim, flickering light, as though one were watching a man walk towards a mirror. The likeness between the two men at the first glance was wonderful. Closer comparison revealed great points of divergence. Landon was less massive in build than Jack, his face weaker and coarser from indulgence and dissipation. There was a harder look in the eyes, a less kindly turn in the corners of the mouth; the nose, broadened and thickened by drink, lacked the classic straightness of Mowbray's. A clever replica, lacking the strength, purity, and charm of the original, would have been the verdict of an artist on comparing the two. While it would be difficult to mistake the one for the other when they were together, it would be easy to do so, if not too well acquainted with them, when they were apart. Landon was hot, weary, and, of course, thirsty.

"Well, how goes it?" asked Landon listlessly.

"Drink this, and talk after." Jack dipped some water from the bag and handed it to Landon.

"Why, that's quite sweet! Where did you get it?" asked Landon.

"Had a little private rain-shower in my own back yard," replied Jack.

Landon drank greedily, draining the dipper dry.

"I wanted that badly. Hulloa, Murphy! What are you doing here?" he inquired of Dan.

"He brought you a letter that looks important, Landon. Come over here to the light."

Landon, looking with interest at Jack, moved away with him towards the lamp.

"A letter for me? From whom?"

"Look and see, old man," whispered Jack.

The letter was in a large official or legal-looking envelope. Landon, sitting with his back to the lamp and opening the outer cover, drew forth three enclosures—one was an open letter, on blue paper, typewritten; the other two were in small white envelopes with a deep mourning border. At the sight of the writing of the first, he started and ejaculated, "My God!"

Jack, who was standing with folded arms against a tree a few yards off, asked—

"What is it, Landon?"

" My mother's writing."

Sal, who had been wakened by Smudgee, had drawn near to her husband. Noting his agitation, and not hearing his explanation, she sneered—

" Who's yer letter from? One of yer gals?"

A dark, angry frown settled upon Landon's brow, and he answered fiercely—

" Get me some tea."

" Not until I've 'eard that letter," answered his wife.

The look on Landon's face was not pleasant to contemplate. Jack was watching him closely, and, fearing an altercation, stepped towards Sal and, offering her his arm, with a bow, minced out—

" Will Mrs. Landon give me the extreme pleasure of taking her in to supper?"

Sal snorted and scowled viciously; but a look in Jack's eyes induced discretion, and, with an angry gesture, she flounced off into the hut.

" Get rid of the others, Jack," Landon whispered.

Jack went to the men, and in a cheery tone said—

" Dan, go to my caboose, and take Bill with you. You'll find some damper and cold mutton. Help yourselves."

The two men strolled away.

Turning to Smudgee, and offering her his arm, Jack addressed her formally, saying—

" Now, Princess, supper."

" Supper! There ain't no bloomin' supper. I know yer!"

" Smudgee, you've the penetration of a diamond drill and the open-mindedness of a prairie. You get there every time. Now then! On with our best court manners, Princess. The real swagger deportment Princess. Deportment! Allons, Princess."

With exaggerated ceremony, Jack conducted Smudgee to the door of the hut and left her.

Landon had scanned the legal letter and opened the two mourning envelopes, but had only read one of the enclosures and a few lines of the other, when he paused and drew from the large cover a photograph, and gazed earnestly at it. It was the portrait of a very beautiful girl of nineteen or twenty summers. A little convulsive catching of the breath, that almost threatened to end in a sob, came from Landon as he scrutinised the picture.

" Jack, come here," he called huskily.

Jack went, and Landon handed him the photograph. Jack's face flushed with pleasure and surprise as he looked at it.

He had led a roving life, and been interested in many women, in love with none. He was a very reserved man and cared little for making friends or acquaintances. He had lived alone for months on the ranches of Texas and in the gullies and cañons of the Rockies. He had no affection for crowded cities, and society, apart from his friends, had no charm for him. His hand was ever ready to help others, but he asked and wanted nothing in return. He attracted people more than they did him. He was deeply attached to Landon and his daughter Smudgee; beyond these two, there was not a soul he could claim as a friend, as he knew friendship, and he had not a relative on earth. In spite of all this, he was to others a most companionable man. Never boisterous in spirits, he was always bright and cheery. Hard to pro-voke, but, when roused, he was terrible in his wrath, as many who had crossed him had cause to remember. He had never known a home-life or a parent's care. His father had married a beautiful girl against the wishes of her family. They had disowned her. Jack's father, Matthew Mowbray, was a poor lieutenant of cavalry, and his wife's people were furious at her choice. They loved each other, and were, for the time, happy. When Jack was born, the young mother quietly gave up her life, and her broken-hearted husband hated this innocent cause of her death. He turned from the rosy, warm babe to the cold, white girlish figure that was lying so quiet and calm among the lilies on the bed, ordered the nurse to take the child away, and locked himself in the death-chamber. It was hours before he left it, and when he did so, his face and manner were changed entirely. He looked years older. Every line of tenderness and softness had vanished from his grey face, and a sternness was there which was not good to look upon. When Jack grew up he was sent to school, which he never left, even in holiday times; he had no home to go to. His father was on service in India, and for years he never saw him. When he was sixteen, the news came that his father had been killed in action, and that he must now shift for himself. A few hundred pounds were placed to his credit with a lawyer, and he was absolutely alone in the world. From that time he had been a wanderer. He had no purpose in life—no one to live for. He had made no successes. Not that he had not the power or the opportunities; he had the one, and could make the other —often did; and as often stood aside to let another take them. He preferred the struggle to the achievement. He simply did not care enough to take advantage of his chances. He could stand looking on with indifference, mixed with contempt, and wonder at the rush of others for wealth; then, turn aside and seek quiet elsewhere. Women had loved him. It gave him no joy to know this. He pitied them and went his way. He began to marvel at his own immunity from heart attacks, and wondered whether there was really such a thing as love in the world,—or, if it did exist, whether he was capable of feeling it. He had passed weeks and weeks among the Rockies without seeing a human face. The vast silence of those giant peaks spoke to him as no human voice had ever spoken. The rushing torrents sang songs to him, the whistling winds among the lofty pines played to him. The sunrises and sunsets wrapped him in a delicious languor of sensuous rapture, while the glorious nights, when in the clear, rarefied air the stars gleamed like small moons, and the moon shone larger than it ever shines elsewhere, filled him with a great peace, and still greater reverence. He forgot he was alone; he remembered not he was a wanderer; he was in the companionship of the mighty Mother, Nature—at home in the presence of her glorious works. But the joy of blood-relationship and real-soul affinity he had never known. His love for Landon was that of a strong brother for a weak one; his affection for Smudgee that of a man for a child-sister. Such sensations as he now felt on looking at the portrait in his hand he had never known. He did not attempt to analyse them; he was lost in them, oblivious to all else. When Landon spoke to him, his voice seemed to come from a distance.

" Well, Jack; well?"

" How lovely!" sighed Jack.

" My sister."

" Your sister?" asked Jack, in intense surprise.

" Old man, I never told you I have a mother and sister in England. I have not seen either of them for twenty years. Haven't seen her since she was a toddling kiddie," and Landon pointed to the photograph upon which Jack's eyes were still fastened. " Read that to me. I can't. The letters all run together," said Landon, handing Jack one of the letters.

Still holding the portrait, Jack sat down, shifted the lamp, and read aloud the missive to Landon.

" ' My dear brother, my dearest Jack, my darling old brother whom I have never seen,—at last we have traced you, or at least the Sydney lawyers have. As we cabled you through them, Sir James is dead——' "

Jack looked up at Landon for information, and Landon answered—

" My stepfather."

" Did you get the cable?"

" Not till now. It was in the letter."

Jack went on reading—

" ' Sir James is dead. His death was terribly sudden, and we feel it deeply. He was always kind to me, though he was cruel to you.' "

Jack paused once more.

"Sir James Walgrove married my mother within two years of my father's death. My father died a ruined and broken-hearted man. The old home, Landale Abbey, was mortgaged up to the hilt to Sir James, whom I always instinctively hated, and believed to have deliberately beggared my father. They both loved my mother; she loved and married my father. Sir James hated my father for this, and drew him into all sorts of plausible but rotten schemes, and broke him. When my father was out of the way, he renewed his suit with my mother. She, poor soul, was penniless, and only remained at the old home by the mercy of Sir James. For her children's sake, she married him. Once master, he made my life a hell. He knew I hated and suspected him. One day he made some insulting remark about my dead father. I flew at him like a mad thing, kicking and biting for all I was worth. He strapped me to the bedstead, and thrashed me nearly to death. I never left my room for a week. As soon as I could crawl, I crept down to my mother, told her I meant to leave the house, never to return to it while her husband lived, and swore never willingly to look on him again. She begged and prayed; I was steel. I kissed her and little baby Sybil, and left the house, found my way to the docks, and shipped as cabin-boy to Sydney, and have never seen home since. Now——"

"Your enemy is dead."

"Yes; he is dead. Go on."

Jack read on:—

"'He is dead, dear brother, and you must try to forgive him, and come home at once. Do not delay a day. Darling little mother is fading away for want of her boy. Dear Jack, she has never ceased to grieve and pray for you, and taught my baby tongue to lisp a prayer each night for you. Dear Jack, you must come back at once—must—must—must!—to save her darling life. Oh! dear Jack, brother of mine, whom I have never seen, whom I do not know, I cannot lose dear mother; and I shall lose her if you do not come. She calls for her boy by day and night. Come to her, dear. We shall be so proud of you, for we know you have done nothing to stain the dear old name, to cause the mother to regret that she has had a son, or the sister to blush that she has a brother. Dear, ill-used Jack, come home. The photograph of yourself never leaves mother's sight by day, and she puts it on her breast at night. Of course she puzzled a little over the splendid fellow at first, but she said she could still see the boy in the portrait of the man. I send my portrait, dear. I hope you will like it. Have you not got a big little sister? And her heart, Jack, is as big as herself with love for you. God bless you, dear, and send you quickly and safely home. All these little dots are kisses for you, dear brother Jack. Your anxious, eager, longing little sister, SYBIL.

"'P.S.—There's just the sweetest girl that ever lived dying to see you. She is half in love with you already, and you *must* fall in love with her. Everybody does. She is my dearest, dearest friend. Her name is Lorna Mannerly. Once more—*come home.*'"

There were tears in the eyes of both men as Landon asked—

"Well?"

"God bless her! What does the mother say?"

Landon handed the other note to Jack.

Jack read—

"'My boy, my son, come to me, and save my life. Come, my boy; come.—MOTHER.'

"Dear chum, I congratulate you."

"Do you?"

"Of course you'll go at once?"

"Of course I shall fly to the dear little mother and my pure, innocent sister, and show them the son and brother who has so worthily upheld the old name! Never done anything to stain it, to cause the mother to regret or the sister to blush! Show them the miserable wreck they are to take such pride in. The gambler, the bank-robber——"

"Go easy, Lan; that has been paid for," interrupted Jack.

"Yes; and how? By *your* sacrifice. Shall I tell them that too? Tell them how you suffered for my sin? Tell them that I am a drunkard and an incurable opium fiend? And Sal? Sal, the wife of Landale of Landale Abbey! Sal, the refined, the pure, the chaste! Show her to the 'sweetest girl already half in love with me'! Show them Sal Berker, the dissipated wanton, who picked me up in Pitt Street, Sydney, drunk; married me drunk; spent her honeymoon with me drunk; lived with me drunk; will die with me drunk. And show them Smudgee, the elegant, the cultured Smudgee, who calls me father, and who might with equal justice call any other dozen men by the same name! Jack, Jack, dear old honest, self-effacing Jack!—what have I done? *What have I done?* Tell me! And for God's sake, man, tell me, *what I am to do!*"

Jack, after a pause, muttered—

"You must go home."

"And kill my mother?"

"You'll kill her if you don't."

Landon held out his hand for the letters and photograph, which Jack gave to him.

After a moment, Jack said with decision—

"You've got to go home, Lan."

"And Sal?"

There was an unwonted ring of hardness in Jack's voice as he replied—

"Let her stop behind and drink herself to death. She'll do that anyway, and better here than at home with them."

"You're a bit hard on her, Jack."

"Hard be hanged! She's been your ruin; made your life Hades. If she had any love for you I'd forgive her; but she has not. She's as empty as a corn-shuck. An idle, selfish, sensual animal, without a wish or thought beyond her own gratifications. Think of her in any refined home! She'd be wretched herself, and make every one about her miserable. There'll be plenty of money, I suppose?"

"Twenty thousand a year, the lawyers say; left to me 'as an act of restitution.' I was not far wrong about Sir James. He wronged my father, and seeks to make compensation to the son. Too late, Sir James! Too late! The son is ruined beyond redemption. Killed body and soul."

"Nonsense! Leave Sal behind. Provide as handsomely for her as you like, as long as she remains out here; and you go home and save your mother's life and your sister's happiness."

"And Smudgee?"

"Put her in a school, away from the mother's influence. She'll polish up; Sal, never."

"That doesn't settle it, Jack."

"What next?"

"That Wurramurra Bank business," replied Landon, in an ashamed undertone.

"Oh! that's forgotten and done with," hastily answered Jack.

"No, it is not, and either of us may be arrested at any time. I was the culprit, you the sufferer."

Three years before this night there had been a robbery at Wurramurra. A party of bushrangers had "stuck up" the bank there. The clerks and cashiers were either pinioned or cowed with revolvers, and the thieves got clear away with their spoil. Landon, who had been drunk for weeks, was led into the scheme, hardly comprehending what he was doing. He was sent into the bank to engage the clerks in conversation until the rest of the gang could cover them with their guns. He was sobered by the time the robbery was over, and, declining to share in the plunder, left the others and wandered into the bush. Jack was at the time travelling down from a station to Sydney. On his arrival, he read of the robbery, and found to his amazement that the name and fairly accurate description of his friend, Landon, was given as being one of the participators in the affair. He had not been in the city an hour before he was arrested as Jack Landon. He denied the identity, but was not believed. The cashier and clerks swore positively to him as one of the men who had entered the bank and distracted the attention of the clerks. Jack knew perfectly well that he could prove an *alibi*, but that must mean the discovery of his friend Landon. In his usual strangely unselfish, self-sacrificing way, he thought not of himself, but of his friend and his wife and child. He simply pleaded "Not guilty," was disbelieved, and sentenced to three years' imprisonment. After a few months he escaped, and went in search of Landon, with whom, in the recesses of the "Never-Never Land," he had remained hidden.

Landon had accepted the sacrifice, and in sheer shame plunged deeper and deeper into dissipation and drink, until Jack's escape brought them together again. Then, under his influence and care, he had kept sober for some time.

Landon continued—

"You didn't serve out the whole of that sentence. You escaped, and there's still a reward out for John Landon's capture. Here, in the bush, I am safe. Show my nose in a town and I'm done for. You can't take my place a second time, Jack." Landon spoke with his head in his hands, as one ashamed of himself. "And, even if I escape that and get home, there's the drink."

"You've been all right for weeks."

"Yes; because you've kept me sober, watched me like a nurse, and kept the drink from me. But you've only scotched the snake, not killed it. At home, with no end of money, without you, and the drink all round me, I should be off in a week."

" Not you. All things will be different. You'll have
the dear old mother, the sister, England, and a beautiful
home."

" I can't. I haven't the courage or the will. I'm done."

The utter hopelessness and conviction of the man's
tone and manner struck a chill into Jack's heart. It was
true, the man was " done." Years upon years of drinking had sapped his will-power and destroyed even the
wish to live cleanly and soberly. The responsibilities
the new position in life would thrust upon him frightened
him. The knowledge that if he could get drink he would
get drunk appalled him. He was naturally a kindly man,
and had, in spite of his terrible fall, an innate pride that
revolted at the thought of the shame he would bring
upon his mother and sister ; and he shuddered and shrank
from the prospect of the pain he would cause them. The
fear of meeting them, of coming into contact with their
refinement, was overwhelming. He had not the " courage"—he had not the " will"—and he was " done"! It
was an awful ending to an ill-spent manhood. Jack's
heart ached for his friend. He asked, in a sad tone—

" What will you do, then ?"

" Send you in my place."

" What ?"

" You went to hell for me ; go to heaven for me.
They'll never find you out."

" And your mother ?"

" You'll save her life, Jack."

Jack put the next question in a barely audible whisper.

" And your sister ?"

" She will be happy in her mother's happiness. Old
man, it's kismet. I'm not long for this world. I've
had an uncanny feeling of going for a long time, that
grows daily stronger. Don't laugh and tell me not to
heed such impressions : we don't heed them enough."

Jack was the last person to laugh at such presenti-
ments. He had communed too much with Nature for
that, and he said sincerely—

"I don't laugh, Jack. But you're all right, and will go home and be a new man."

For a moment or two there was silence; and then, with a far-away look in his eyes, Landon answered—

"Yes, Jack, you've hit it. *I shall go home and be a new man.* But, old chum, I wish God would be very good to me, and let me be of use to some one before I start. I should go with a lighter heart."

"Don't talk of going that way, old chap," said Jack huskily.

"Jack, you've got to listen to me and do what I say. God'll work it out His own way, but you've got to go home in my place, and comfort my mother and sister. They won't find you out. They will expect you—not me. A year ago I sent them your portrait. I was ashamed to send my own, which spelt drink in every feature. That's what Sybil means in her letter. It was in your picture my mother saw the likeness of her boy—what her boy might have been, a cleaner, better man than he is. Mother is expecting her son in the original of the picture she places on her breast o' nights; and, Jack, old chum, we mustn't disappoint her."

"My God! lad, what have you done?" Jack asked, in a voice choking with emotion.

"The best act of my reckless, ill-spent life. Sent the mother and sister a son and brother whom they can love and never blush for."

For some time both men were silent, each busy with his own thoughts. Jack was sorely tempted. For the money he cared nothing; it had no attraction for him. But the home life! How he could love such a mother! How he could worship such a sister! His mind went back over the long vista of years—yearning in vain for one really loving caress from one of his own blood, for one hour of peace by a hearth that he could call his home. Now he could, if he chose, have all that he had so long missed. One little word would give him all that he had so longed for. What harm would he be doing? What sin would he be committing? He wronged no one. Surely not the mother, whose life he would save! Nor the sister who lived for this mother, and whose heart would break if she lost her! Nor the son and brother who was begging him to take his place! For the little wrong he might be doing, surely he could atone a thousand-fold by his love and devotion to the dear ones whom he was deceiving? Could he live and never see the sweet sister, with that lovely face, that tender, loving soul? His heart beat rapidly, the blood surged to his head as he thought of seeing her—living in the same house with her—having, as her brother, the right to guard and shield her. If he did not go, Landon would not. Long he argued with himself, trying in vain to stifle the conscience which would not be silenced.

Landon anxiously awaited his decision.

"Well, old man?" he asked timidly.

"I must not do it, Lan; it can't be right," Jack replied weakly and hesitatingly.

"It is right, Jack, it is! It means the salvation of those two lonely women; it means peace, comparatively, to me. Do you suppose I have not suffered, or felt no remorse for the pain I have caused them? If I did not know—absolutely know—that I should break their hearts if I went, should I ask you to take my place?"

Before Jack could answer he heard a footstep, and turning saw Wong-Lung, a Chinaman of uncertain age, approaching him. Wong was dressed in old corduroy trousers, very old boots, a faded blue china slop, and a sailor's ragged straw hat.

"What's the matter, Wong?" asked Jack.

"Allee samee bushee fire—come alongee—muchee klick," sang Wong in his high treble.

"Where?" cried the two men in alarm.

"Allee samee Tlomsonee sleckshun—Tlomsonee man say, Damn Chinaman, tell two Jackies come much klick, or sleckshun plenty soon all in hell-ee."

The men started as they saw the red glare of the

advancing fire, heard the distant shouts of the workers who were trying to beat out the flames. Jack was instantly alert. Turning to Wong, he said—

"Go and tell Bill; he's in my hut. Hurry, Wong, for once in your life! Hurry!"

"Wong go plenty klick," said he, as he started on a funeral-like trot towards Jack's hut.

"Come, Lan, old man; let's save the poor devil's home if we can," Jack said.

And the two friends started at a brisk run for **their** neighbour's house.

CHAPTER III

LANDON GOES HOME

JACK and his companions had about half a mile to go to reach Thompson's homestead. The fire was advancing with terrible swiftness. The roar and crackle of the burning bush and trees were increasing. Parrots, mopokes, magpies, and other birds flew screeching over their heads; cattle and sheep, rushing from the flames, sent them dodging behind trees to avoid being trampled to death under their hoofs; kangaroo rats, wallabies, squirrels, rabbits, and snakes were darting through the undergrowth, hurrying panic-stricken anywhere from the universal enemy.

As they neared Thompson's homestead, they heard his voice shouting out directions to the men who were helping him. Not a word was spoken by the friends. They knew what was required of them, and went to work with a will. It is an unwritten bush law: Every man's hand against fire. Men and women rise from their beds and gallop miles to assist a neighbour to fight the dreaded foe. They need no entreaty, and ask no thanks. The brave, generous, and hardy people willingly risk life and limb for their friends to-night, knowing they can rely on equal devotion to themselves on the morrow.

Tearing down large branches of trees, Jack, Landon, Tom, and the others joined the long line of men who had arrived before them. With these branches they beat at the advancing flames. The long drought had dried up everything; there was no water, so that the task was almost a hopeless one. The fire would be checked in one direction, only to gain in another. The sparks flew thickly round the workers, singeing and burning them as they fell. They were blackened with smoke and charcoal, half blinded with the glare and the heat, nearly choked with the dense smoke and the cruel thirst; but they worked on. There had been little or no air stirring for days; now, to their horror, a breeze began to rise, blowing the flames towards them. A large hayrick caught. Nothing could be done to save it; it must go. Next the shearing-shed was alight. There was no water—that was doomed. There were but a few hundred yards between these and the stables and cow-sheds, where the most valuable breeding animals were kept. They were in danger. The cattle were bellowing, the horses neighing, whinnying, and screaming. Thompson and one or two of his helps rushed over, opened the gates, loosed the terrified animals, and they plunged away wildly into the scrub.

Fiercely the men fought, but steadily the fire was gaining on them. There was a narrow creek between the outbuildings and the homestead. In ordinary times, there was a fair volume of running water in it; now, there was not a drop. There was nothing to check the flames when once a building caught. The wind carried sparks and even burning branches towards the homestead.

Poor Thompson looked half crazed with despair. Born in the bush, the son of a small selector, he had from childhood lived a life of incessant toil, slaving ceaselessly to help in the general welfare of the family. Bush-clearing, ploughing, sowing, reaping, sheep-shearing, fence-raising, horse-breaking, cattle-tending, milking, slaughtering, and the thousand and one other things inseparable from such a life had been his lot since boyhood. It had been his father's fate: it was his. He had seen his mother with a child in one hand, milking the cows with the other. When his father was down with fever, he had seen his young sisters working with plough and harrow, cutting up carcasses for food, wood-chopping, milking, using up their young lives doing the work of men, and attending to the household duties as well.

Falling in love with the pretty daughter of a neighbouring selector, he had married her, and, leaving his father, had started in life for himself. By never-ceasing industry and rigid economy, he had enlarged his stock and holding year by year, until he was the possessor of a capital farm, a sheep-run, and a comfortable home for his ever-increasing family. All the labour of his life, and all the fruits and profits thereof, were represented in his sheep-run, his barns, stacks, stock, and homestead. The bulk of his stock were dead or dying through the long drought, the run was a charred and blackened desert, the stacks and barns were blazing furnaces, and now his very home was in peril. The despair and anxiety of the man were terrible. His boys were struggling with the men in the work of salvation. His wife, with a six-months'-old baby on her left arm and a branch in her right hand, was feebly beating at the burning, withered-up grass. She gave a scream, as she saw the wind bear a burning brand into the clump of trees that surrounded the house. She knew those trees would burn like tinder—they were dry, and their destruction was certain.

Jack ran for an axe, and, calling on some of the others to follow, rushed for one large tree which had been planted so near to the house that if it fell it must fall upon the roof. Savagely Jack and Thompson plied their axes at it, while others ran for ropes to help to pull it over. Fortunately, the tree was young, the trunk slender, but the branches were now alight, and in a few moments it would be a mass of flame. Slash, slash fell the axes on the hard wood, and the chips flew in clouds. The fire was gaining. This particular tree gone, the house might be saved.

Fiercely the men tugged at the ropes. " Pull, boys! Pull for your lives!" yelled Jack. The burning embers fell upon the brave fellows, scorching their bare arms and hands, singeing their hair and beards. Still they fought on.

As Thompson's family increased, extra rooms had been found necessary, and these had been added to the original house. Unlike that, which had a corrugated iron roof, they were covered with a bark and brush thatch.

A young fellow of twenty-five swarmed up the lattice-work of the porch, sprang like a cat upon the roof, and threw the brand away from it, burning his hand as he did so. The thatch had caught. With his felt hat he was beating it out. It was Tom Hewley, a comparatively new chum, who held Jack in affectionate esteem.

With the energy of despair, the men plied their axes. The poor wife and mother stood, dry-eyed and terror-stricken, clutching her baby to her heart, unconscious of everything except the horror of the ruin which had fallen upon the husband she loved. Still the men hewed on—still the fire spread. With scorched faces, smarting eyes, parched throats, and blistered hands, they struggled on. At last the tree was yielding! " Pull! Pull now!" screamed Thompson; and they did pull. The tree was tottering. Thompson, half blinded by the sparks, did not see a large projecting branch falling right over him. Landon did, and, rushing at the distracted man, he dragged him from the impending death, only to be caught in it himself. The tree toppled over; the branch pinned poor Landon to the earth, the weight of it crushing in his chest. " God *had* been very good to him. He had been of some use at last."

He was quite insensible. Carefully the men rescued his poor, mangled body, and, on a rude stretcher of branches and leaves, they bore him to his home, Jack running on ahead to prepare the wife and child for the reception of the sad news.

When Wong had warned Bill and Dan, he returned to Landon's hut, and, sitting on a stump, he warmed a piece of opium at the lamp, carefully turning it to get it well heated, produced a small pipe from the inside of his slop, and began to smoke himself contentedly into temporary bliss, smiling happily. Wong's smile was a curious one. It began very slowly, spread gradually over the bulk of the face, and then, as if repenting its own existence, it would instantly disappear, while the old vacant look of Mongolian apathy took its place. He was breaking into that smile now.

Lifting his eyes towards the scrub at the back of the hut, the smile disappeared. Putting his pipe inside his sleeve, he slid off the stump on to the ground, and, on his hands and toes, wriggled backwards behind some scrub and lay there motionless.

A man was cautiously approaching the hut. He was a disreputable, dangerous " sundowner," or tramp. His face was stamped with vice and knavery; his mouth was set in a shaggy beard of a dirty red; his eyes were small and cunning, his whole manner furtive and vicious. Creeping up to the tree from which the water-bag was suspended, he took a long drink, and smacked his lips with much satisfaction. Hiding behind the tree, he gave a low, peculiar whistle. The door of the hut opened. Sal came out, with a white, scared face, and peered into the shadows eagerly and anxiously. The man repeated the whistle. Sal started, and stood trembling. The man came forward into the moonlight. He was limping from weariness and sore, wayworn feet. With a cunning leer upon his villainous features, he stared at Sal, who ejaculated—

" My Gord !"

" Glad to see me, old gal?" he asked jeeringly.

" Nat !"

" You bet !" he answered, with a look of triumph at the frightened woman who stood shrinking before him. " Thought you'd bushed me for life, eh? But I've done me time, an' there's nothin' more agin me."

" Nothin' more?" Sal was regaining her courage, and asked this question with a sneer.

" Nothin' that's known."

" What are yer 'ere fur?"

" You," he replied brutally.

" Me?"

" Yus. You put me away, and I'm 'ere ter git even."

Sal made a movement as if to escape in the direction

in which her husband had gone: Nat stopped her, and drew a knife.

" Bail up, and shut yer face, or I'll do yer before yer bloomin' fancy man can git wivin a mile o' yer!" And he moved threateningly towards her.

" I didn't put yer away," said Sal sullenly.

" Yer a liar! Yer did," retorted Nat, glaring at her savagely.

" What are yer goin' ter do about it?"

" Git even wiv you an' your mash, Jack Landon."

" Wot's *he* done?"

" Robbed me o' you, me wife, me pure an' hinnercent wife, an' left me broken-'earted an' in quod," whined Nat, in affected emotion, then breaking into a chuckle at his own humour.

" He married me square."

" Oh! he did, did he? Then that's bigamy fur you, my beauty, anyway."

" Well, what about it?"

" 'E's got ter pay fur it. I wants the oof."

" You won't git it 'ere. There ain't none—wuss luck!"

" Then 'e'll 'ave ter git it."

" Fur you?"

" Yus."

" What fur?"

" Ter shut me mouth about 'im an' you. If he wants you, he must pay me ter keep out o' his way."

Sal laughed bitterly, saying—

" Why, you fool, he'd pay anything ter be shut o' me. 'E 'ates me."

" Rats! Why's 'e sticking ter yer, then?"

" Well, yer see, 'e's a gentleman—not one of our sort, Nat."

" Bly me! That's good, that is!" sneered Nat.

" Yus; it's funny, ain't it?" said Sal, with a half laugh.

" Yus—if it's true."

" Don't worry. It's true enough. An' 'e ain't had a roaring old time wi' me, neither," chuckled Sal.

" You bet! Nobody never did wiv you, Sal—not fur more'n five minutes at a time. You're a pretty warm member—leastways, you was in my time."

Smudgee, who had been left in the hut, here called out—

" Muvver!"

" Who the blazes is that?" asked Nat, in astonishment.

" Your daughter," Sal calmly answered.

" My what?" queried Nat, in wild astonishment.

" Your daughter," she repeated.

" Oh, come off the earth! What's yer givin' us?" asked Nat incredulously.

" It's straight, Nat. You was in fur two years, and I planted it on ter 'im, but it's yours all the same. I didn't find it out afore you was nabbed."

" Well, I'm jiggered! Let's 'ave a look at 'er."

Sal hesitated, and Nat roared out—

" Call 'er! D'ye 'ear?"

Sal, still doggedly staring at Nat, said—

" Come 'ere, Smudgee."

" Who's 'e?" asked Smudgee, as she stood at the door, with her arms akimbo.

" Shall I tell 'er?" asked Sal.

" No. I'm a poor traveller, miss, an' I'm bushed, an' the bush is blazin', as you can see—and smell; an' this kind-'earted lydy is goin' ter 'elp me, 'cos I'm starvin'."

Smudgee noted the cadger-like whine in the man's voice, and took an instinctive dislike to him. Her sense of humour was strong, and her sarcasm at times particularly keen and biting. Quietly folding her arms, she regarded Nat steadily, and then said, in mock pity—

" Poor feller! An' all our sham-pager-ne is run out—an' all the 'ock an' lager's gorne that sour ye'd never drink it! And the baker's gorne and burnt the steak-and-kidney pie, and the custard—there! you'd never touch it, the cook's so overdone it. An' the jelly's——"

" 'Ere, 'ere! put the brake on! What's yer givin' us?"

asked Nat, astonished at her volubility, and annoyed with her humour.

"Nothing, my poor man. I wus tellin' yer what we couldn't give yez," replied the unabashed Smudgee.

"Git 'im some damper," ordered Sal.

Smudgee lifted her hands in affected horror.

"Damper! A real gentleman like 'im eat damper! Pore feller! Oh! 'ow 'ard is life! Pore man!" And, pretending to wipe the tears from her eyes, she went into the hut.

"She's an 'ot un, she is! That kid 'as got somethin' in 'er. She gets that from me." And Nat expanded his chest with parental pride.

"You believe it, then?" asked Sal.

"Bly me, I do," answered Nat, with conviction. "She's the werry spit o' my sister Hariminter at 'er age, wiv a bit o' my particular style and superior manner chucked in. What d'ye call 'er?"

"Smudgee."

"Ah! A pretty name!" sneered Nat. "Quite airys-tercratic and fairy-like. Was she baptized as sich?"

"No. Loocy."

"Ah! That's a bit common. I'd a fancied Harra-beller or Clementeener meself. I think she'd look Harrabeller. Jest send her off while we chin it a bit. Hurry up; your bloke may come back." He looked round anxiously.

Smudgee returned with some damper, and with an assumption of a very superior manner, she said—

"'Ere ye are. Excoose me fingers. The butler is cleaning the best silver sarver in the pantry."

"Ain't ye afraid o' me?" growled Nat, with affected ferocity.

"Not much I ain't!"

"Ah, I likes yer all the better for it. Come an' kiss me, my little darlin'."

"Garn wash yer face," was the reply of the unmoved Smudgee.

" Water's too scarce, me pet. Yours ain't none too clean, if it comes to that."

" No; but yer see yer out wisitin', an' I'm at 'ome," replied Smudgee loftily.

" Werry much so, me darlin'."

" Not so much o' yer darlin's, if yer please! Yer see, I'm a bit pertickler about my acquaintances."

Sal interrupted her, saying—

" Fill a tin o' tea an' take it to your father. Know where 'e is?"

" Yus. I seen 'im go wiv the others to Thompson's selection, to fight the fire." Smudgee still stared stonily at Nat.

" 'Urry up, then!"

" 'Urry up!" echoed Smudgee. " Who's a-talking? The Emperor of Roosher? Look 'ere; you be civil to my muvver, or I'll fetch my farver, and 'e'll knock the saw-dust out o' yer. We're a werry select family, we is. You 'ear *me!*" And Smudgee, with a switch of her one short garment, strode off majestically into the hut.

" 'Er father'll kill me, will 'e! Does the kid take me for a blooming sooicide?" Nat chuckled.

" Now, what are yer 'ere fur? Let's 'ave it straight an' quick," asked Sal, now quite herself again.

" I'm 'ere on the make. There's several ways o' doin' it, but yer bloke's in the lot. Either 'e pays me ter tyke yer off his 'ands, or 'e pays me ter let 'im keep yer. See?"

" 'E'll pay for neither. 'E's got nothin' ter pay yer with."

" Then I gits 'im another way. 'E's wanted!"

" Wanted!" repeated Sal, in amazement.

" Yus. 'E was sentenced to three years for being con-cerned in bailing up the Wurramurra Bank. 'E only served a few months, and then escaped—did a clean bunk. There's a reward fur a hundred quid out fur 'im."

" When was this?" asked Sal.

" In '92."

" You're dotty !"

" Wot ?"

" Why, 'e's never left me."

" I tell yer, I wus in Berrima wiv 'im."

" Not you, I tell yer; 'e's never left me since we wus married," replied Sal, with a coolness that carried conviction with it.

Nat stared with surprise at Sal, and then spluttered out—

" But I seed 'im, I tell yer! What the blazes does it mean? Is 'e twins?"

After a moment's silence, Sal clapped her hands together in sudden enlightenment, and cried—

" Jack Mowbray !"

" Who the deuce is 'e?" asked the puzzled Nat.

" 'Is pardner—'is double."

" Two on 'em alike?"

" Yus—outside; but one's a man, the other—" Sal shrugged her shoulders.

" Which is the man? Your bloke?"

" No, the other."

" Jack Mowbray?"

Sal nodded her head.

" 'Ev you tooked 'im on too?"

" Don't fret. 'E 'ates me more'n Landon."

" Seems as if they both knew yer, Sal," Nat chuckled.

" P'raps."

Wong had been straining his ears to catch the conversation, but his limited knowledge of the slang language of the speakers, and the distance at which he was lying, made it difficult for him to follow it. He crept stealthily nearer, on his hands and knees. Unfortunately, a twig snapped, and Nat, darting forward, saw him. Dragging him into the moonlight, he shook him violently, and shouted—

" Now, you blasted Ching-Ching, wot 'ave yer 'eard? Tell me, or I'll squeeze cold tea out o' yer! Come on! Own up !"

Wong's head wobbled from side to side as he gasped out—

"Wong no talkee welly muchee. No bleath him got. White feller allee muchee too stlong—he chokee me."

In a fury, Nat knocked the helpless Mongolian down, and then, with a vicious kick at him, roared—

"Take that, you mooching mongrel! And that! and that!" he went on, accompanying each word with a savage kick. "And that——"

But here a pair of strong hands grasped him by the back of the neck; he was swung violently round, and received a straight blow on the nose that sent him reeling on to his back, where, for the moment, he lay still, absorbed in the contemplation of what seemed to him to be myriads of constellations. When his vision was relieved of the dazzling astronomical display, he looked up with a pair of very watery eyes at Jack, who was his assailant, and ejaculated with surprise—

"Jack Landon!"

"No; Jack Mowbray! You cowardly bully!" said Jack to Nat, as he helped up Wong, who was ruefully rubbing the places where he had been kicked. "Clear out, before I give you something worse!"

"I want to speak to him," urged Sal.

"Some other time, Mrs. Landon, please. I've bad news for you.

"Wong, go and keep Smudgee long way off—no come here some little time. Go."

Nat slunk away into the bush, and Wong muttered—

"Wong lemember this white feller plitty long time— Wong go plitty slow along—not quitee well—him pain some got—here—where klicks come along." And, rubbing himself, he slowly limped into the hut.

Jack looked half pityingly, half resentfully at Sal. He cordially disliked the woman. She had tried hard to draw him into an intrigue with her. He had repulsed her with anger and contempt. His rebuff only made the woman more persistent.

Finding him alone one evening, sitting smoking in the shelter of the gully, she had stolen up behind him, flung her arms round his neck, and drawing back his head, had kissed him on the mouth. Jack's answer to her endearments was a push, which sent the woman reeling into the stream, from which he fished her, with her ardour damped for the time, and her anger at fever heat.

"If you ever dare to touch me again," said Jack, his eyes blazing with anger, "I'll wring your neck, and tell your husband why I did it!" And he strode off into the bush, leaving the drenched and furious woman cursing him as he went.

Strangely enough, this had the effect of making the jade respect Jack as she had never respected her husband; and, when her rage subsided, she was as near being in love with him as she had ever been with any one in her dissipated life.

Despising her as he did, Jack remembered that she was a wife, and that he had to tell her that her husband was dying. The man's natural goodness and tenderness made him relent towards her, and, with more softness than he had ever before shown to her, he said—

"Mrs. Landon, there's been a terrible accident."

"What's the matter?" asked Sal.

"Landon—your husband——"

"Well, what's he done?"

"We've saved Thompson's homestead, but—well, you must be told—the big tree outside it was burning; the only chance to save the house was to cut it down and pull it over. Just as it was falling, poor Thompson, who was nearly frantic, got in the way of a big branch. Your husband ran in under it, pulling Thompson clear; but it fell on him and pinned him to the ground, crushing his chest. I—I fear—poor Landon——" And Jack hesitated, almost broke down, but with an effort continued, "He can't live. It's no use pretending that you care much; but let him die in peace. Don't make a scene."

"I ain't a-going to make no scene," said Sal surlily.

The sad little party of rescuers, blackened and grimy with smoke, bore Landon to the door of his hut.

"Gently, boys, gently!" urged Jack. He got some water and held it to Landon's lips, and dashed his forehead and temples with it. Bending close to Landon's ear, he asked—

"Lan, old man, can you hear me?"

"He spoke a minute ago, and asked for you," whispered Tom Hewley.

"I'm here, Lan, old chum. It's Jack. Do you know me?"

"Hadn't we better carry him inside?" asked Tom.

Landon stirred slightly, and muttered—

"No—no! Don't move me—pain—too—bad. Jack —s-send—them away—want—to—s-speak——"

"Boys, clear a bit. He wants to speak to me."

The men retired. Sal moved as if to go to Landon's side. Jack motioned her away, and bending over Landon, said—

"All right, old man. What is it?"

In broken sentences, with great difficulty, Landon gasped—

"I'm booked, Jack; this is God's way out of it. You'll go—home—in my—place."

"Lan—I—I can't," half sobbed Jack.

Earnestly and eagerly Landon spoke again.

"Swear you will, Jack! I can't die in peace—if you don't. Swear you will—go—for my mother's sake—and —Sybil. It is for them—it is right—take a dying man's word—Jack—for God's sake—promise! You must—you must—promise!"

It was cruel to torture the dying man further, and Jack, scarcely thinking of what his promise meant, only wishing to spare his friend pain in his last moments, whispered—

"I'll go, Lan."

"Swear it."

"I swear it."

" Thank God! Take the letters—in breast—dear pal— Jack—God—was good—to me—He let—me—be of use —to—some one—Look after Smudgee—tell Sal—I forgive——"

Jack beckoned to Sal to come near to her husband, and she came, half ashamed, and, with a sniffle, said—

" I'm here, Landon."

But she was too late. Landon had " *gone home.*"

CHAPTER IV

THE BUSH PARSON

THE day had not dawned when Jack, who had scarcely slept the whole night through, saddled his horse and rode off to the home of the nearest clergyman to try to induce him to come and perform the funeral service over the body of his dead friend.

The Rev. Walter Benn was a worthy, hard-working minister, whose parish was the size of a small English county. Preaching in one district one Sunday, and in another forty or fifty miles away the next, he was like a bush doctor—you never knew where to look for him. But when you found him, it was to find him ready for any good work, at any time and at any self-sacrifice. Jack's ride was sixty miles out and back.

He rode alone. His eyes were filled with the glories of the sunrise; but alas! it rose over a scene of death and grim desolation—a death for which the whole earth seemed draped in funereal black. With the blackness of mourning there reigned the silence of the tomb. Charred skeletons of animals and birds bestrewed the path in all directions. Here and there were a few trees, which had somehow escaped the full fury of the flames and still held a few dry, light, yellowish-brown leaves. It was as though an "avenging angel" had passed over the land and swept it and all that had lived upon it into ashes. Jack's thoughts were his only companions, and they were almost as sombre as the landscape through which he rode. He was filled with a great and enduring sorrow for the loss of his friend. He had really loved the reckless wastrel, and he loved but few. He thought over all the years of their intimacy, and of the many good qualities and better instincts the man possessed. He cared nothing for his want of success in the world, but grieved bitterly for his wasted life and his untimely death. He felt a deep and tender pity for the two sweet women who were anxiously expecting news of the son and brother who was awaiting the lonely burial in this charred, withered, and desolate corner of the " Never-Never Land." He pictured them in their English home watching for the cablegram which would announce the news of the receipt of their letters, and the date of the sailing of the vessel which was to bring him to their arms.

Jack had the letters and the photograph of the sister in a bag round his neck, in the inside of his shirt. He could feel the picture of the lovely girl beat time against his heart to the rattle of his horse's hoofs, and a choking sob rose to his throat as he thought of her grief if she should learn of her brother's death. He was torn between his oath to his lost chum, and his inborn sense of right and wrong; dragged by his desire to share in the love of the mother and sister to keep his word—pulled by his innate code of honour to break it, and to confess to them the truth, and comfort them as best he could. Letting the reins lie loose on his horse's neck, he drew the photograph from its hiding-place and earnestly studied it. What a refined, soulful face it was! What love and tenderness shone through the large, luminous eyes! Jack carried the portrait to his lips, and kissed it with the reverence of a devotee at the shrine of a saint. No thought of breaking his oath could linger in his mind a minute while his eyes were on that lovely face. It swept away every doubt and every vestige of indecision. Come what may, he must see her—must be something to her— be of some solace and service to her and her mother. Then came the thought of Sal and Smudgee. How was he to do justice to them, and yet keep them in ignorance of the deception he was about to practise? As Landon's widow and daughter, they were clearly entitled to their share of the inheritance, and they must have it. Yet how to explain to them the accession of so much wealth without exciting suspicion? Men did not give away thousands a year to people of Sal's stamp from motives of charity or generosity. If he went to England and carried out his promise, how was he to meet the embraces of the mother without shame, and, above all, how to encounter the eyes of that exquisite creature, the sister, without showing in his face the degradation he felt at the fraud he was practising?

Then, how were all the details of the scheme to be compassed? Apart from the mother and daughter, who was there living who remembered Landon as a boy? How would they receive him? Unused to duplicity, he shuddered at the thought of the hypocrisy he must be guilty of—not for a day, a week, a month, a year, but for the whole of his life. Not only to tell, but to live a lie! No; he could never go through with it. And yet, his oath. That dear mother's life, that dear sister's happiness. Again he looked at the portrait. Ah! Yes, he would go—he must. Had not Landon told him it was right? It was *God's* way out of the misery his friend had brought upon those who loved and waited for him. So, to and fro, Jack tossed the shuttlecock of conscience between the battledores of inclination and duty.

Presently, he began to leave the burned country behind. He had reached the limits of the fire. The bush here was parched and dry, but it was not burned to cinders. He had ridden some twenty miles. Easing up his horse and striking away from the track, he went down a steep incline, where there was a gully with a little water still trickling lazily down between the stones. Dismounting and going to the bed of the stream, he drank and filled the water-bag he carried at his saddle. Returning to his horse, he filled his own mouth with the water and spurted it into the nostrils and jaws of his hot and thirsty steed. He did not dare to let it drink; it had too far to travel. This he repeated several times, and the poor beast caught at what little moisture it could, eagerly and gratefully. Thoroughly washing out its mouth, and patting its head and neck affectionately, Jack mounted and continued his journey.

He had left the ordinary track now, and was making one of his own. It was growing intensely hot; there was little or no shade, and in the sun it must have registered over one hundred and forty degrees. Mile after mile the jaded man and brute plodded on. He was nearing his destination; he was out of the bush again, and into a clearing. Away on a rise he could see a low, flat, wooden hut, with a corrugated iron roof. The hut and roof were both white-washed, and stood out clear and strong in the bright morning sun. Giving a loud " Coo-ee!" he waited anxiously for an answer. Presently he heard it, and a man's figure came from the rear of the house.

It was the Rev. Walter Benn. He had been cleaning his horse. He was in his shirt and trousers, with turned-up sleeves, and held a curry-comb in one hand and a horse-brush in the other. He lived alone, without servant or help of any kind. He was a queer little figure, not more than five feet three in height, and very spare in build. His face, which was clean-shaven, was thin and ascetic-looking. His eyes were keen and fearless, although one of them had a most unclerical black ring round it, which Jack wondered at, but asked no questions about. His frame was sinewy, and as supple as steel. As he walked towards Jack, his step was light and springy, his look kindly, and his manner alert.

" Good morning, Mowbray," he said cheerily. " It is Mowbray, is it not? Not Landon? Ah yes, I see it's Mowbray. What's the matter? No bad news, I hope? Eh! Well, well; come in, and let me give you some breakfast. You've had none, of course. Nor your horse? Well, turn him loose for a bit, while I go and boil some tea and eggs. I've got plenty of damper and some cold mutton."

Seeing Jack was about to speak, he stopped him, saying—

"Your news will wait until you have had something to eat and drink. If you want some water to rinse your horse's mouth and wash the dust from yourself, you'll find it in the barrel at the back there. Go easy with it. It's rather scarce nowadays, but take what you want." And he rattled on, all the time keenly watching Jack, and trying to gather from his manner what the trouble was that had brought him to his door.

When Jack had loosed his horse's saddle and rubbed him down, he went into the house and found the reverend one, still in his shirt-sleeves, lifting out the eggs from the saucepan. The billy was boiling on the hob; damper, milk, and butter were on the table. Sinking to his knees, Mr. Benn uttered a short morning prayer, to which Jack listened reverently, hat in hand.

" Now, fall to, and do not spare it."

Jack drank greedily of the tea, but felt little appetite for the food. This Mr. Benn noted, and formed his own conclusions. The trouble was serious. It was neither a baptism nor a marriage he was to celebrate. It was death. He went steadily on with his breakfast, talking of all sorts of things likely to interest Jack; but not until the meal was over did he ask him what his errand was. When he learned the truth, he gave Jack an affectionate little pat on the shoulder, saying—

" I must go back with you, Mowbray. We must bury the poor fellow to-day. To-morrow I have a wedding at Mollinson's at ten; a funeral at Dennis's at four. That's a good sixty miles to cover in all, and I must be back for my evening class at half-past six. The next day is Sunday, and I have two sermons with twenty-five miles between the two. So it must be to-day. If you're rested, we'll start at once. Your horse is not too tired, I hope, as I've only one, you know, and he can't carry us both. Your twelve stone and my seven stone ten would be too much for my ' Jimmie' in this intense heat. He is rested, you think? That's right." And the little man bustled into his black coat, picked up the bag which held his cassock

THE BUSH PARSON

and books, put on his black straw hat, led the way to the horses, and the two men were soon in the saddle, cantering back towards Woolloogolonga Gully.

Jack was silent and thoughtful, but Mr. Benn kept up a constant little ripple of bright and cheery conversation, his quick eye noting and taking in all that they passed on their way.

"So poor Thompson has suffered, has he? I'm very sorry. A decent, honest, hard-working fellow that. He will feel his loss keenly. Poor chap! Dear, dear me! This bush life has its drawbacks; and yet, how the native-born ones love it! Grumble as they may—and I must say they have cause to grumble—yet how they stick on, and how few of them can stand city life who have been reared in the bush! Looking at this black eye of mine? Nice thing for a reverend father, is it not? No, I did *not* rub it against the door-post nor against the branch of a tree. It went up against a fellow's fist. Those young blackguards, the Crowdons—they must be mad, surely, or they'd never play such pranks. Mischievous beggars that they are! What do you think, Mowbray? The eldest Crowdon— that big bully, Jabez—came over last Sunday with their pair-horse buggy to drive me to the morning service at Big-Tree Creek. Like the innocent I am, I took the un-wonted courtesy for a sign of coming grace. I was soon undeceived. Directly we started, he set that pair of wild black horses of his at a full gallop—you know what the road is like! Well, the way we bumped and jolted, swayed and swerved, was wonderful to contemplate. All the time, Master Jabez was yelling and shrieking like a Choctaw Indian. I saw his game. It was to frighten me and prevent me from holding the service. Well, I didn't like it much, but I sat tight and waited, thinking if I took no notice and accepted it all as a matter of course, he'd grow tired of the fun. Not a bit of it! You know the timber fence, just above the horse-corral near Crowdon's boundary? Hanged if that bully did not whip his horses into madness, and make a full charge at it! Over went

55

the horses, clearing it like birds; but the wheels struck the fence, and the shafts were wrenched off. Jabez jumped forward, and fell on his hands and knees. I shot out at the back, turned a somersault, and landed in the scrub, a bit hurt but no bones broken. When I got breath, I went for Master Jabez, and——"

" You got that black eye?" smiled Jack.

"Yes, but not without some fair exchanges," said the little man. " I called to inquire after his health yesterday. His nose is not what it was, by any means, and he has a *pair* of black eyes. I didn't look well in the pulpit, I fear, but they tell me I preached an uncommonly good sermon. The text was, ' If a man smite thee on the one cheek,' &c. &c.; but I wove in a little of ' Spare the rod and spoil the child,' thus giving an entirely new tone to the old text, which some of those who had come up in time to witness the end of my somewhat discursive argument with Master Jabez fully appreciated."

" I'm glad that you pasted the ruffian, Mr. Benn. But, my word!" said Jack, as he eyed the diminutive form beside him, " you gave away a lot in weight. He must be at least two stone heavier than you are."

"Yes, quite," coolly replied the reverend gentleman; " but, you see, the poor beggar had never been taught, while I was the ' Bantam Champion' of my year at Oxford. You see, he hadn't the ghost of a chance, really. I say, Mowbray," he rattled on, " this has been a big blaze indeed. Hullo! there's Finlayson yonder. What's he doing there?" And he looked towards a man who, black and grimy, was sitting on a stump, smoking and looking over the blackened plain.

" No—yes! Why, Mowbray," he whispered, " this *was* his farm, of course! Here's the road, and there's the three boulders. This is awful! Not a vestige of the place left!"

He rode up to the disconsolate figure, and, jumping from his horse, put his hand on the man's back, and said affectionately—

"Finlayson, this is bad indeed! But your people and family—are they safe?"

"Aye, they're awa' tae M'Donald's, wha's gi'en them hoose-room, till—weel, weel—" And the man faltered.

"Until we can get something from the Relief Fund, and start you afresh, eh, Finlayson?"

"Na, na; I'll hae none o' their damned charity, meenister. Ma land's ma ain yet, and if they'll lend me eno' to get some seed an' some eemplements, an' maybe a horse an' coo or twa on mortgage at four per cent., I'll pay them back iv'ry bawbee. But I'll tak none o' their charity." And the sturdy, brave fellow looked away into the distance.

"I'll see to that, Finlayson. Come to me to-night, and we'll talk it over. I'm not going to pity a man like you. I'm going to thank God that there are such men left in the world."

The two rode on quietly, and even Mr. Benn's tongue was silent for a time. Presently he spoke again.

"That man's a hero," he said. "This is the second time he's been utterly ruined. Years ago he took up a selection at Boolonga. The rabbits got on to the land and ate him nearly out of house and home. He tried everything to exterminate them, in vain. He fenced below and above the earth, but they got round and under the fencing and went on increasing. A dry season came, and he thought he would kill them out with thirst. He fenced in the water-holes. They rushed at the fence in thousands, and died struggling to force their way through it. Hundreds upon hundreds gasped out their lives with the water in sight, and the heaps of dead made steps for those that followed. Over them, they climbed the fences and got to the water, and afterwards to the poor fellow's young crops, which they devoured to the last blade of corn and grass. Nothing that he could do would stop them. The Rabbit Board fined him for not taking proper precautions to destroy the pests, and a travelling sheep-salesman sued him for killing his sheep with the poison he had laid down for the rabbits. Between them they ruined him. He left Boolonga and came on here. And now, look!" And the little man waved his hand over the desert of charcoal in deep sympathy.

"Poor devil!" sighed Jack.

"Oh, he'll come out on top yet," said Mr. Benn hopefully. "Such men never go under."

.   .   .   .

It was hours after Jack's departure before Sal opened her eyes, and when she did so, it was with a dim consciousness of something having occurred on the previous night which was not altogether of a pleasant nature. What was it? As she yawned and stretched herself, she remembered. Landon was dead. She sat up with a sudden start, and began to think. What difference was this to make in her life? Her real husband, Nat Rudder, was, she guessed, lurking somewhere in the bush, waiting the opportunity of seeing her again. Could he help her?

When she first met Landon, he had told her, in a fit of drunken confidence, that he was entitled to a fortune and large estates. The woman's cupidity was aroused. He was evidently a gentleman, and he spoke as one who speaks the truth. Sal had pictured herself living as a lady, with her own house and servants, unlimited dresses and finery, races and amusements galore, and plenty of entertaining companions. She never lost the hope that the fortune would ultimately come, and this hope was the mainspring of her comparative faithfulness to her husband. She dreaded the old life of the streets—not for any dislike to the vice itself, but for the discomfort and inconvenience it entailed. When Jack joined Landon as a partner, her existence had an added interest. As much as she could love anybody, she loved Jack. She knew that he despised and disliked her. Accustomed as she was to be admired and sought after by men of her own class, his cool, contemptuous indifference piqued and excited her. Her dreams were enlarged, and her ambitions for the future widened. She saw herself a widow with an immense fortune, living a life of luxury, with Jack for her partner, either as husband or lover—she cared little which. That Landon had not inherited his patrimony was only an incident—a trifling delay—the fortune would come eventually, if not in his lifetime, then after it. Better that he should be out of the way. She, with her daughter, would inherit the property, and be free to do what she liked with it.

But now that Landon was dead, Nat had returned, and of Nat she was afraid. He had a nasty habit of thrashing her when in his cups, which Sal shiveringly remembered and silently cursed him for. If she was to capture Jack, how was she to shake off Nat? Sal sat nursing her knees and pondering. Nat was not easy to shake off, if he saw anything to be made by his holding on. Now that Landon was dead, his scheme of making something out of his fears or desires necessarily fell to the ground. She had no money to give him, but her good looks still remained, and on them Nat would trade. And she knew him well enough to feel sure that, if no better merchandise was to his hand, he would trade on them to the fullest extent. With Nat dominating her, what chance was there for her with Jack? How was she to live? Nat would not work for her. Where would Landon's fortune come from, if it ever came? How was she to set to work to learn the truth about it? Could she work at all without Nat's assistance? How was she to begin? She had neither money, education, influence, nor friends. Neither had Nat, but he had great cunning and any number of unscrupulous pals, who could nose about and pick up handy scraps of information for him, which, pieced together, would prove serviceable to her. Then she remembered the letter her husband had received the day before. What was that about? Where was it? She rose and searched the room, vainly, of course, for the letters were in Jack's possession, and he was miles away. She thought they might still be on her husband's body. She did not like the idea of looking upon the dead man's face, but she must know if the letters were there. She shuddered and paused. More than once she started towards the little back room, where the body had been taken, but her courage failed her. She would ask the men, before the body was removed for burial, to search it. No. She had better look for herself. Calling up all her resolution, she went into the darkened chamber, and, uncovering the rigid form, which was still dressed as in life, passed her hands nervously over the breast pockets, not daring to raise her eyes to the face of the dead man. The letters were not there. Hurriedly she replaced the cover and scuttled back to her own room.

She had come to the conclusion that the letter was in Jack's possession. If so, how would it be possible to learn the contents? She knew it would be useless to try to induce Jack to tell her, if he did not do so of his own accord. As she sat turning the matter over in her dull, heavy-brained way, her daughter approached her. Smudgee was unusually quiet and thoughtful. She had made an effort at tidiness which, if limited, was at least earnest. She had pulled her hair into something like order, had rubbed most of the dust off her person with a bit of rough towelling, and from somewhere she had unearthed a few yards of black tape, a portion of which she had twisted round her hat, and with the rest had made a kind of plaited necklace. Smudgee was in mourning. Approaching her mother, she said, with some anger—

"Ain't yer goin' ter wear nothin' fur mournin' fur 'im?"

"Mournin'!" echoed Sal. "Wot are yer torkin' of? Do black silk dresses and crape grow on trees? Where'll I get mournin' from?"

"Seems to me," said Smudgee scornfully, fondling her black tape necklace, "that anyfink black 'ud be better'n nuffink."

"Ah!" sarcastically replied Sal. "An' a coach an' four, with plumes and mutes, 'ud be better than a 'and-stretcher; an' a marble tomb better than a hole up yonder, in the burnt-up scrub. But wen yer can't get what yer want, yer must take what yer can git, seems to me."

" Well, ain't yer goin' ter do nothin'?"

" Yus; I'm goin' ter bile some tea, an' git some break-fast." And with that parting shot, Sal strode away into the hut.

Smudgee looked after her mother with an expression of puzzled regret. She was a loving little soul, and very tender withal towards all who were weak and suffering. She had learned of Landon's death during the night, and had cried herself quietly to sleep in her lonely, unnoticed way. She had known Landon's weakness; knew he cared little for her; but she saw much that was good in him, and if she felt little real love for her supposed father, she had at least an affectionate regard for him. Her mother's callousness hurt and angered her. She had balanced, in her own clear-seeing way, the father and mother, and her father had all the best of the analysis. Surely her mother might make some show of respect for her dead husband! If she did not, she herself must try to make up for the mother's neglect by her own endeavours; and she wandered off into the bush to search for flowers or leaves wherewith to deck the lost one's grave.

Smudgee strolled on. The fire had left nothing, Thompson's way. She took another route, and, gathering a few belated blossoms here, a bunch of wattle there, and some half-dried leaves still further on, she turned back with her arms full—hot, dusty, tired, thirsty, and hungry, but with no thought of herself or her own troubles in her mind; only an aching, yearning longing to do something to show her regard for the memory of the man who only yesterday was her father. Her little heart was throbbing with pain, her brain puzzled with the ever-unanswered question, " Whither away?" Where had he gone? Was he still hovering round the wretched hut that constituted his home? Could he see the brutal indifference of the woman who had been his wife? Could he understand her own wish to do honour to his memory? She hoped he could. Not for any gain or credit for herself, but that he might know that there was some one left in the bush who remembered all that was good in him and had forgotten all that was evil.

Smudgee's sense of justice was acute to painfulness. She could never hit anything smaller or weaker than herself, and she now deemed it cowardice and meanness to remember anything of so helpless a thing as the still, cold, unconscious remnant of her father, that was awaiting burial in the hut yonder. As she wandered on, she tried to enlarge and exaggerate all the little acts of kindness and goodness she could remember Landon doing, and put away, with a shudder, all his faults and failings, grieving for them as if they were her own, while all the excellences she placed to his credit alone. The remembrance of his weaknesses caused her remorse, as though she were primarily responsible for them. She felt like going down on her knees and praying for pardon for them.

The clatter of horses' hoofs aroused her from her reverie, and, looking up, she saw Jack and the minister cantering towards her.

"How are you, Miss Landon?" asked Mr. Benn, as he rode up to Smudgee.

"Fusty as——"

Jack coughed warningly, and Smudgee did not complete her answer.

"What have you got there, Smudgee?" questioned Jack, indicating the mass of flowers and ferns in Smudgee's arms.

"Sumfin' fur 'im," answered Smudgee simply. And the two men looked at the little tattered figure, and back at each other, with moistened eyes.

" 'Ev yer bin all the way ter fetch the parson, Jack?" said Smudgee, indicating Mr. Benn.

"Yes," assented Jack. "Give us your hand, Princess, and up you come."

Jack held out his hand. Smudgee gathered up her treasures into her right arm, and, offering her left arm to Jack, was lifted lightly and easily up beside her faithful knight.

"So you know all about it, Princess?" Jack was holding the child closely to him.

"Yus; I 'eard it all in the night, wen they was puttin' 'im in the room. I say, Knight, it was just like you to go off wivout yer breakfus' ter fetch the parson."

"How do you know that I went without my breakfast, Princess?"

"'Cos I watched yer go," answered Smudgee softly. "Say, Jack, do yer think 'e knows yer went?"

"Who, Smudgee?"

"My farver," she whispered.

"Why do you ask?"

"'Cos I'd like ter think 'e knew you wus doin' somfink fer 'im, though he *wus* gorn."

"Then we will hope he does know, and knows, too, that you are thinking of and doing all you can to show your love for him."

"I dunno about love, Knight," answered the truthful Smudgee. "P'raps I dunno what love is. I ought ter 'ave loved 'im best, 'cos 'e was me farver, but somehow I never did. I allers thought fust o' you, Knight, wen I woke o' mornin's, muvver next, and 'im last. Was that wrong, Knight?"

"I'm afraid it was not quite right, Smudgee. But you were always very good to him, so that you'll be forgiven, I'm sure."

After this they were silent for some time, Jack pondering still over his mission to England and his dear friend's relatives, while Smudgee was trying to puzzle out the insoluble mysteries of life and death.

"I wish I'd bin better ter 'im when 'e was 'ere," sighed Smudgee as she saw the hut, where the body was lying, loom up in the distance.

CHAPTER V

IN WHICH SMUDGEE AND JACK ARE PARTED

LANDON's grave had been dug under the remains of some trees, denuded now of every leaf by the fire, but only waiting the blessed rain to spring into blossom and sweetness again. The earth was black and scorched here, as elsewhere, the dug-up soil standing out red against the charred surface.

The little procession was wending its way towards the lonely resting-place. Jack and Thompson, Tom and Dan were carrying the body, Sal and Smudgee were the chief mourners, if such a term can be used under such circumstances. Bill and a few of the station-hands followed. Mr. Benn had donned his cassock, and, with head bared to the scorching sun, led the way.

When the party had gathered round the grave, Mr. Benn began the service, and, as he read simply, the beautiful words went home to almost all who heard them. When he came to the lines from the Psalm, " O spare me a little, that I may recover my strength before I go hence and be no more seen," Jack recalled his friend's prayer to " be of some use " before he " went hence and was no more seen," and was thankful that the prayer had been answered.

Smudgee dropped her poor offering into the open grave when all was over, and turned away, biting her lip to stop the sobs that rose to her throat, and threatened to choke her.

Jack took Mr. Benn to his hut, gave him some tea, and then the good little minister galloped off to his multifarious duties elsewhere. When he had gone, Jack went in search of Tom Hewley, and, finding him, strolled off into the scrub with him.

SMUDGEE AND JACK ARE PARTED

Next to Landon, Tom ranked closest in Jack's affections. He was by far the best educated and brightest man in the district. Barely twenty-five, he had passed through a strange and chequered existence, and had acquired a knowledge of the world and mankind most unusual in one so young. He had been educated for the law, but, too poor to continue his studies, he had been at intervals travelling-companion, tutor, journalist, secretary, super-cargo, steward, waiter, miner—anything and everything in turns, but nothing long. Jack had taken to him, and felt he could trust him, as indeed he could, for he was as true as steel to his friends, and as secret as the tomb when necessary.

Jack wanted some one on whom he could rely, to go to England with him, and help him in the task he had undertaken. There were so many things to do—so much to learn—so many dangers to face, that, without some one on whom he could rely, the task looked hopeless. He had determined to trust Tom and ask him to accompany him home.

Tom, he knew, had no ties to hamper him. Like himself, he was alone in the world, ready for anything that might turn up. He had been chumming with Jack and Landon on this claim for months—had failed and almost starved with them. If there was no unknown reason why he should not return to England, he would take him as private secretary and companion. It was to broach this question and sound Tom that he had sought him out. Landon's death and the recent funeral service and burial had saddened Tom, who was unusually quiet and silent.

The evening was closing in rapidly. In a few moments the sun would be down, and the night would fall. Jack felt some little difficulty in opening the question with Tom, but he found assistance in an unexpected way. It came from Tom himself, who said suddenly—

" Jack, I must own up. I heard what Landon said to you."

" When?" asked Jack, startled.

5   65

"As he was dying," replied Tom.

"Well?"

"I think Landon was right, if you can go through with it."

"I never thought you could hear what was said."

"I have quick ears, Jack."

"I can trust you?"

"What do *you* think?"

"I think you are an honest, faithful fellow, and I *will* trust you," answered Jack. And he did. As they strolled through the scrub, he unfolded his scheme.

"I want a friend to help me. I shall, of course, encounter many dangers and risks when I meet with Landon's people. There may be many old tenants, friends who knew him intimately as a boy, who will have to be brought to see in me what they recollect of him. There will be the house, grounds, and neighbourhood to study and learn, for the memory of his birthplace and home could not possibly pass out of a man's mind. To betray the slightest ignorance would be to excite the greatest suspicion. In all that, you could be of help to me. I shall want a private secretary, and no one could suit me better. I can pay you as well as any other employer, and we could still be friends. What do you say, Tom?"

"That you are a good fellow, and I a devilishly lucky one, and I'll go with you and work for you with pleasure, my dear Jack. I suppose it will be conspiracy, according to the strict letter of the law, but, as I heard poor Landon's dying entreaties that you should undertake the task, my conscience does not prick me—so be hanged to the law of it! When do you think you will start?" Tom asked.

"There's nothing to keep me here. To-morrow will see us on the road to Sydney. We can catch the express from Wallangarra, and be in Sydney in time to see the lawyers on Monday morning early."

"What about funds?"

"I can manage well enough until I see Martin &

Martin, who will honour my signature to any amount, they tell me in this letter."

"What about your signature, by the way?" queried Tom.

"Landon told me that they had never seen his writing; and, oddly enough, there is as much resemblance in our general handwriting as there was in our faces. I don't think that will give me much trouble, while the fact that his mother and sister have accepted my portrait for his, will relieve me of much anxiety as to their recognition of me as Landon. I shall have to be careful when we get to Sydney. I don't think there is much fear of being recognised while I wear this beard, but it would be hard luck if I should be caught for that old Wurramurra Bank business. I could prove an alibi, I think, but it would be difficult to hunt up the witnesses after this lapse of time, and we might be delayed for months. We must avoid that if we can."

"Well, I must say you are in as tight a corner as any one could wish for. A more innocent villain it would be hard to find. An escaped convict, liable to re-arrest for a crime he never committed, and an unwilling conspirator, liable to imprisonment for fraud! A nice respectable employer for a poor orphan like myself, I don't think!" laughed Tom.

"I'm afraid I'm a bad lot, Tom, but I'll balance it out somehow," said Jack feelingly.

"Oh, don't get remorseful. You have not done much wrong up to now. If everybody had as clean a slate as you have, the Recording Angel would not have quite so busy a time of it."

"What do you think we had better do about Sal and Smudgee?"

"Lose the one and plant out the other, I should say."

"Sal is not so easily lost. What's worrying me is this. They are entitled to a share of Landon's estate, and I intend that they shall have it; but how am I to give it to them without arousing their suspicions?"

"By Jove! that's a teaser. Through your lawyer, of course,—but——" and Tom rubbed his head in a puzzled way.

"Yes," continued Jack, "there's that 'but.' I can't tell him that Mrs. John Landon is my wife, because Mrs. John Landon knows perfectly well that Mr. John Landon, her husband, is dead and buried. Large yearly incomes are not, as a rule, shot at people's heads without cause or reason. What excuse can I give for shooting this one at Sal? True, she knows nothing of the name of Landale. She knew him as Landon. Yet that is not enough to keep her off the scent. If she once begins to suspect, she may get on the track of the whole business, and then——Well!" And Jack paused, lacking the words to express Sal's conduct under the conditions and circumstances.

"Um," pondered Tom. "You'll have to be a distant relative of poor Landon's, a grandfather or grandmother interested in his wife and family. Hang it all! Sal is not such a fool as to quarrel with a relative who makes a rich woman of her, is she?"

"One never knows what a drunken, hysterical woman will not be fool enough to do. I see no end of trouble through this same income for Sal. She'll have a high, ungodly old time with it, that's certain. And Smudgee? what effect will it have on her? Poor little kid! There's a heap of good in that child. What a cursed shame to let it go to rot, as it must with such a mother as Sal! Poor little Princess! I shan't like parting with her," sighed Jack.

"No! she'll not like parting with you. You are her best friend. She'll lose a lot when she loses you."

"Poor little neglected kiddie! I wonder where all the goodness that is stored up in her comes from? Landale and his ancestors, I suppose."

"How can one tell? It is not a child's father and mother alone that are responsible for its character. It is the product not of one but of hundreds of generations.

'Like mother, like daughter' is a huge fallacy, like many another proverb," Tom said. "What do you think of allowing them in the way of an income?"

"It's difficult to decide. My determination is to touch no more of the money for myself than is necessary to keep up the position of head of the family. All else that comes to me I intend to invest and leave to Landale's sister, Sybil, and his daughter, Smudgee, either at my death or when necessity arises. It is theirs, not mine. It certainly should not go to Sal, who really ruined his life, and shall not, if I can prevent it."

"If you are bowled out, as Landale left no will, it certainly must go to Sal and Smudgee."

"And so turn out his mother and sister from their home?" asked Jack.

"Unless Sir James Walgrove made some other stipulation in his will."

"That shall never be, if I can help it," Jack answered fiercely. "If there were no other reason for my carrying out Landon's wishes, that would be sufficient. Think of those two dear women being turned out into the world for such a creature as Sal! Ugh!" Jack shuddered.

"No! the chaste Sal has certainly no moral right to dispossess Lady Walgrove and her daughter. We need waste no remorse over the fair Sally. But we must not shut our eyes to the fact that she is the heiress—or one of them."

"No! we will not forget it. I will be just to her, be sure, if not for her own sake, for Smudgee's. Poor Smudgee! I dread saying good-bye to her; but it has to be done."

As he parted from Tom for the night, Jack said—

"Keep well, Tom, and be up bright and early in the morning. To-morrow must see us on the road to Sydney."

In the morning Jack sought Sal, and told her he was leaving Woolloogolonga for ever that day. This was a piece of news Sal was not prepared for, and she turned pale and felt a sudden shock at her heart that took her breath away and left her speechless. Strangely enough, the possibility of being parted entirely from Jack had never entered into her calculations. She stared at him in a dazed and helpless kind of way, and Jack spoke again—

" You have no money, I suppose?"

" No," Sal whimpered out. " Where should I get money from?"

" Well, you can get some from me for the present. What do you intend to do? You'll not stay here, I suppose?"

" What is there here for me to stay for?"

" Nothing, so far as I can see. Where will you go?" asked Jack.

" Where are you goin'?" questioned Sal eagerly.

" That does not concern you, Mrs. Landon," replied Jack sharply.

" But it does, Jack!" whined Sal. " You're not goin' ter throw us over, are yer? Think o' poor Smudgee!"

" I am thinking of her, and I am not going to ' throw you over,' as you call it. I will see that the wife and child of my dead chum do not come to want, be sure of that. But for the future our roads lie wide apart. It is more than probable that we shall never see each other again after to-day——"

Here Sal interrupted him with a cry. She was a vulgar, slow-witted kind of creature, guided entirely by her animal instincts. She felt hunger, thirst, cold, heat, fatigue, desire, pleasure, rest, and repletion. Those sensations ruled her. She was happy or unhappy according to the gratification of her bodily feelings, or the reverse. In losing Jack she was losing something which added to her comfort and pleasure, and she cried out aloud at the prospect.

" I won't let yer go!" she screamed. " I won't! I'll kill myself—kill you—kill Smudgee! I love yer! Yer know I love yer! Yer can't be so crool! I love yer, I tell yer!" And the excited, hysterical creature beat her hands on her breast and sobbed violently.

Jack, very wisely, let her sob herself into something like calmness before he spoke again. Then he said—

"Mrs. Landon, let there be an end to this. Nothing in the world could ever make me respect, much less care for you. As the widow of my friend, you will command my services in any matter that concerns your welfare or the welfare of your daughter. I will take care of you both, and see that you want for nothing necessary for either. Beyond that, I will have no communication with you, under any circumstances."

"Do you think you're goin' to give me the shake like that?" yelled Sal, her face now crimson with rage. "Not much yer ain't! Not if Sal Landon knows herself!" And the half-crazy woman launched herself into a sea of invective and abuse, delivered in language so varied and picturesque that it became, as the newspapers have it, "entirely unfit for publication."

Jack was a prey to very varied feelings. The contempt he felt for Sal as a woman was tempered by the thought that he was wronging her. Could he but have known that Sal was not Landale's wife—that Smudgee was not his daughter—all would have been plain sailing. But, unfortunately, he did not. He tried to soothe her. Sal, who knew nothing of the inward working of his mind, took this partial relenting as a sign that she had made some impression upon him, and renewed her endearments. At this Jack sickened, and, repulsing her angrily, he said—

"Stop this nonsense, please. Try to remember, will you, that your husband was my friend, and that he is scarcely cold in his grave. I am going to find Smudgee and bid her good-bye. Let me have some address where I can send you assistance. Take care of your child and lead a sober, decent life, if you can."

Sal sulkily named Sydney Post-Office as her address,

and Jack strode away, leaving her in a fury of rage and baffled desire.

The parting with Smudgee was not to be so easily accomplished. He found her studiously poring over a sheet of an advertisement page of the *Australasian,* in which scantily-clad ladies displayed the relative merits of combinations, corsets, cosmetics, curling-pins and fluids, shapes, hair-renewers and hair-removers, fat-producers and fat-annihilators, blush-providers, and—and—well, other things which the eye masculine should not even peep at.

She sighed wofully as Jack approached her, and said—

" Seems to me a woman's a pretty expensive thing to make, Knight. I've read this paper till I'm nearly blinded, and I knows all of it by heart, and if it takes all these things ter make me inter a woman, I shall hev ter remain Smudgee. Look at this—and this! Wot der they want 'em fur? That gits me!"

" They don't want them, as a rule, Smudgee, but fashion tells them they do—and that's the same thing."

" Look at the shape o' this woman. Where's she put herself? She seems to be bustin' out everywhere where she oughtn't. How's she do it?" asked the scornful Smudgee, pointing at an advertisement for a new corset. " You'll never ketch me makin' such a objeck o' myself as that."

" I sincerely hope not, Princess. You will always be the same dear, natural little girl that you are now. And if I ever meet you when—when you have grown up, I shall, I am sure, find in the woman the same honest soul I knew as a child."

Smudgee looked at Jack wonderingly for a moment, as though unsure that she had heard him aright, and then she whispered—

" If ever you *meet* me! Wot der yer mean, Knight? You're never goin' ter *part* from me, are yer?"

" Yes, dear Smudgee; I must. I'm going away." Jack's voice was low and a little unsteady.

Smudgee started to her feet, and stared at Jack with

wide-open eyes glistening with tears. The tone of his voice told her more than his words. She felt that something serious had happened—something that was to make a great change in her life. What could it be? Her heart was beating wildly. Something had caught her by the throat; she could not speak. The paper she had been reading fluttered to the ground. Slowly she went to Jack, and pushing him gently down on to a stump, she knelt at his feet, put her arms over his knees, and, hiding her face on them, she whispered—

"Go on. Tell us wot it is."

It was a hard moment for Jack, one of the most trying he had ever experienced. How was he to tell her? What had happened, indeed! His friend, the child's father, was dead, and he was going to take his place in the world, and leave that friend's daughter to the mercy of her dissolute and worthless mother. His conscience smote him sorely, and, as he stroked the tousled head, he swore silently to himself that he would never wrong the poor, trusting little being of a penny. What was due to her should be hers, to the last farthing; and, so far as it was possible, he would watch over her.

"Tell us! tell us!" repeated Smudgee.

"I hardly know, Smudgee—how to make you understand."

"You go on. I'll understand quick enough, Jack."

"You see, Smudgee, your father's death has made it necessary for me to—to—well, to break up everything here, and go—away."

"Where to?"

"Well, out of the bush altogether—perhaps out of the country. You see, I only came here because your father was my chum—one of the very few friends I had in the world; and now that he's gone——"

"What about me, Knight? Ain't I one of your few friends?"

"Indeed you are. But you see you're a girl, and in your mother's care."

" Pretty kind o' care, ain't it?"

" Still, she is your mother, Smudgee."

" Yus, I know she is. *When* do yer go away?"

Jack paused. It had all been so sudden—it seemed cruel to tell her that this was his good-bye, and yet he must do it.

" I must go to-day, little pal."

" Go away to-day? *Right* away?"

" Yes."

The childish figure was trembling violently. Jack held her two hands tightly in one of his, and with the other he continued to caress her hair.

" Am I never to see you again?"

" I hope so, Smudgee."

" When?"

" I don't know."

" Soon?"

" I'm afraid not."

" Take me wiv yer!"

" That is not possible."

" 'Cos I'm a gurl?"

" That's one reason."

" Wot was I made a gurl for, I wonder?"

" To make some good fellow happy when you grow up to be a woman, I hope."

" Some good feller! Oh, yus! Likely, ain't it? Wait a bit, Jack. I ain't quite got it inter my 'ead that you're really goin' away. I feel a bit stunned like, an' I've got a big lump like a heavy stone 'ere." And she beat her heart. " An' it's kind of liftin' higher up, inter me throat, an' stiflin' me. I—I *can't* believe it! You're such a kind chap. Yer can't be so hard an' unfeelin' as ter leave me! Don't, Jack! Dear Jack—dear Knight! don't—don't! Please—*please,* don't!"

Smudgee did not cry. No tears fell, although her eyes were moist. She shivered as if with cold, her breath came in loud gasps, as if, as she said, she was being stifled. Jack was sorely grieved for the poor waif, and tried all he knew to comfort her. But only one thing could do that, and that was impossible. He could not take her with him; and he could not stop with her. He must go. To prolong the parting with Smudgee was cruel to her and to himself. He rose, and lifted her up to him, saying—

"It's got to be, Smudgee. Nothing can alter it. I will write to you sometimes, to the Sydney Post-Office; and you will write to me to the address I shall send you later on. Now, be a brave little woman, and bid me good-bye."

Smudgee's hands were clasped and unclasped in feverish excitement. She looked at Jack with her pleading eyes in speechless entreaty. He kissed her on the forehead, and, in a choking voice, said—

"Be brave and good. I shall never forget you, Smudgee. Remember that. Good-bye." And he went hastily from her.

Smudgee stood where he left her, looking after him until he disappeared among the scrub. As he turned round for the last time he waved his hat. Smudgee did not stir. She watched him out of sight, and then fell in a little heap with her face to the earth. *"The train was gorne."*

CHAPTER VI

JACK LEAVES WOOLLOOGOLONGA GULLY

IN order to avoid another encounter with Sal, Jack asked Thompson to take charge of the money to defray her expenses to Sydney and provide for her wants until he could draw some funds from the account at Martin & Martin's. Thompson agreed readily. In a few hours they were at the station, had secured sleeping-berths, and were dashing through the darkness on their way to Sydney.

Jack's heart was heavy. He had a sincere, half-fatherly, half-brotherly love for Smudgee, and her grief had deeply affected him. The knowledge that he was deceiving her, and going home to take up what he believed to be her inheritance, added to the pain he felt in parting from her. It was a puzzle indeed he had to unravel, and the more he thought of it the more difficult the solution became. If Sal had not blocked the way, he could have taken the child to England and watched her education and upbringing until she was old enough to be entrusted with the fortune which he intended her to have. But, unfortunately, Sal did block the way, and that most effectually. Jack slept but little, and was glad when the journey was over.

Arriving in Sydney, Jack and Tom drove straight to the Australia Hotel. After much cogitation, they had decided that the larger the hotel they stopped at, the less likely they were to be noticed, and they had telegraphed from a station on the road to the manager of the " Australia" for accommodation. Passing through the crowded vestibule to the clerk's office, they got the numbers of their rooms, and were shown to the elevator and conveyed upstairs.

Early as the hour was, a man far gone in intoxication stumbled into the lift. He was showily dressed, and wore much jewellery. As he sank to the seat with a jolt, Jack with difficulty suppressed an exclamation. This Tom noticed, and when they were alone he asked the cause.

"That fellow who got into the lift just now—the drunken one—knows me. He was in Berrima prison with me. His name is Grimes. He was in for two years, and has been released since I escaped."

"He did not recognise you?" asked Tom.

"No; he was too drunk to see me," replied Jack.

"Let's hope he will continue so until we start for Auckland."

The friends had decided that the route *viâ* Auckland, Samoa, Honolulu, and America would be better than the six weeks' voyage in one ship, with the same people, by the Suez Canal way. Their fellow-voyagers would have less time in which to observe and gossip about them.

"The bibulous Grimes doesn't know *me*," said Tom. "If necessary, I will scrape acquaintance with him, and fill him up nightly until we sail. I don't think, by the look of him, that it would take much to persuade him to drink with me, although I should imagine it would take a lot of whisky to 'fill him up.' However, as money is no object, I will try, if you like."

"Better let him alone, and avoid him," replied Jack.

The hotel was very full. The fourth test match of the English and Australian cricketers was in its third day, and thousands of visitors had been drawn into the city to witness it. This influx of strangers made it all the more safe for Jack. He would attract less attention.

Mr. Grimes, however, was a danger to be reckoned with—and avoided.

After breakfast, the two friends started off to interview Messrs. Martin & Martin, the solicitors employed by Lady Walgrove to search out and convey her letter and the other messages to Jack.

It was a most respectable firm, carrying on business in Macquarrie Street. Passing in to the outer office, scribbling his name on a piece of paper and handing it to the clerk, Jack asked that it might be at once sent to the head of the firm. This was done, and soon the two companions were seated in the inner office occupied by Mr. Martin senior.

Mr. Martin was a quiet, dignified man of about sixty years of age, with a keen pair of steel-blue eyes, iron-grey hair, and rather long side-whiskers. He was tall and portly, moved and spoke slowly, weighing his words carefully, and not using a superfluity of them. He had shaggy, bushy eyebrows, and wore glasses, over which he peered occasionally in a piercingly questioning way that was hard to meet by any man who was endeavouring to deceive him.

Neither Jack nor Tom felt too comfortable in his presence. He held out a large, strong hand to Jack, as he said—

" Mr. Landale, I presume?"

Jack felt a peculiar sensation pass over him, as he heard himself addressed for the first time by the name of his dead friend. It was not without a little difficulty that he answered—

" Yes."

Mr. Martin was watching him closely, and Jack had to nerve himself to endure the scrutiny. As Mr. Martin did not speak again, Jack was compelled to do so; and he said—

" Allow me to introduce my friend and secretary, Mr. Hewley."

Mr. Martin looked steadily at Tom, and offered his hand, saying—

" Please sit down."

Jack summoned up his courage, and, feeling that the sooner the business was over the better, drew out the letters sent to Landale, and, placing them on the table beside Mr. Martin, said—

" I received your letter, Mr. Martin, enclosing these from my mother and sister, also this portrait of my sister, which, of course, you have not seen."

Mr. Martin quietly received the photograph, and, after looking at it carefully for a few moments, turned his eyes upon Jack, as if to compare the two, or try to discover if there were any points of resemblance between the faces.

Jack bore the examination fairly well, but was glad when Mr. Martin broke the silence with the remark—

" An extremely beautiful girl."

" She is indeed," replied Jack, naturally and enthusiastically. " And now, to—to business."

Mr. Martin murmured the one word—

" Pleasure."

Jack rightly accepted this as an invitation to continue, which he did.

" It is my intention to go home at once, Mr. Martin. My sister tells me that my mother is far from well, and is fretting a great deal for me."

" Not unnaturally," observed Mr. Martin.

" Of course not. I—I"—Jack stammered a little here—" I am afraid I have not been too good a son, Mr. Martin."

" It would be hard to be that," was the quiet reply.

" Quite so," acquiesced Jack. " There is nothing a son could do that could repay the love of a good mother."

Jack's eyes glistened, and his voice had a tremor in it which did more to raise him in Mr. Martin's estimation than the most eloquent speech could have done. There was a more kindly tone in his voice as he said—

" I am glad to hear that you believe that, Mr. Landale."

" I am aware that I have hardly acted up to my belief, Mr. Martin. But the circumstances were peculiar. Are you aware why I left my home?"

" Lady Walgrove has told me."

" I swore never to return while my stepfather lived, you see, and—well——" Jack hesitated and was silent.

" Mr. Landale, it is neither for me to question your motives, nor to express any opinion upon your conduct. I am charged by Lady Walgrove with a duty which I am only too glad to fulfil."

THE NEVER-NEVER LAND

Jack had impressed the old lawyer in a manner which surprised him. He was deeply prejudiced against him before his arrival. He expected to meet a drunken, dissolute blackguard, reckless and heartless. He had encountered many in his business. Scores of such cases had passed through his hands. Sons of wealthy parents who, having disgraced themselves and their families at home, were sent out to Australia to hide their misdoings and save their relatives the shame of meeting them. Mr. Martin had many wastrels on his books to whom he was deputed to pay monies, on condition that they remained in Sydney. There are so many hundreds of these vagabonds in every large city in the Colonies—and in Australia particularly—that they are classed and known as " Remittance men." These fellows turn up regularly and eagerly on remittance-day to receive the allowance meted out to them, instantly to disappear and gamble or drink it away in a few days; cadging, borrowing, or swindling until their next receiving date arrives.

These creatures are a nuisance to Australia and a disgrace to England. The practice of dumping all that is depraved and vicious into the Colonies is one to be most severely condemned. They are the cause of half the offences perpetrated against the laws there. Men are sent from home because they are useless and a nuisance, and they are not, as a rule, improved by the change. If they were compelled to earn their living, it would not be so bad; but the mistaken kindness of allowing them enough to live on robs them of the incentive as well as the necessity for work. They simply loaf from one drinking-bar to another, sinking lower and lower in the moral and social scale themselves, and dragging others down with them. They haunt the hotels where new-comers from England are staying, using their credentials of birth and connection as a means of provoking pity, lying as to their condition and circumstances, and borrowing money on notes of hand that they never dream of taking up, or on promises they never intend to redeem. Too often they are sons of reputable and well-known fathers, whose names are used as a guarantee for monies obtained by them. Sometimes orders to those fathers to refund the amounts they extort from the unwary are given, which are naturally and very properly repudiated. For the one genuine case of undeserved hardship for young arrivals in the Colony, there are ninety-nine impostors. They are a curse to the Colonies, to their families, and themselves. Parents may be sure, if their sons will not work and live honestly and cleanly at home, that they will never do it in Australia while they can beg, borrow, or steal enough to keep body and soul together. Decent Australians loathe and despise them, and they, in return, do nothing but abuse and decry the country and its people. More bad feeling towards Englishmen is aroused by these parasites in a month than can be allayed by their more reputable countrymen in a year. They are a cause of incessant friction between the native-born Australians and the settled English, while they are a pest to governors, consuls, and all Government officials. Trust a tramp, swagger, sundowner, penniless gaol-bird, but never trust a " Remittancer" is the advice of all who know the tribe.

If parents want to kill the future of their sons, to make the chance of their redemption utterly impossible, they cannot do better than to send them to the Colonies and allow them enough to live upon. Let them work as scavengers, labourers, sandwich-board men—any occupation at home, so that it entails labour—they may improve sometimes. As " Remittancers," never.

It was a being of this stamp that Mr. Martin expected to meet in Jack. He knew the species thoroughly. Hence his surprise on finding that Jack was a clean, reputable, wholesome, and seemingly honest and lovable man. It was thus that Jack impressed all with whom he came in contact. What puzzled the lawyer was the apparent want of sympathy with his mother and sister. He knew, of course, that Landale had not written to them for years, for the portrait of Jack that he had sent home was unaccompanied by a line of writing save that which appeared on the back of it, viz.: "Your loving son, Jack." This bespoke a carelessness, if not callousness, that seemed utterly foreign to the kindly-natured man who sat before him. Certainly he could not understand it. Jack had disarmed his suspicions by his naturally honourable bearing and manner, and it never entered his mind to doubt that it was Landale who was speaking to him.

"I quite understand that my conduct must appear strange and, to some extent, unaccountable, Mr. Martin; but there have been reasons which no longer exist, that made it kinder, perhaps, to—well, cut adrift from those dear people altogether. Young men form ties, and—and——" Here Jack was getting on dangerous ground, and he hesitated and paused.

"Ah! Some woman—some disreputable connection," thought the astute lawyer. But he did not say so; he contented himself with remarking, in a kindly manner—

"Whatever that reason may have been, Mr. Landale, I am glad for your own sake, and for the sake of your mother and sister, that it no longer exists, and that you can now go home and be a comfort to them."

"I hope and trust I may prove that," replied Jack, so earnestly that the clever but kindly lawyer was touched and moved.

"And now, how did you discover my whereabouts? He—that is—I mean—I passed as Landon." Here, again, was extremely thin ice. Did Mr. Martin know that a man called Landon had been sentenced to imprisonment, had escaped, and had now a reward for apprehension hanging over his head? If he knew, did he associate that man with himself, and, if he did, would he move in any way to help, or evade the law?

As a matter of fact, Mr. Martin had utterly forgotten the bank robbery and all connected with it. He was not a criminal lawyer, and took little interest in criminal cases. Jack was safe so far.

"I found you out through an accident. A client of mine had some dealings with a man named Thompson, a selector of Woolloogolonga, whom you know. This client wanted to take over Thompson's place, and went up to make inquiries, and look it over. He learned from Thompson that three or four men had his permission to live on the ground rent-free, and among them he mentioned Landon. The similarity of the names struck me, and I sent on the letters. You exactly resemble the portrait sent home, a copy of which I got from Talma; here it is."

Mr. Martin opened a drawer, and took out a photograph of Jack as he appeared before he grew his beard.

"You have grown a beard since then, Mr. Landale, but that does not disguise you from me, nor did it from my client, who recognised it immediately as the man he had seen at Woolloogolonga Gully."

Here was a puzzle for Jack. Had this client seen him or Landale? He might refuse to recognise him as the same man.

"Who, and where is this client?" asked Jack. "I should like to meet him."

"His name is Carter, and he is now in Queensland," replied Mr. Martin.

Jack and Tom breathed more freely.

"Now, Mr. Landale, as I have another engagement, let us settle what is necessary as quickly as we can. You want money, I suppose? How much?"

"Five hundred pounds will do, I fancy. I have a few accounts to settle, and the passages to pay. I can hardly do with less."

"Mr. Landale, you can as easily have five thousand as five hundred pounds. It is your own money. I will write the cheque, and send my clerk round to the bank with you, to save you the trouble of identification."

This Mr. Martin did, and after a few other details had been settled, Jack and Tom left the lawyer's office and went to the bank.

As they passed the offices of the newspapers, the crowds gathered round them recalled the fact that an international cricket match was being played. Large placards, on which were the names of the cricketers, were in the windows, with blank spaces for movable numbers. Every run was instantly telegraphed from the ground to the office, and immediately registered on the placard, cheer after cheer going up when some favourite cricketer made an addition to his score. Patiently in the broiling sun did these enthusiasts, pestered by the flies and dust, watch the progress of the game, as reported in the windows. No one passed who did not pause to see the state of the score.

After leaving the bank, securing their passages to San Francisco, and making some necessary purchases, the two friends drove up to the cricket ground.

An international Cricket Match in Australia is well worth seeing. It is played on a beautiful ground, before an assemblage often numbering over thirty-five thousand people, the larger number of whom are charmingly-dressed ladies. When the friends arrived on the ground it was crowded. Stand after stand looked like huge baskets of flowers, the variegated costumes blending their colours in harmonious accord, while the constant movement of thousands of different-tinted fans gave the effect of clouds of butterflies hovering over the blossoms. An Australian girl is the keenest critic on cricket that exists anywhere. She is an authority on all its science, understands to a nicety all its details, and her excitement over a closely-contested international match is delightful to witness. She is taught to play the game in the schools, and there is not a point scored or missed that escapes her keen and critical eyes.

After the loneliness of the bush, the sight of the immense concourse of people struck the two friends into silent wonderment. The attitude of the crowd, too, is one to excite the deepest interest. They are there for cricket, and they watch the game in breathless suspense and silence, broken with a roar of applause at a good hit or fine bit of fielding.

"What a wonderful sight, Jack!" said Tom. "What a curious people we are! Here are thousands of men who have left their business to sit in the blazing sun to see these fellows rush about after a leather ball; and all these pretty girls really interested in the game, and understanding it, too! Where outside of the British Dominions could such a thing happen? We are certainly a strange race."

"We may be," replied Jack. "At all events, here are nearly forty thousand people doing no harm to anything or anybody, except to their business and their complexions. There is nothing degrading in the exhibition, if there is nothing ennobling in it. At least it is better than torturing unhappy bulls and disembowelling a lot of worn-out horses. If it is not an intellectual sport, it certainly is an innocent one. Our national game is probably less harmful to the players and spectators than any sport in the world."

The two friends thoroughly enjoyed the unique scene, and for a time Jack almost forgot his troubles in watching it.

In the evening they had a sail in the glorious harbour. Sydneyites may be forgiven their love and enthusiasm for this wonderful series of land-locked bays. Wherever the eye is turned, it is greeted by scenes of exquisite beauty. On a fine day the sky is blue, the water a deep sapphire, the cliffs brownish-white, the foliage a dark green; the well-built houses are beautifully placed in every direction, many white, with red roofs, bringing instantly into mind scenes in Italy and the Riviera of the south of France, which it rivals, and sometimes outshines.

Thoroughly tired out with the excitement of the day's work, the two friends went to bed, and slept, undisturbed even by visions of Mr. Grimes, who snored in drunken stupor but a few yards away from them.

CHAPTER VII

THE COMING OF WONG

THE next morning dawned terribly hot. There was a wind blowing, but it came laden with the heat of the northern deserts, where the aboriginals were dying of thirst and starvation; where, in rainless Queensland, out of a season's total of twenty-one millions of sheep, fourteen millions had perished from the same causes; where the heroic, if almost heart-broken, settlers had, in a gross rental of one hundred and twenty-five thousand pounds, a deficit of over one hundred thousand pounds.

Accustomed as they were to the hot sun of the northern bush, the damp heat of Sydney nearly prostrated the two men. Every window was closed to keep out the hot air, but still they felt half-stifled. It was one hundred and ten in the shade, and the humidity was that of an overheated vapour-bath. It was almost unendurable. But Sydney is a place of climatic surprises. There was a sudden lull—a stillness—a darkening of the sun—a vivid flash of lightning—a roar of thunder—a sudden rush of wind from the south, followed by a dust-storm, which filled the air and drove the people into door-ways and shops for shelter. Windows were blown in, chimney-pots and sign-boards hurled to the ground; horses were frightened, shying and bolting; the temperature fell in a few minutes from one hundred and ten to seventy-two. Hailstones, the size of pea-nuts, rattled on roofs, windows, and on the flying pedestrians, who were now shivering with the cold. Flash followed flash of forked and sheet-lightning, peal upon peal of roaring, crackling thunder deafened the ears. It was as if pandemonium had broken loose. A " southerly buster," as the natives call it, had arrived; that was all. Welcome, if somewhat

86

violent " southerly buster," you come suddenly and depart as quickly! You are a blustering, rowdy, noisy, dangerous article, but you are blessed among the blessed to any one who has sweltered for days in Sydney at one hundred and ten in the shade.

Jack threw open the windows of his room when the storm subsided, saying—

" The ' southerly buster' is busted, Tom. Come out on the balcony here and cool off. By Jove! but this is a relief indeed. Why, look! If there is not half an inch deep of hail still on the ground!"

Jack leaned over the balustrade of the balcony to look into the streets, and then gave vent to an exclamation of surprise. As well he might, for opposite to him, with the well-known open smile upon his yellow face, stood Wong.

" Look there, Tom!" he said.

" Well, I'm blest if it is not that imperturbable, immovable heathen Chinee, Wong! What is he doing, and how on earth did he get here?" Tom asked.

" I'll go down and see," said Jack. And he motioned Wong to remain where he was.

The caution was unnecessary. Wong would not have stirred for a week. He had been waiting for Jack ever since his arrival by the morning express.

" What the dickens do you want, Wong?" Jack queried, as he walked up to him.

The Chinaman smiled wider than ever, and answered—

" Wong no stopee Woolloogolonga now one Jackee go dead, and another Jackee go muchee long way off."

" Well, what do you want?"

" Wong wantee go away with Jackee—and wlork for him allee timee."

" Work for me! How?"

" Me washee-washee you—me cookee-cookee you—me dlessee-dlessee you—me allee samee eblerting you. Me wlant to go along o' you plitty bad."

Beckoning Tom to go down, Jack took the Celestial on into the Arcade and questioned him further.

"How did you pay your fare here, Wong?"

Wong smiled and said,—

"Railaway pleoples no askee Wong for flares—ley no see Wong—Wong lilly bit hidee, allee timee."

"How?"

"Me lidee on le axleys allee timee."

"Well, well, you blessed old fraud! You must be sore from head to foot," said Jack compassionately.

Wong's reply was to smile and gently rub himself.

"Here, go and get something to eat at one of your Chinese restaurants. But don't eat Sydney rats, Wong. They are too loud, even for a Chinaman. After your meal, get some decent clothes—English, mind—and come along here, and ask for—for—by Jove!"

Jack stopped. How was he to account to Wong for his change of name?

Tom saw the difficulty, and added—

"Ask for Mr. Thomas Hewley. And, see here, you blooming old pirate! Answer no questions, and say nothing—do you hear?—nothing of us to any one, or I'll tan your yellow hide into top-boots. Savee?"

"Wong savee welly muchee."

"See you do. And come back at four o'clock, see? One—two—three—four."

"Wong clum backee—one—two—three—four times all along."

"No, you blessed old Mongolian! Come one time only, at four o'clock. Savee now?" asked Tom.

"Me muchee allee lightee now," replied Wong.

"Now, go and eat, wash, and get your new clothes," said Jack, as he handed the delighted and astonished Wong five sovereigns. "Off you go, and don't forget four o'clock."

Wong smiled, and shuffled quickly off down Castlereagh Street towards the Chinese quarter, and the friends returned to their rooms.

"Well, well, isn't that like a Chinaman? He's bilked the railway people without a qualm of conscience, and yet he is faithful enough to me to risk his neck to follow me. How did he find out I was staying here?" asked Jack.

"From some of his countrymen who wash or work for the hotel, most probably," answered Tom. "A Chinaman will find out anything he wants to discover. But what are you going to do with him?"

"Take him with me. He'll make an invaluable servant, and, as I shall want one who will be faithful, and never gossip, I consider Wong a real good find."

Wong was punctual to a minute. Tom was waiting for him, and hardly recognised him. Wong had on a quiet suit of English cut, navy blue, a stiff white shirt and collar, a black tie, and a hard bowler hat. Leading him to Jack's room, he left him and Jack together.

"And now, Wong, do you know where I am going?" asked Jack.

Wong shook his head, and said "No."

"Allee samee where I go?"

"Allee samee—Wong go along—allee timee."

"Why do you want to go along with me?"

Wong smiled, but made no reply.

"Is it because I shall pay you plenty money?"

"Wong no wantee plenty money. Me go along—welly lilly dollars."

"I may go all round the world."

"Allee samee."

"Where did you first see me?"

"Me first see you in Slan Flancisco."

"What?" asked Jack in amazement. "In San Francisco?"

Wong gave an assenting nod of the head.

"When and where?"

"Long timee back—Market Street, F'lisco. Melican man tly to knifee Wong. Jackee plitty klick stlop Melican man—so." And Wong pantomimed the delivery of a straight left and the tumbling over of an imaginary antagonist.

Jack recalled the incident, which he had quite forgotten. A drunken bully had drawn a knife on a Chinaman against whom he had collided, in Market Street. The Chinaman had tried to avoid him, in vain. The ruffian blamed Wong for the collision, and would undoubtedly have stabbed him but for Jack. Wong had been drawn to Jack by that strong personal magnetism which so strangely attracted almost all who came in contact with him; had watched him often, and had done many little things for him at odd times. All this had passed out of Jack's mind, but Wong had remembered.

"Why the dickens didn't you tell me this at Woolloogolonga?" asked Jack.

"Jackee no talkee—Wong no talkee."

The extraordinary reticence of the average Chinaman—out of his own circle, at least—has often been commented upon. Here was this strange creature content to follow the man who had saved his life from San Francisco to Australia—for that is what Wong had actually done, taking a passage steerage on the same vessel, after exchanging the certificate for landing with a fellow-countryman. This is habitually practised, the difficulty of distinguishing one Chinaman from another making the fraud easy.

"Well, well, well!" mused Jack. "Then you followed me here?"

Wong nodded his head.

"When?"

"Allee samee boatee—*Moana.*"

"Well, if you are not the most mystifying creature I ever met, I have certainly forgotten who is," said Jack, regarding Wong curiously.

Wong smiled.

"How did you know I had come on here?"

"Smludgee tellee Wong."

"How is Smudgee?"

"Smludgee lilly sick."

"What is the matter?" asked Jack anxiously.

"'Cos Jackee go alonga away."

"Poor little woman!" Jack sorrowed to think she was grieving for him, but it could not be avoided. He determined to write to her that very day, and expend some of the first of the money he received out of the estate in purchasing presents for her and her mother.

As to Wong, Jack had already decided. He was just the sort of servant he wanted. If he could be so silent for years on such a matter as he had now, for the first time, mentioned, there would be no fear of his gossiping over others.

"Well, Wong, we are off to-morrow back to San Francisco, in the *Alameda*. I must see about your passage and permission to land."

"Wong 'mission can get—no tlubble."

"Oh, indeed! You swoppee with another Chinee feller?"

"Yes, allee samee, for lilly few dollars."

"Well, I suppose that's all right for a Chinaman, but as you happen to be my servant, we'll act on the square allee samee, my faithful Mongolian," said Jack. "Now, give us a sample of your work. Packee allee my clothes. Savee?" And Jack pointed to a very disorderly array of wearing apparel, linen, boots, and shoes, which had been sent to him on his orders.

And Wong again astonished Jack by folding and packing the articles with a neatness and deftness that might have excited the envy of the valet of a fashionable Belgravian.

CHAPTER VIII

JACK GOES SHOPPING

JACK went off alone to Anthony's Stores, the Bon Marché or Whiteley's of Sydney, and, interviewing the head of the Ladies' Costumes Department, told her of his desire to provide an outfit for two ladies. Describing the general appearance of Sal and Smudgee, he asked her to do her best as to colour, style, and approximate fit.

"What do you wish me to send?" asked the manageress, not at all averse to prolonging her interview with handsome Jack.

"Well—dresses, &c. &c. The usual things—such as—well, you know—such as ladies generally wear," was the slightly indefinite and vague reply.

The manageress, with truly feminine love of seeing mere man floundering in his masculine ignorance, urged him on to further confusion by saying—

"Well, ladies wear so many things."

"Exactly! That's what I mean," stammered Jack. "I want them to have all of them."

"Rather a large order, sir. 'All of them!' I'm afraid you hardly know what that means."

"No, I'm sure I do not," blushed Jack. "Well, don't send all. Send enough."

The manageress was smiling. Certainly, Jack was entertaining. His honest, handsome face was blushing beneath the tanned skin. He was fidgeting and stammering. He looked so deliciously helpless that not only the manageress, but several other young ladies came up, stared at him, whispered amongst themselves, and seemed so deeply interested that Jack felt very like giving in and running away. However, his affection for Smudgee gave him courage, and he stuck to his guns. The manageress and the other ladies formed themselves into a small committee, and talked things over, leaving poor Jack standing wonderingly, uncomfortable, as strange and previously unheard-of articles were mentioned and discussed by the now excited fair ones. Woman-like, they all wanted to shop for Jack themselves. This lady suggested one thing—another something else. "What were the queer things they were talking of?" Jack asked himself. It was an awful time for him. The ladies would get their heads together in a little circle, all talk at once, then turn and stare at him—smile, and get their heads together again. Then the manageress asked him sweetly—

"I suppose you would like two or three sets of each?"

"Eh? Oh yes, of course; two sets of each."

What were "each"? Oh! If he could only get out of this, never would he go into a ladies' department again as long as he lived! He must end it. With all the dignity left in him, and with truly masculine helplessness, he said—

"Will you kindly let me have the bill, please?"

This was too much for the ladies, and they burst into merry laughter. Jack failed to see the joke, and made matters worse by saying he was really in a hurry and must have the bill at once.

Never did the ordering of one trousseau occupy such a little time—and Jack was ordering two. He was looking so obviously unhappy that sheer womanly pity awoke in the bosoms of the fair ones, and quickly a long list—a very long list—of articles was made, which Jack barely looked at and determinedly declined to read through. There was another delay while the prices were settled and the bill was prepared. Then the names had to be given for the different articles—Miss Lucy Landon this, Mrs. Landon that. Scores of parcels, baskets, boxes, &c. &c., were to be divided between mother and daughter. But they were getting on, and Jack was beginning to breathe a little more freely, when the manageress threw him back into dire confusion by opening various card-board boxes and disclosing some dainty, lace-trimmed, essentially feminine articles, saying—

" Of course you'll see the things, sir ?"

" No, no! I'm d—— that is, I'd rather not—I mean, I haven't the time. Please tell me what the total is."

The total was of a nature to astonish Jack, and send him on another visit to Martin & Martin's and the Bank of New South Wales.

The rest of the day was spent in letter-writing, preparations for the voyage, in paying into the Bank of New South Wales a hundred pounds to the account of Sal, and another interview with Mr. Martin.

On Wednesday, Jack, Tom, and Wong sailed from Sydney in the *Alameda,* en route for San Francisco.

CHAPTER IX

IN WHICH SMUDGEE FINDS A RELATION

WHEN Smudgee fell fainting, after parting with Jack, Wong had gone to her assistance. When she recovered, it was to see his kindly face looking down upon her.

" Lilly better now ?" he asked.

" Wot's 'appened, Wong?" said Smudgee weakly, sitting up and holding her head, which was throbbing with pain.

" Me not know. Me see you allee tum-lee down when Jackee go along."

" Yus ; that's it ! Jack has gorne, Wong—gorne away !" And Smudgee sat with her chin on her hands, looking very white and wan. " 'E's gorne, an' is never comin' back. 'E's gorne ! 'E's gorne ! The train is gorne !"

Wong's face wore an expression, for once, of a quite decided kind. It was one of the deepest concern and grief.

" Where he gone along ?" he asked eagerly.

" Dunno. I dunno," wailed Smudgee. " 'E said 'e was goin' out o' the bush for ever, an' 'e went."

" You plitty better now ?"

" I'm all right now," answered Smudgee, in a dull, apathetic way.

" Len Wong go allee along plitty klick—bym-bye." And without another word, he shuffled off into the bush.

Learning that Jack had gone to Thompson's, he hurriedly got his belongings together, and followed him there—only to learn he had left for the railway station in Thompson's trap. Without the slightest hesitation, he started to walk through the bush after Jack ; but, when he arrived, the train had departed. Learning that Jack had booked to Sydney, he determined to follow him. This he managed by concealing himself on goods-trucks, and riding under the carriages on the axles or buffers, or in any other way that chance provided, getting off before the train stopped, and waiting his opportunity of slipping on again before it started.

Worn out and sore, he arrived in Sydney, and, going to the Chinese quarter, learned from a laundryman—a fellow-countryman—that a person resembling Jack was stopping at the Hotel Australia. He immediately took up his post opposite the hotel entrance, and so caught sight of Jack on the balcony, as already described.

When Wong left her, Smudgee walked slowly and disconsolately home. How changed it all seemed now! Her father dead—Jack gone away! All the light seemed to have gone out of her little world, and she was in darkness. Her mother was sitting outside the hut, in a furious temper, with no one on whom she could vent it. She turned upon Smudgee angrily—

"Where yer been ter all day, eh? Don't yer know I'm all alone 'ere, eh?"

"Yus, I know, well enough—and you ain't the only one," said Smudgee mournfully. "I'm alone too. Jack's gorne."

"I could ha' told you that. I know it well enough. I—I——" And she paused. The expression of Smudgee's face was so piteously sad that her anger subsided, and she continued, in a tone almost of tenderness—

"Well, don't fret about it. It can't be 'elped. He's gone—and a good riddance!"

"'Old yer tongue!" said Smudgee fiercely. "'Old yer tongue if yer can't say nuffin' good about 'im. 'E was our best friend—your best friend—best friend of 'im as is gone—an' we shall never git another like 'im. 'Ullo! Wot der yer want 'ere?" she suddenly exclaimed. And Sal looked up to see Nat standing looking at them both.

"Wot do I want? I wants somethin' to eat and drink —and I want it pretty quick. Wot yer got?"

"Nuffin' fur you, so git out," replied Smudgee. "An'

git out quick, or you'll be moved out. So go afore there's trouble."

" I go wen yer mother tells me—not afore, my young friend. An' I don't think that'll be in a hurry, either."

" Tell this sundowner to 'ump 'is bluey somewhere else—an' 'ump it quick. We don't want none o' 'is sort 'angin' round us."

" Mind yer own business!" snapped out Sal. " 'E'll stay 'ere as long as I like. It ain't none o' yer affairs. Go an' make some tea, an' come an' tell me when it's ready."

" Oh! that's it, is it?" asked Smudgee, in contemptuous anger.

" Yus, that's it. An' let's 'ear no more tork about it. Go an' do it," said Sal.

" I'll go and make the tea ; but if that fly-blown swagger thinks I'm goin' to wait on 'im again, 'e's mistook. This ain't a 'otel for busted sundowners like 'im, an' if it wur, I ain't goin' to do the waitin'." And Smudgee, with a look of intense scorn at the dilapidated Nat, went into the hut.

" You've brought 'er up beautifully, Sal ; there's no gittin' over that. She's a credit ter yer."

" Never mind whether she is or not—you ain't been much troubled by 'er, anyway," sourly retorted Sal. " Wot's yer come back fur?"

" Fust place, 'cos I'm your lovin' 'usband, an' the only one yer got at present—must make yer feel kind o' lonesome, arter bein' accustomed to two! Second place, 'cos I'm starvin' and want some tucker. So, if yer don't mind, I'll go inside an' nibble a bit o' somethin', while our obedient daughter boils the bloomin' billy."

They both entered the hut, to Smudgee's intense annoyance. The billy, or kettle, was boiling upon the fire, and she was putting the tea into the pot.

Eyeing Nat with supreme disdain, she poured the hot water upon the leaves, saying—

" There! I've made the tea. 'Elp yerself, an' much good may it do yer! If yer can take yerself off when yer've 'ad it, do. An' when yer've gone, I'll come back and clean the room up. It'll want it."

Smudgee went out, and her mother saw her no more for some hours.

Nat chuckled as Smudgee left the room, remarking—

"Well, as I said afore, she is an 'ot un, is my daughter Loocy. I've 'eard people say as 'ow blood will tell. I believe it. There's all my spirit of independence in that gal. Wot I likes is, there ain't no bloomin' prewaricatin' about 'er. She sez wot she means, an' means wot she sez. Just like me. I can see myself exackerly in that bloomin' kid. Tell yer wot, Sal. Me an' 'er'll git on like a 'ouse afire arter we've been together a month or two," said Nat, helping himself to a huge piece of damper.

"Wot yer mean by a month or two? Do yer think yer goin' ter stop 'ere?"

"Not much I don't. But I think you an' me is goin' ter chum up agin. Yer a fine woman yet, Sal; a bit heavier, but a fine woman still, an' it's quite like ole times seein' yer sit there at the 'ead of my table. Ye'll sit there many a day yet—but not 'ere, old gal—not if Nat knows 'is little self. We'll 'ump ourselves down to Sydney, if you please; but by rail, my gal, by rail."

"Ah! and where's the fares to come from?" asked Sal, who was quietly waiting for Nat to indicate what he intended doing.

"The fares'll come from you. You've got a quid or two, I'll bet. Fust thing we'll do'll be to get to the nearest telegraph office, an' wire to Sydney as 'ow Jack Landon, *alias* Jack Mowbray, is ter be 'ad fur the askin' at Woolloogolonga Gully; and that nets us a clean 'undred quid—which'll be a pretty fair starter."

"If you ever dare to 'arm a 'air o' 'is 'ead," said Sal threateningly, "I'll—I'll——" And Sal, like many another prophet of what might, or was going to, happen, stopped on the threshold of her prophecies and was silent.

"You seem pretty badly struck on that Jack Mowbray, seems ter me," Nat growled.

"Look 'ere, Nat, Mowbray is——"

Here she was interrupted by a " Coo-ee!" and, going to the door, saw one of Thompson's stockmen coming towards her with a letter.

" Well, wot is it?" she asked.

" Mr. Thompson sez, ' Tyke this ter Mrs. Landon, and tell 'er Mr. Mowbray said she would 'ear from 'im again at Sydney Post-Office,' " replied the man, with that indescribable, half-cockney accent and tired drawl of the uneducated Australian. The denizens of Whitechapel or the now happily-extinct Seven Dials never did, nor never could eclipse this dialect.

Sal hastily opened the letter the stockman brought her, and uttered an exclamation of delight, for in it were four five-pound notes of the Bank of New South Wales.

" See here, Nat," she exclaimed, " there are two reasons why you won't interfere with Jack Mowbray. One is that he's gorne away, and another is that we'll get a 'undred pounds to let 'im alone. Here's twenty from him, to begin with. And he sez, ' I'll find plenty more awaitin' me as long as I behaves meself and is good ter Smudgee.' "

" Wot? Twenty quid! Ah! Let me look—let me feel 'em in my own hands—only let me feel 'em! Oh! ain't they just 'eavenly to the touch! The blessed mother o' New South Wales, let me kiss the face of yer!" And Nat rubbed the crisp notes on his dirty and evil-looking face.

Sal watched him with undisguised contempt. Her association with Landon and Jack had taught her something, if very little. She missed the refinement inherent in both—their easy grace and mutual contempt of money. Nat's grasping greed disgusted her. She did not find her first husband improved by his absence. Save that he was of use to her, she would have found means to have got out of his way, but he was likely to be of help, and she intended to avail herself of his services. She snatched the notes from Nat's hand, exclaiming—

" Hand them over. They are mine, if you please."

" Well, ain't we goin' 'arves, Sal? Yer ain't goin' ter be stingy ter yer lovin' 'usband, are yer?"

" No, I ain't," retorted Sal. " I'm goin' ter 'elp yer to a lot, but you'll 'ave ter do somethin' fur it."

" Course I will. You bet! But wot's 'e sent yer this fur? Wot's 'e goin' ter send yer more fur?"

" That's wot I want ter know. 'E said as 'ow the widow and daughter of 'is old chum should never want for anything," answered Sal.

" That's all right, but where'll 'e get the money from? Has 'e struck it rich out 'ere?"

" No; 'e's been workin' with Landon for years, an' they neither of 'em 'ad any luck. There's somethin' at the bottom of this business that we've got ter find out; an' if you've got any sense you'll keep straight and 'elp me to do it."

Nat's evil eyes glistened as Sal told him of the inheritance that Landon had spoken of; of the letter he had received; of her suspicions of what it might have contained; of its disappearance and her belief that it was in Jack's possession.

" It's a 'undred to one that's why 'e skipped so quickly," said Nat, who was clever and cunning, as Sal knew.

" That's my idea too."

" 'Old on!" Nat continued. " This wants a bit o' thinkin' over. If there should be any fortune left to Landon, you—'Ev 'e left a will?"

" Not a scrap of paper, as far as I know. I've searched all over."

" Then all 'is property would go to 'is heirs, eh?"

" That's it," answered Sal; " that's just it!"

" Which would be his wife and daughter?"

" Naturally. Mrs. Landon and her daughter Loocy."

The expression of Nat's face grew, if possible, more cunning than ever as he continued—

" Which is you and your daughter—if—if——"

" Exactly—if you hadn't married me first."

Nat uttered an oath, and said—

"Blast them marriages! They *never* come to any good. Wot wus we fools enough to go and string ourselves up like that fur?"

The two whom "Heaven had joined" were quite in sympathy over this matter. Sal was mentally cursing herself for that same act of folly, now bitterly repented.

"Well, we must have been a pair o' mugs."

"So useless! And it cost a quid too."

"Well, of all the bloomin' jugginses! The only excuse we've got is that we wos both blind drunk."

After a pause, in which their evil brains were both working in their separate ways—Sal's slowly and ponderously, Nat's quickly and alertly—Nat whispered—

"Sal, there's not so many as knows it. No one in England, I should say. Wot prevents my bein' yer brother an' workin' the thing out between us?"

"Yer've 'it it, Nat! But you'll 'ave to act square all through."

"Wot yer mean?"

"I mean that it's a big thing, and I ain't a-goin' ter give away chances. Yer'll have ter be my brother—and nothin' else. Smudgee 'as eyes in the back of 'er 'ead. We can't do without 'er in this business, an' she'd blow the 'ole thing in a minute if she got 'old of it. Yer'll 'ave ter act square—deal square—all through; square ter me an' square ter Smudgee. Now you've got it."

Nat was far too clever not to see the wisdom of this advice, and he made no show of disagreeing with it.

"Right, old gal! You've got a better 'ead-piece on yer than yer used to 'ave. You're as right as rain, and square it shall be."

Nat's declaration immensely relieved Sal's mind, for she still had that wild, unreasonable hope that if she got this fortune she could yet bring Jack to her side.

"Yer right, Sal; dead right. An' this werry night we'll tell Smudgee she's found a' uncle, which 'is name is Nat Berker."

THE NEVER-NEVER LAND

Meanwhile Smudgee, all unconscious of the coming increase in her family, was lying brooding dismally in the scrub, some distance from the hut. How her little life had changed in a few hours! Before her father's death she had practically no cares. Her parents' lapses from sobriety affected her but little. She had seen the shearers and stockmen often the worse for drink; it was no special sin in her eyes. She was as free as a bird to come and go into the bush, within certain limits; and she had Jack to teach her to read and write, tell her fairy stories, of which he had an unlimited store, and for which she had a never-waning interest. She was happy. And now? What was there to live for? Her mother? She knew that without some restraining influence she would be seldom sober, and, under the influence of alcohol, Sal's temper was not lamb-like. She knew, too, that her mother would never stop in the bush, but would go to a town where there would be no difficulty in obtaining drink; and they would be cooped up in some small, ill-smelling room or house, away from any surroundings that were pleasant to look upon or live among. And this evil-looking sundowner, who was he? He was not hanging round for any good purpose. Oh, if Jack were but here to advise her! What was this man to her mother? When her mother told her he was a stranger, she knew that she was lying. The man spoke to her mother with authority, and with the manner of an old acquaintance; and had he not said that " he would not leave until her mother insisted upon it, and he didn't think that would happen in a hurry"? Oh, where was Jack? Why couldn't she run away and find him? She was a girl —that was why. If she only knew whose fault *that* was, she would have something to say to the delinquent concerning it! The fact of her being a girl had robbed her of Jack. He had said that was the reason she could not go with him. And so Smudgee's thoughts ran on, until, in her excitement and loneliness, she called aloud—

" Jack, come back! Do! If yer don't, I shall die. I can't stand it."

SMUDGEE FINDS A RELATION

Sound travels easily in the silent bush, and her voice was heard by Sal, who exclaimed—

" Whoever's that gal torkin' to ?" Going to the door, she gave a loud " Coo-ee !" which Smudgee refused at first to reply to, saying to herself, " Oh, you coo-ee away and be blest! I ain't agoin' to answer !" But, as her mother repeated the summons, and was coming directly towards where she was lying, Smudgee rose, and said ill-temperedly—

" Well, wot is it now ?"

" Yer jest come in, will yer ?"

" Wot fur ?"

" I'll tell yer when yer come."

" 'As that blessed sundowner 'umped 'is bluey yet ?"

" No, 'e ain't; and wot's more, 'e ain't agoin' to, neither. You jest come along, miss, without any more nonsense !" And Sal took the reluctant Smudgee by the arm and led her to the hut, where her newly acquired relative was awaiting her.

" So yer still 'ere, are yer ? Seems ter me, any man would 'ump it when he wus told straight he was not wanted. Wot right hev you to come and plant yerself on us like this ?" queried the scornful and indignant Smudgee.

" Tell 'er wot right, Sal," suggested Nat.

" Well, the fact is, he's yer Uncle Nat," stammered Sal.

" 'E's my uncle wot ?" asked the now astonished Smudgee.

" Yer Uncle Nat."

" So 'e's my Uncle Nat, is 'e ? 'Ow long's 'e bin my Uncle Nat ?"

" All your blessed life, my little pet," drawled Nat.

" 'Ow'd yer come ter recklect it ? Seems as if it 'ad struck yer sudden, don't it ? Yer didn't seem ter remember much about bein' my relation day afore yesterday. 'Ow's that ?" sneered Smudgee.

" Well, yer see a good deal 'appened day afore yesterday, an' there warn't no time," answered Nat.

"Oh, indeed! Wasn't there? 'I'm your Uncle Nat' is four words," and Smudgee ticked them off on her fingers. "And 'I'm a poor traveller, miss; an' I'm bushed, an' the bush is blazin', as you can see and smell, an' this kind-'earted lydy is goin' ter 'elp me 'cos I'm starvin',' is about thirty or forty. 'Ow'd yer find time to tell me that, eh?" And the sharp-witted Smudgee put her arms akimbo and stuck out her chin with a vigour that fairly staggered Nat and left him for a moment non-plussed. "Are you goin' ter answer?" asked the re-morseless Smudgee. "'Urry up, and don't make up any more lies than yer can 'elp, 'cos they don't take me in. I know yer!"

"Well, yer see, me little dear," Nat began. But Smudgee cut him short, saying—

"None o' that! I ain't yer little dear, and ain't likely ever ter be—uncle or no uncle. Now, if yer've made up yer bloomin' lies—and yer've taken yer time about it—let's 'ev 'em."

"Well, my little——"

"Wot?" blazed out Smudgee. "Little wot? Let's 'ev it! Little wot?"

"Little lydy."

"That's a bit better."

"Wot I was agoin' ter say when yer nearly snapped me nose orf wus that yer didn't give your poor old uncle much encouragement to tell yer who 'e wus, the day afore yesterday; an', come to that, yer ain't over-affectionate to-night. An', arter all, uncles is uncles—an' when one's got 'em, they 'as ter be put up with."

"Like measles, or 'oopin'-corf, eh? But, yer see, my good man, people as 'as sense don't go round a-huntin' for 'em, an' ain't too glad when they come unarsked."

And Nat began to realise, as many others had done before him, that Smudgee was by no means an easy young person to placate when justly incensed, nor a very gullible one. Smudgee was truthful herself, and was unpleasantly quick to detect falsehood in others. She did not believe in Nat's avowal; she was perfectly well aware that her mother and this stranger were bound by some tie of which she was ignorant, and she determined to quietly watch until she discovered what it was. Smudgee could be patient when she had an object to attain; and she had one now. A greater one than she knew of, or could even imagine.

CHAPTER X

IN WHICH MR. GRIMES BECOMES TROUBLESOME

THE A. & A. steamship *Alameda,* carrying Jack and Tom to San Francisco, was two days out to sea from Sydney.

The weather had been very rough, and most of the passengers preferred to hide their woes in the seclusion of their cabins. On the third day the sea was calmer. The morning dawned with a golden mist enveloping the whole of the ocean. The albatrosses had caught up with the ship in the night, and they were floating, skimming and soaring gracefully, and seemingly lazily, after and around it. The sailors were slushing and washing the deck. A passenger came out of a deck-cabin in his pyjamas, and yawningly inhaled the pure, fresh air; then stepped on the raised cover of the hatchway to avoid the stream of water from the hose. It was Tom.

Looking up, he softly anathematised the unfortunate fowls in the hen-coop placed on the roof of his cabin. The purser strolled up, with his pipe in his mouth, and saluted Tom with a cheery " Good morning."

" How did you sleep, Mr. Hewley?"

" I didn't sleep," replied Tom.

" Bad sailor, eh?" asked the purser, with an air of sympathy every ship's officer thinks fit to assume towards unfortunate passengers.

" No! I am not, but those wretched chickens are. They have kept me awake the whole night. Every bird must have been ill, and each was telling the other how bad it felt, and how they wished the wind would change, and what a pitcher the *Alameda* was. You never heard such a racket. Cluck! Cluck! Cluck! Schr-r-aw! Schraw!

Sch-sch-sch-r-r-r-aw!" mimicked Tom, giving an imitation of the sea-sick fowls which convulsed the purser, who, sleeping far away from the hen-coop, by design, could enjoy the joke of Tom's description, knowing he was secure from a like disturbance.

"See here," continued Tom, "I'll swop cabins with you. What do you say?"

"No, I think not," good-humouredly answered the purser; "unless you care to do my work. You see, all my papers and books would have to come with me, and your cabin wouldn't hold them."

"The cabin won't hold me much longer, if those birds don't get their sea-legs. Are they doing the whole journey to 'Frisco with us as passengers, or do we land them at Auckland?"

The purser's eyes twinkled as he answered—

"No! you will observe their numbers grow 'small by degrees and beautifully less.' Much depends upon the weather, and the appetites of the passengers. There are not so many now as there were, and there will be fewer still after dinner to-night. Mr. Hewley, you are a good trencher-man, I have noticed. You go on as you've begun, and that coop will soon be empty."

Tom made a wry face, and said satirically—

"Oh, thanks! Thanks very much; but I do not think I am quite so fond of chicken as I used to be," and went off to his bath.

As the day wore on, the decks were gradually peopled. Men and women crept up, one by one, looked round with a nervous, doubtful stare at sea and sky, hurriedly withdrawing their eyes from the bow of the boat, as she pitched rather low and soared a trifle high. It was a glorious morning, but still a little lively. The colour of the sea had changed from an emerald green to a bright blue. The passengers formed themselves into separate groups. Three middle-aged females sat with faces close together, whispering the current gossip of the ship. Characters and reputations were torn to shreds and tatters as, with evil eyes and tightly-drawn mouths, these tattle-mongers chattered on.

Leaning over the bulwarks was a party of men, telling funny stories. A little farther off, a green-and-yellow-faced young fellow was leaning over the bulwarks doing something else. By the midship-hatchway two young men were playing with two girls at deck-quoits. Farther up the promenade was another pair, engaged at shuffle-board. Two stewards appeared at the door of the saloon stairs, carrying an arm-chair, in which was seated a young soldier returning from Africa to his New Zealand home, helplessly crippled for life. He had been shot in the thigh; his horse had been killed, and had fallen on him. He had lain insensible all through a night; when found in the morning, he was paralysed from injury to the spine. He was handsome, dressed in khaki, and had a constant small crowd of sympathising young women round his chair. He was repeating, for the twentieth time, to the twentieth inquiring girl, how he was wounded and rescued. Like Othello, he was loved " for the dangers he had passed," and he was quite prepared to love the long line of Desdemonas, " that they did pity him." Children were playing and squabbling all over the deck. Demure maidens dropped books and handkerchiefs for willing swains to pick up and thus give opportunities for small flirtations. Hearty, healthy damsels, who ate voraciously in their cabins, picked daintily at tiny wish-bones of chicken and nibbled biscuits or dry toast handed to them by admiring manhood. Rugs that would flap in the wind had to be tucked under pretty feet. A handsome, half-caste Maori girl was smiling and showing a set of teeth that a duchess would have bartered a year's income to possess. A newly-married couple in the first stage of honeymoondom cooed and languished at each other in dreamy happiness. Flying-fish darted about, casting gleams of brilliant incandescence over the purple waters. A shoal of porpoises gambolled and frolicked round the vessel, mocking with their wonderful speed its comparative slowness. Some, swimming but a few feet ahead, seemed deliberately daring the sharp cut-water of the bow to catch them if it could.

Jack and Tom were leaning with their backs to the bulwark opposite the saloon entrance, when, to their horror, the red, pimply face of Mr. Grimes appeared, and Jack found that gentleman regarding him with a pair of fishy, puzzled eyes, in a drunken stare.

Jack's first impulse was to move away, an impulse he instantly checked. Mr. Grimes lurched unsteadily towards Jack, and said—

"Excoosh me; we've met before, I think?"

Jack drew himself up, and stared stonily at the man as he replied—

"I think not."

"Yesh, we hev—shertinly—wash yer name—eh? Tell us yer name."

The vessel rolled suddenly as Mr. Grimes asked this question, and shot him into Tom's arms. Tom got a good grip of him, ran him backwards with a little more force than was absolutely necessary up the deck, and landed him rather suddenly on a hard wooden bench. Mr. Grimes was a trifle shaken. Before he could collect his befuddled and scattered senses, Jack had strolled out of sight.

"Say—who's your friend?" spluttered Mr. Grimes.

"What friend?" queried the wide-awake Tom.

"Friend here jist now—friend I spoke to."

"Oh! That one? That's Captain Prisms, of the Royal Mounted Marines. He's just going to join his ship at Timbuctoo. He's very deaf, very dangerous, has just had scarlatina, and is sickening for the jim-jams. Take my tip and don't go near him; he's not safe," rattled out the lively, mendacious Tom.

Mr. Grimes' eyes rolled in a befogged endeavour to follow Tom's glib and rapid delivery. Failing to grasp its meaning, he fell back mechanically on his oft-repeated formula, and stuttered—

"Lesh have another."

"Well," assented the playful Tom, "just one more before we part. Let's go to the smoke-room."

"What's your favourite lotion?" inquired Tom.

"Branny—branny."

"Two brandies and a split soda," ordered Tom of the smoke-room steward.

"No—no—so—soda," hiccoughed Mr. Grimes. "Take mine neat—soda—spoils branny—no flavour—branny doesn't—bite—doesn't bite with soda."

Mr. Grimes was in a bad way. He had been steadily drinking for months, and for days had been swallowing raw spirits. Tom saw this, but had no particular desire to keep him sober. In fact, in Jack's interest, he was quite prepared, as he said, to fill Mr. Grimes up full and keep him so—if he could.

The purser, looking in at the smoke-room door, beckoned Tom out, and whispered—

"Mind what you are doing with that fellow, Mr. Hewley. He's a bad lot; had a pretty severe attack of delirium tremens last night. The doctor had to dose him. A little more of this kind of thing, and we shall have to put him in irons."

"Do, Mr. Purser, do. Put him in irons and keep him in 'em. He's a nuisance, and will be frightening all the women into hysterics. Put him in irons, and fasten them as tight as he is."

"We can't do that while he keeps quiet. The doctor has reported him to the captain, and he is being watched," replied the purser.

Tom left the wretched drunkard and went to find Jack, to whom he retailed what had passed between himself and Grimes. Jack could not resist expressing a wish that Mr. Grimes would be put in irons—at any rate, until they got clear of New Zealand. He suggested to Tom that he should ask the purser where Mr. Grimes was going. Tom asked, and found to his dismay that he was booked through to San Francisco. Jack discussed with his friend the advisability of forfeiting their passages, landing at Auckland, and taking another steamer later on.

However, Mr. Grimes settled their difficulty in his own peculiar way. He drank steadily on until the purser ordered the bar-steward to refuse to serve him. This so enraged the half-crazy man that he created a disturbance and was put out of the smoke-room. He reeled to a chair on deck and sat quite quiet for a moment. Then, as if possessed by some demon, he rose and, striking an unoffending, unprepared passenger who was in his way a violent blow in the face, he ran to the bulwark rails, and, before any one could stop him, leaped overboard. Without a moment's hesitation Jack sprang into the sea after him. There was a great shout of " Man overboard!" raised. The deck was crowded. All rushed to the side, but nothing was to be seen. The two men were already far astern. As soon as Jack came to the surface of the water, he swam away from the ship's side to clear the blades of the propeller, and then looked around him. At first he could see nothing of Grimes, who was in the trough of a wave, the crest of which Jack was mounting. He was a strong swimmer, and a few strokes brought him within reach of Grimes, whom he caught by the collar of his coat with his left hand. The madman struck at Jack, and then, clutching him by the waist and twisting his legs round him, dragged him under water. It was a terrible moment. Madness had given Grimes increased strength. Strong as Jack was, he could not shake him off. His breath was giving out. He must be free, or drown. Gathering together all his energies, he struck Grimes full in the face, again and again. The instinct of protecting himself made Grimes let go his hold, and, with a kick as he sprang upward to the light, Jack thrust the man from him. Coming to the surface he breathed once more, and again looked round for the drowning drunkard. Presently Grimes rose for the second time. Now Jack was more cautious. He swam to the back of Grimes, and, waiting a favourable opportunity, seized him by the hair, pulled him vigorously towards him, throwing Grimes upon his back. Floating, but kicking out strongly with his feet, he kept himself and the man from sinking. He could only see the sky, and knew nothing of the direction in which he was going. He knew it would take some time to lower a boat and row to him, as the *Alameda* was going at fifteen knots an hour, and the way upon her would take her far ahead. How long could he keep up the struggle? Not much longer, he feared. And then, the sharks with which these seas were infested! That was another horror. But it never entered his mind to abandon the poor maniac, who was now, fortunately, fast sinking into insensibility.

Still no sign of rescue. In the struggle below the surface Jack had swallowed a lot of water, and began to feel sick and dizzy. His arms and legs seemed to be weighted with lead. Every stroke was now less strong than the last and more painful to him. There was a rushing sound in his ears, then a ringing of church bells, a vision of a peaceful English village, a rush of old recollections, a dreamy sensation of far-away pain, a sudden darkness, and then—oblivion.

CHAPTER XI

THE moment Jack jumped overboard, Tom sprang to the side of the vessel, detached a life-buoy, and threw it after him. But Jack, who was already many yards away, did not see it. The captain turned his vessel round and steamed back. The way on the boat drove her past the men. A boat was lowered. Without waiting for permission, Tom jumped in, anxious to help in the rescue of his friend. The crew were pulling with all their strength towards Jack and Grimes, who were struggling for life a quarter of a mile astern. After rowing for a few minutes, Tom gave a startled cry, saying in a tone of dismay—

" My God! Look there!"

The men looked, and bent to their oars with renewed energy, for what they saw was the dorsal fin of a shark, slowly following in their wake a few boat-lengths away from them. Tom's face was ashen grey. The shark had probably noticed either the splashing of the men as they leaped into the sea or that of the boat, and was swimming in search of prey.

" Pull, for God's sake, boys!" cried Tom, in an agony of dread.

The men needed no urging. They knew that the lives of two fellow-creatures depended upon their exertions. At present the shark seemed content to follow them at a distance; but at any moment he might see the men, then nothing could save them.

Tom was standing up in the bow directing the rowers and steersman. He could now see Jack. He redoubled his cries and entreaties for them to hasten. Jack's strength seemed to him to be failing. Would the boat never reach him? Looking back, Tom saw to his increased terror that the fin of the shark was no longer visible. In which direction was it now going? Vainly Tom strained his eyes; he could see no trace of it. Nearer and nearer the boat was approaching the men. The tension was almost unbearable. Tom's heart was beating so violently that it almost stopped his breath. They were now within a boat's length. Tom was leaning over the side of the boat ready to grasp at his friend. They were alongside. Tom and one of the crew were stretching out their hands to seize the half-drowned men, when there was a piercing shriek, the two men suddenly went down, and the foam churned up by the propeller around the boat was reddened with blood. All were speechless and motionless with horror. Who had gone? One or both? Tom, recovering, looked down into the deep as far as he could. Was that something rising? Yes; the body of a man! Who was it? With a cry of joy, Tom recognised Jack.

"Quick, men, quick!" he shouted. "Bear a hand here!"

Two of the sailors started to Tom's help, and Jack was pulled on board, insensible, but alive and unhurt.

CHAPTER XII

JACK REVISITS AUCKLAND

THERE is much beauty in and around Auckland. The harbour is delightful. The view from Mount Eden is a glorious and weird one. The Mount itself is an extinct volcano. From its summit—the top of the crater—several other silent volcanoes can be seen. At the foot of this eminence are the pretty suburbs of Auckland; in the middle distance is the city, and beyond that the bays, the hills, and the gulf.

Jack, now fairly convalescent, strolled into the city. Nearing the square of the Art Buildings, Tom called out—

" Look, Jack! There's old Wong. Where is he off to ?"

" Going to hunt up some relations or countrymen; there are plenty of them up yonder. He'll be going to have a chin-chin with some of them, I expect."

What Wong was really doing ashore was the " hunting up" of some of his countrymen to assist him in acting as a bodyguard to Jack while he remained on shore. Wong feared his master's arrest.

However, Jack was not molested, and in a few hours they were again on board, and were sailing for Samoa. Out of the Colonies and under the American Stars and Stripes, Jack's fears of arrest were gone. He could breathe freely. He was safe.

As the land receded from sight, Wong came up to Jack and handed him his pocket-book.

" Where did you find this ?" asked Jack.

" Allee samee in clabin—soon no him find at all if leavee him along. Bletter purser him hab."

" Thanks, Wong. It was careless of me. I'll let the

purser take care of it." Going to the purser's room, Jack confided the pocket-book, which contained the money he had drawn from the bank in Sydney, to his keeping. While writing the receipt and placing the money in the safe, the purser said—

"That's a good Chinaman of yours, Mr. Landale."

"Indeed he is," Jack assented. "A real good one."

"I'll bet on that," continued the purser, "and I've had some experience with Chinamen, dead and alive."

"What do you mean by ' dead'?" asked Jack.

"Well, when I was on the *Goptic,* then in the China service between San Francisco and Hong-Kong, I had to carry one hundred and three dead Chinamen from 'Frisco to be buried in their own land. You see," the purser continued, lighting a long, fat cigar, " when a Chinaman dies there, they put him in their burial-ground until there are sufficient to make a consignment in bulk, as it were. The coffins are all most carefully numbered, and have the name and home address of the defunct Mongolian inscribed in Chinese characters on the outside. The longing for home burial is so strong in a Chinaman's breast that one of the first uses he makes of his savings is to insure the return of his body to China, in case of dissolution. On this particular trip, somehow or other, I lost one of the parcels. The one hundred and three dead passengers were reduced to one hundred and two. When the time came for their disembarkation, I discovered the loss and was in the dickens' own quandary, for I knew that there would be trouble. I handed out the hundred and two to their several relations, who carried them off to their last lodgings, and, meanwhile, instituted a vigorous search all over the hold for number one hundred and three. As ill-luck would have it, number one hundred and three's family were the first to arrive on our getting into port, and began their inquiries for their particular package almost before we had let go the anchor. As we swung the caskets up, in half-dozens at a time, this precious old family party would amble up and watch the operations, waddling to read the inscriptions as they were placed in long lines on the quay. As my consignments got nearer and nearer delivery, and there was no sign of their relation's case appearing, they eyed me with more and more malevolent interest. I began to ooze perspiration from every pore. Had the wretched old Mongolian 'goner' been a case of diamonds I could not have funked the loss more. What had become of the blamed thing?

" ' Number one hundred and one—number one hundred and two. All out !' shouted the supercargo. The bereaved Ching-Chings looked at me ferociously, and the head of the family, a wizened old fellow who looked like the carved head of an umbrella gone yellow with age and neglect, shuffled up to me and said, ' Nlumber one lundred and flee?' ' Well,' I swaggered, feeling deucedly uncomfortable. ' What about it?' ' Nlumber lundred and flee no hab got? Nlumber lundred and flee must hab got. Allee samee lemand note,' and he handed me the receipt for the wandering old corpse. It was right and regular enough.

" ' Yes, that's all right,' I said, as briskly and cheerfully as I could. ' Allee lightee! No, no allee lightee—me no lundred and flee hab got.' ' No, I know that. But we've got him away in a special place, to takee muchee care—see? Come along to-morrow, and hundred and three you get. Savee?' ' Lundred and flee me wantee now,' he squeaked. ' Yes, no doubt, but don't worry. You get him allee samee to-morrow. Come along at ten—no, say two. Savee? At two, and you get him allee lightee. Run along, I'm busy.'

" But run along they would not. They stuck to me like hungry leeches, followed me whenever and wherever I stirred. At last I went to the captain, and, confiding my troubles to him, asked him to order the whole family off the deck. He did so, but they all squatted down on their haunches, watching me anxiously from the dock. All over that blamed ship did we search, but never a hundred and three could we find. What had become of the departed, and whither he had departed, we could not find out.

"When darkness set in, I sneaked off in the boat and foraged out an old rascal of a dealer in Chinese curios, whom I had known and dealt with for some years, and asked him at what price he could supply a dead China-man. A sufficiently startling question even for a China-man, but my old acquaintance, Lung-Tong, never moved an eyebrow. All he said was, ' How longa him be dead?'

" ' Doesn't matter,' I answered. 'Anything over three months gone will do.'

" ' Allee lightee. Me get him.'

" ' What's the figure, old man?' I asked.

" ' Two hundred and fifty dollars.'

" ' Two hundred and fifty Chinese devils! Do you think that I am buying dead Chinamen at the price of Circassian beauties?' I roared. 'Fifty dollars is the last cent I'll give, and that'll take the gilt off half this voyage's gingerbread.'

" ' Flifty dollars no hab. Two hundred and flifty must hab—no tradee else.'

"Well, for two mortal hours did I do battle with that old scoundrel over the price of that heathenish corpse. At last, utterly worn out, and getting more and more into a funk for fear I should lose my billet, as I had lost the corpse, never again to recover it, I consented to give a hundred dollars, if the article was delivered on board before daylight next morning. Lung-Tong agreed, and I went back to the ship a little easier in my mind, if a little more uneasy in temper. There were the whole of the family still waiting their blessed old kinsman. They had never moved. About four in the morning a large crate arrived, under the convoy of Lung-Tong and four other Celestials. On unpacking it in the hold, there was the coffin, duly labelled one hundred and three, and, in Chinese figures, the deceased one's name and address, which they had copied from my list. I dirtied some of the newness off the characters, and bruised the case a bit, to give it an air of travel. When daylight came, only too anxious to be rid of the watching eyes of the family of 'a lundred and flee,' I had them aboard, and, handing him over, got my receipt.

"I asked the head of the family, pointing to the coffin—

"'Some relation?'

"'Y—les.'

"'Father?'

"'Nlo.'

"'Uncle?'

"'Nlo.'

"'What then?'

"'Me glan-mother.'

"'Great Scott!' I yelled. Rushing into my room, I locked myself in. His grandmother! Lung-Tong had sold me the remnants of a middle-aged man! How anxiously I prayed for the ship's departure, no one will ever know. As we cleared out, a mob of some two hundred Mongolians, naked to the waist and bent on trouble, rushed to the dock's edge, bearing sticks, and yelling for their 'glandmother.' I got transferred, and have never dared to show my nose near Hong-Kong since. I afterwards learned that the corpse Lung-Tong had sold me was own brother to the head of the family of the missing 'glandmother.' This, of course, would account for some of the excitement of his family on the wharf. What had become of 'glandmother' I never learned. Whether there had ever been a 'glandmother,' or, if there had, whether she had really embarked at 'Frisco, only the Joss of Josses could tell."

CHAPTER XIII

IN WHICH JACK'S PRESENTS ARRIVE

IT did not take Nat long to decide that the sooner he was in Sydney, the sooner he would be in a position to prosecute his inquiries about the Landale legacy. It is difficult to extract anything out of drought-parched gum-trees, but to drain information from them respecting landed estates sixteen thousand miles away is impossible. To Sydney he would go. There were all sorts of things in Sydney that appealed to Nat. He knew that there he could get water to drink, and even, if he desired it very much and had the wherewithal to pay for it, something a little stronger and more congenial to his palate. Then, there were certain attractions in the neighbourhood of Pitt Street, in very uncertain company, where a man of his parts and a well-lined purse could " do himself pretty well," that he had long longed to revisit.

Nat had gone through many things in his time, and many pockets. There were few things he liked better than winning at poker and picking a favourite at a ten-to-one chance. There was a little racecourse outside Sydney, where he was in the habit, in the old days, of not only picking the favourite but of what he called " stiffing it," which was to put obstacles in its way of winning. All sorts of little methods were employed for this purpose, none of which was too vile for the unscrupulous Nat.

Better than that did Nat like the higher game of Flemington and Randwick. But these required more capital than had been his for many a year. Jack's promise to provide for Sal and Smudgee, and the prospect of sharing in Landon's inheritance, opened boundless visions for his future. He saw himself an owner of racehorses which he could " run in and out," and " stiffen " or not, at will, to his own exceeding profit and amusement. Unlimited field-days of sport and measureless nights of dissipation were his, with a little trouble and patience. He was, in imagination, already in possession of the fortune; but it was borne in upon his mind that he must at least get to Sydney to enjoy it. In order to avoid the quick-eared Smudgee, he went off for a walk with Sal into the scrub, where they discussed their prospects and plans.

Meanwhile, Jack's presents, despatched to Woolloogolonga Gully, to the care of Mr. Thompson, were nearing Sal's hut.

Smudgee was sitting at the door, sadly ruminating over the loss of her father and her friend. When the cart containing Jack's purchases arrived at Sal's place, Smudgee came from the hut, and, looking at the large number of boxes and packages, asked the man in charge—

" Wot yer got there? Is Thompson's moving?"

" No; they's presents for you," was the answer.

" Presents for what?" asked the wondering Smudgee.

" 'Ere, ketch 'old," said the man, handing out hat-boxes, dress-baskets, paper parcels, one after the other, in such numbers that the astonished Smudgee fairly gasped for breath.

" Is all these for us?" at last she asked, as the last of the pile left the hands of the man.

" Well, carn't yer read?"

" Yus, I can. Presents for us!" she murmured.

" An' 'ere's a letter for you, too."

" Letter! Give it to me!" Smudgee was trembling with excitement. She had never received a letter before, and she saw at once this was in Jack's handwriting. Her heart gave a little jump as she took the note, but she mustered up enough self-command to say—

" Thanks, young feller. Tell Mr. Thompson as we are much obliged for 'is kindness."

" Ain't yer goin' ter remember the carrier?"

" Yus, young man, to me dying day. And when I

opens me bank account, and gits me cheque-book, yer'll 'ear from me. For the present, good morning."

With a grunt and a muttered grumble, the man drove off.

Smudgee stared at the envelope for fully five minutes before she could bring herself to open it. With trembling, nervous fingers she at last did so, and then read her very first letter, which was as follows :—

"DEAR LITTLE PRINCESS,—I told you I would not forget you. I have not. Herewith you should receive some boxes and parcels. They contain dresses and—and other things for your Highness's wardrobe and for that of your mother. I am afraid they will not all fit, and there may be some things among them you do not want, and others that you *do* require may be missing. You see, I have not had much experience with princesses' wardrobes, and the young ladies at the stores where I bought them were a little confusing." ("Hussies! Wot did they do, I wonder? Wish I'd been there!" interjected Smudgee.) "But I have done my best." ("Bless 'im, I should think 'e 'ave!" said Smudgee, kissing the letter.) "If it is not a very superfine best, you must put it down to my lack of knowledge, not to my want of will. Write to me care of Martin & Martin, Solicitors, Macquarrie Street, Sydney. God bless you, dear little woman, and make you happy. —Affectionately yours, JACK."

Smudgee burned to attack the undoing of the parcels, but she yearned still more after Jack, and not until she had carefully read his letter through a second time did she cut the first string and open the first of the boxes. It contained a new hat—such an one as Smudgee had never seen, never even imagined. She scarcely dared to touch it. Putting it gingerly and carefully in the box, she opened one of the dress-cases.

"Ooh! Ooh! Ooh!" was the only thing she was capable of saying; but the amount of admiration she contrived to throw into these few sounds was wonderful. Box after box was opened and investigated.

"Well 'e might say there might be some things I do not want. Wot is this for? 'Ow do I wear that?" she asked of the air, as she took out one strange garment after another. There were dresses and hats, shoes, belts, gloves, and wonderful things in cambric, lace, silk, linen; brushes, combs, hairpins, needles, cotton, button-hooks, powder-puffs, collars, handkerchiefs, blouses, a gold chain and locket, and—oh! luxury of luxuries—a silver-backed hand-glass. This was too much. Smudgee put on one of the hats, looked eagerly at herself in the precious glass, and then burst into a fit of sobbing, thus shedding the first tears since Jack bade her good-bye.

"Oh, Gord bless 'im! Gord bless 'im! Ain't 'e good! Ain't e' an angel! If 'e could only see me in all these lovely things! But 'e can't—'e can't!" she sobbed to herself.

She had opened all her own parcels, and spread them on the stump and fences, but she had religiously abstained from touching those containing her mother's presents. When Sal returned with Nat, it was to find a weeping Smudgee, surrounded, as it seemed to them, with a perfect equipment for a George Street millinery establishment.

"Well, I'm blest!" ejaculated Nat, as he stared at the wondrous array of colour and material.

Sal stood speechless for a moment, dazed with astonishment. Then running eagerly from one box to another, she examined the articles with the most intense interest and admiration.

"Wot's it mean? Wot's it mean? Whose is they? Where'd they come from?" she asked breathlessly.

"It means Jack's an angel. They're mine, and they come from Anthony's, Sydney," answered the literal Smudgee.

"And there's none for me?"

"Yes; all them's yours." Smudgee waved her hand towards the rest of the packages.

Sal rushed from one to another, not knowing which to open first.

" 'Ere, Nat! Don't stand there like a stuffed pig! Git out your knife, and cut some o' these strings. 'Urry! 'Urry, will yer?" she shouted.

" It's a bloomin' millinery store, that's what it is! A bloomin' Anthony's Store—nothink less," chuckled Nat, cutting the strings and opening the various parcels.

" Oh, look at this, Smudgee! Look at this! I say, Nat, did you ever! Did you ever!" And she grabbed at one thing after another, as a hungry dog will at too large a dish of succulent bones.

If there is one thing a woman really revels in, it is the opening of packages of personal adornments, especially if she is ignorant of their contents.

" 'Ere! 'Ow's this? Eh? Look at me! Jist look at me! Did yer ever see?—Well, there! *Do* look!" she implored of the others, as she swung a gorgeous cloak round her handsome figure, and strolled up and down, looking over her shoulder at it. Suddenly she caught sight of Smudgee's looking-glass, and screamed out, " Give that to me! 'And me that glass! Oh, my! Oh, ain't it becoming! 'Ere, 'old this, while I try this on!" And she gave the glass to Nat to hold, as she dragged out a hat and tried to balance it on her head.

" Carn't yer stand still?" she yelled at Nat.

" I'm a standin' still," replied Nat. " It's you wot's jiggerin' about."

" 'Old the glass still! 'Ow can I see the effect if yer don't?" Sal was dodging Nat's unsteady holding of the mirror, in the frantic endeavour to catch sight of herself in it. Not until she had examined every article and tried all the tryable garments on, did she pause. Then she sat down, with as many things as she could hold in her arms, and began to think of which she should wear first.

Smudgee, who had been watching her and noting the articles as they were snatched out, one after another, said quietly—

"Well, ain't yer got nothin' to say about '*im!*'"

"About who?" asked Sal.

"About 'im as sent yer all these things."

"Ain't 'e sent no letter?"

"'E sent one ter me."

"Ter you! Ain't 'e never sent none ter me?"

"Not as I knows on."

"Wot's he say? Might hev writ a line, I should think," grumbled Sal. "Wot's 'e say ter you? Give us the letter."

"'E says them things are fer you," replied Smudgee.

"Well, give us the letter. 'Ere, give it us—and give it quick."

"I shan't. It's mine—not yours—and I mean to keep it," resolutely answered Smudgee.

Sal's eyes blazed with anger. She was furiously jealous of the extra attention shown by Jack to her daughter. Dropping the things she was holding, she strode over to Smudgee, and made a snatch at the letter. Smudgee thrust it into the bosom of her frock. Sal thrust her hand out and caught hold of Smudgee's dress, and tore it open. Smudgee, fearful of losing her treasure, bit at her mother's hand savagely. Sal, with a cry of pain, fell back, yelling,

"Yer little beast! Yer beastly little brute! I'll skin yer!"

But Smudgee had picked up an axe, and stood with flashing eyes awaiting her mother's onslaught.

"If yer take this letter from me, I'll kill yer," she said quietly.

The mother quailed. She was what Smudgee could never be—a bully and a coward. She was afraid. She hesitated—glared about her—then seized the hat that Smudgee had tried on and so admired, and tore it to shreds, using fingers and teeth in her mad endeavour to destroy it. Smudgee grieved over her hat, but she had saved Jack's letter.

Nat had not interfered. He had a gradually growing

respect for Smudgee which, combined with the knowledge of her value as the principal lever by which the Landale estates and fortune were to be turned over in his direction, made him extremely cautious and disinclined to cross her in any way. He determined to go to Sydney next day. There was little to arrange—less to hinder them—and on the next evening, at six o'clock, a splendidly-dressed, handsome woman, and a gorgeously-arrayed girl of some twelve summers, accompanied by a particularly disreputable-looking man, took their places in the train and were soon rattling away to Sydney. They were the transformed Sal, Smudgee, and their relative Nat, still in a state of grub.

CHAPTER XIV

AMONG THE SAMOANS

SAMOA, the beautiful island immortalised by Stevenson, was the first port the *Alameda* stopped at after leaving Auckland. Its soil is now rendered for ever sacred by the fact that all that is mortal of the great story-teller lies in it. Jack, who was a lover of Stevenson's works, held it a duty to visit his grave and scatter some flowers about it. Had Stevenson lived, Samoa would have been under British rule. He loved and laboured for it. He died—it passed from us.

Jack was entranced with the beauty of the island, the splendid physique of the natives, the loveliness of the women, the strength and dignity of the men. As soon as the boat anchored, a number of canoes were hitched on to its sides, and Samoan men and women came up, hand over hand, easily and freely, to the promenade deck. Handsome girls, prettily decorated with flowers, sprang over the bulwarks, offering strings of opalesque and glittering sea-shells, bananas, Tappa mats, fans of beautifully woven grass, charmingly dyed in variegated colours, rings cut out of solid tortoise-shell, into which little bits of cut silver were dexterously stamped, and other curios for a few cents. The joyousness, carelessness, and happiness of these children of Nature acted like a mental tonic upon Jack and his fellow-travellers. Soon all on board were infected with their childlike good spirits, and were joining in the general enjoyment.

At intervals along the deck were placed buckets of water, with tin pannikins, for the use of the natives. One handsome woman filled one of the cans, lifted up the skirt of her dress, and, placing it over the top of the can, used it as a strainer—the primitive filter of the untutored natives. Another girl was standing at the door of the purser's cabin asking for a drink. Unthinkingly, he handed her a glass of iced water. She drank; then, clapping the skirt of her dress to her mouth, ran screaming up the deck. She had never known contact with ice; she thought she had been scalded.

Jack had brought with him a large box of chocolate bon-bons. To console her, he gave her a handful of the sweetmeats. She soon forgot her trouble in the enjoyment of the hitherto untasted delights, and eagerly munched them. Like a lot of children, men and boys, women and girls, rushed at Jack and grabbed at the delicacies, screaming with triumph if they succeeded in securing a few, and glibly complaining if they failed. Not a vestige of chocolate was left; even the box itself was seized and fought for. Packets of American chewing-gums were despatched as easily as though they had been cream méringues. What pangs and groans they produced afterwards, it is not possible even to conjecture.

Jack and Tom went on shore and purchased the local newspaper, issued that day, anxious to learn the news of the world since they left it ten days before at Auckland. The leading article of this representative organ was headed—

" Thank God, we have at last got a jail!"

This was a staggerer to Jack.

" Tom," he called, " do read this. 'A jail!' What are the offences? A 'drunk'—with whisky which we have imported and sold to these poor innocents! Fines for not wearing European clothes, which we insist upon their using, to the utter destruction of their health, comfort, and appearance. Stealing bananas. Oh, shades of Justice! We steal their land, put fences round it, and punish them for taking back that which we have stolen! Verily, we are a great and glorious people! These Samoans are communists in the true and primitive acceptation of the term. To refuse a request for any article desired is considered bad manners. There is no idea of personal property. Each and all have, in their creed, a right to all that grows. It is theirs by inheritance. We have higher, nobler codes of honour and probity! We take by force or chicanery their common property from the owners, and thank God when we have erected a jail in which to punish them for taking a portion of what is their own. Ah me! Tom, but we are a queer people!"

"Bully for you, Jack! All the same, we are not going to have Samoa. That is gone as a sop to Germany—oddly enough, the last nation the Samoans wanted as rulers. The purser told me that when that awful storm took place, and the German and American boats were wrecked out yonder, that magnificent fellow, who is a Samoan chief, pulled out of the raging surf a hundred men. But then he had not—and never has—been converted to Christianity."

"Christianity!" answered Jack. "Christianity in its essence and primitive truth is salvation indeed. When we hark back to that and observe faithfully its tenets, we are saved without a doubt. But when do we do this? Oh, when?" And Jack sighed wearily.

As they wandered through the long, picturesque lane, which is the principal street of Samoa, Jack gradually collected a string of curious, open-eyed followers.

To Tom's intense amusement, his friend's habitual good-nature had landed him in a predicament which, at one time, threatened to end in his remaining on the island until another vessel should come along and take him off. He had been distributing his silver coins with an exceedingly lavish hand among the natives, who were bartering shells, rings, models of catamarans, spears, and other Samoan articles, and had collected a large crowd of people of all sexes and ages, who were laughing and chattering around him, holding on to his arms, thrusting their wares into his hands, stuffing his pockets with them in perfect confidence in his honesty. One extremely beautiful girl was trying to unfasten the cummerbund he was wearing.

It was of a rich, oriental blue colour, and the young savage had taken a strong liking to it, wanting it for an ornament for herself. She had on the native dyed-grass costume, fastened round her waist and reaching to her knees. Her hair had been dyed a bright golden-red. Round her neck were three much-worn silk and satin buckled stocks or neckties of the old-fashioned type, in different colours. In her hair was a glowing scarlet hibiscus. She was a curious, but certainly picturesque young person. She spoke no English—Jack no Samoan. The situation was an embarrassing one. She was offering all she possessed for Jack's cummerbund. Jack would have willingly given it to her, but there were at least another dozen ladies who desired it just as eagerly. Giggling and chattering, they were all trying to disengage the much-prized article with so much energy that Jack was in danger of losing not only that but a great deal more of his wardrobe. The intense heat, the contact of so many sparsely-covered bodies, the strong smell of the cocoanut-oil with which those bodies were smeared, made the contest raging around and over him not altogether too pleasant. Matters might have proved somewhat trying to Jack's modesty and self-respect had not an enormous male Samoan approached the group, and, in a few stern words of command, dispersed it. Jack felt immensely relieved. But, alas! his troubles were not over yet. He was wearing a very fine, white, Japanese silk shirt under the coveted cummerbund. This had caught the eye of the giant Samoan, who, in the politest manner possible, requested Jack to give it to him. Had Jack been carrying the shirt in a parcel, he would have parted with it as willingly to the man as he would have given the other article of attire to the woman, but to strip on the landing-place and return to the boat shirtless was more than he could summon courage to do. The Samoan seemed much hurt at Jack's want of courtesy in refusing his request. Then, like the damsel, he began to bargain for it. Meantime, the boatmen were calling upon Jack to embark for the steamer. The surf was rolling in heavily, and their canoe was tossing up and down in a sufficiently dangerous way. With the greatest possible politeness, the Samoan persisted in his attempts to secure the much-coveted garment, and, with equal politeness, Jack refused to strip and give it to him. A crowd had again collected, and Jack's attempts to pass it were frustrated by the comely damsels, now anxiously interested in their fellow-country-man's bargaining. The boatmen yelled; Tom called; all to no purpose. The steamer screamed out her second signal. In desperation Jack seized the chieftain's arm, and, pointing to the boat, roared—

"Boat going—very sorry; give me your address and I will send you a dozen."

The chieftain did not understand Jack's words, but he did his pantomime and the steamship's whistle. With the greatest courtesy he cleared the road, and Jack, with Tom, jumped into the tossing canoe and got safely back to the *Alameda*, followed by many pairs of very wistful eyes —one pair fixed on his Japanese silk shirt, the rest on his oriental blue cummerbund.

CHAPTER XV

WHILE Jack was tossing on the miscalled Pacific Ocean, Nat, Sal, and Smudgee were in Melbourne, whither Nat had gone for the purpose of helping a little syndicate, of which he was member, defraud the public by the means of a couple of horses owned by them. Nat found, on his return to Sydney, that he was a little too well known there to be trusted. Sal had drawn the hundred pounds left to her account by Jack, a portion of which Nat had put on a sure thing at Randwick and won. With his winnings he bought a share in the before-mentioned syndicate, and was looking forward to a pleasant and profitable stay in Melbourne. After putting up at a Bourke Street hotel, with Sal and Smudgee and the members of his enterprising firm, he sallied forth to view the land.

Melbourne did not suit Nat as well as Sydney; still, it was newer ground, and offered a surer and easier won harvest. There were many little games to be played at the Fitzroy racecourse; some, though fewer, at the Caulfield Grounds; and, now and again, though with greater risk, something could be done even at the more fashionable Flemington.

By the time Sal and Smudgee had lunched and dressed, it was nearly four o'clock. Sal took her daughter, and, crossing to Elizabeth Street, turned into the Melbourne Regent Street, viz. Collins Street, just in time to join the fashionable, afternoon crowd there. Sal was in ecstasies. Her handsome face and splendid figure won her a lot of admiration, more especially from the extremely youthful, and the doddering, bleary-eyed, and leering aged ones of the " nobler" sex. Sal was over-dressed, but her blazing beauty carried off the excess of colour which would have swamped a less-striking woman. Her bold return of the admiring glances of the men soon gained her a small string of followers, who played the usual pavement-game of walking ahead and stopping to look in shop windows, facing suddenly the object of their supposed and pretended regard with an assiduity that delighted Sal and roused to fury the more retiring Smudgee.

" Wot's that ole bloke a-starin' at ?" she asked, ostensibly of her mother, but really in tones intended to catch the said " ole bloke's" ears. And they did. " Wy don't 'e go and git 'is whiskers washed? 'E's dyed 'em a pale green."

" 'Old yer tongue, miss !"

" Shan't. Let 'im 'ump 'isself orf, the ole wobbling wallaby !"

The " ole wobbling wallaby" did " 'ump 'isself 'orf," in double-quick time, too. There was not much to be gained by a contest with the mamma of a candid young thing like Smudgee; so the aged Lothario sought the neighbourhood of a sailor hat, a short skirt, and a mass of golden curls hanging over a youthful pair of shoulders.

Sal and Smudgee seldom agreed upon any one point. They were as opposite as the poles, but they were equally delighted with the well-set-up shop windows, and if her mother would have kept her love of admiration and her ogling flirtations within decent bounds, Smudgee might have enjoyed the afternoon. But Sal's brazen effrontery enraged her.

" Don't yer think yer might let the men 'ave a rest now and then ?" she asked indignantly.

" Wot yer mean? I can't 'elp the men admiring me, can I ?" snapped Sal.

" Yer can 'elp gigglin' an winkin' at 'em, anyhow. I know yer !"

" Wot yer mean by ' gigglin' ' and ' winkin' ?"

" Oh ! Yer know well enough. If it ain't stopped, yer

can walk by yerself. I ain't goin' ter 'ev this crowd a-trottin' after my heels—so I tell yer straight!" Smudgee did not moderate her youthful contralto voice, and as she spoke she turned and faced the hangers-on to her mother's skirts with such a flaming face and indignant frown that they discreetly and incontinently took refuge in flight.

If Sal had dared, she would have boxed Smudgee's ears. Her afternoon was spoiled. Here was a duenna of twelve guarding her as if she were a child.

"Now, look 'ere, miss! You keep quiet, or when we get 'ome——"

"Oh! Come off about wen we get 'ome! Wen we get 'ome, you'll do no more'n you do 'ere. Behave yerself, ef yer can. Ef not, I won't be seen with yer. I ain't goin' ter disgrace *myself*. You 'ear *me*."

Collins Street heard a considerable portion of this dispute, and Collins Street was alternately amused and shocked.

"Really," simpered one fair, blue-blooded aristocrat (whose father drove cattle, and, to his credit be it said, drove them so well that he laid the foundations of a large fortune, which a devoted wife, two ditto daughters, and one very undevoted son were now doing their utmost to squander)—" really, if these wretched back-blockers are allowed to infest Collins Street in this way, we will have to cut it."

"Yes," said her youthful attendant swain, " it's gettin' low is Collins Street. I'm gettin' full up on it. Let's go into the ' Vienna ' and I'll shout for you."

It was an exceedingly warm afternoon, and very dusty, so there really was some excuse for the fair aristocrat to submit to the " shoutings " in the Vienna Café—quite the highest-toned restaurant in Collins Street.

But they were not to shake off the " back-blockers " even there, for Sal had been for fully half-an-hour without a drink, and the heat and dust had affected her quite as much as the other pedestrians.

" I'm ready to drop. I've that sinkin' feeling. Let's go in an' 'ave a cup o' tea."

" Ef it is tea, I'm with yer," said Smudgee, " but ef it's whisky, I'm off."

" Of course it's tea. Do yer think I can't be'ave my-self when I want to?"

" You'll 'ave ter want to, as far as I'm concerned. I know yer!"

Sal entered the café, and, sitting down at one of the tables, ordered two cups of tea. While waiting for it to be served, a man who had been following her in the street walked up to the table, and, taking a place beside Sal, ordered coffee for himself. Leaning back in his chair, he gazed at her with an assumption of intense admiration. Sal grew a little uneasy. Dearly as she would have loved to return with interest the approaches of her new admirer, her wholesome dread of Smudgee prevented her. The worst of Smudgee was that one never knew what she might or might not do. The stranger tried to open conversation with Sal.

" Very hot and unpleasant outside, is it not?"

Sal smiled, and was about to reply, but a vigorous kick from Smudgee, under the table, checked the smile and choked the reply. The tea was brought, and the gentleman fussily offered the milk and sugar, say-ing—

" Allow me, madam."

Before Sal's hand reached the articles, Smudgee's had grasped them. With a glance at the stranger, and an-other kick at her mother, she gave her some milk and two lumps of sugar. Sal was crimson with wrath. Her admirer thought she was blushing at his advances, and redoubled them.

" Some cake, madam?" he asked languishingly, offer-ing her a plateful. Sal was at that moment sipping her tea. A kick from Smudgee, under the table, made her swallow more than she intended, and most of it went the wrong way. A violent fit of coughing, a reddened nose, and streaming eyes were the results. The stranger sat in silent, sympathising sorrow, waiting for the paroxysm to pass. Smudgee glared at her mother's admirer, and whispered to her—

"'Old yer breath 'ard, and take a bit o' lump sugar."

The gentleman heard the whisper, and lifted the sugar-basin to hand it to Sal. But Smudgee, taking it from his hand, said inquiringly—

"Are the waiters allowed to sit at table with the customers at this 'ere shop?"

The gentleman started, coloured, and asked—

"Why? What do you mean?"

"You're one of the waiters, ain't yer?"

"No, certainly not!" he replied indignantly.

"Oh! Thought you were—you do it so naturally. Given up business, perhaps?"

"Really! You're mistaken, miss!" he blustered.

"So are you," said the imperturbable Smudgee. "You mistook us for two hinfants as couldn't 'elp ourselves to milk and sugar. Well, we can—and to a good deal besides. You hear *me!* The bill, if you please, miss." And Smudgee turned to the waitress.

"It's paid, miss."

"Paid, is it? And who paid it, pray?"

"This gentleman, miss," replied the waitress, indicating the stranger.

"This wot, did yer say?" holding her hand to her ear.

"This gentleman, miss."

"Oh! That's a gentleman, is it? Dear me! So glad you told me. A new kind, perhaps. We thought he was a waiter. An' 'ow much did the gentleman pay for this?" And Smudgee swept her hand over the table.

"One and six, miss," replied the highly amused waitress.

"One and six? 'Ere, my good man, is two shillings," said Smudgee. "You can keep the change. *Good* afternoon." With superb dignity she took her mother's arm and marched out of the café, leaving the gentleman staring at the two-shilling piece she had left upon the table, and, for once, abashed and humbled.

Out into Collins Street the two went, arm-in-arm. Sal, who was still coughing and gasping for breath, had no choice but to yield to Smudgee's guidance. She had no speech wherewith to protest.

Smudgee had seen as much of the fashion of Collins Street as she wanted for one afternoon. Turning down into Elizabeth Street, she led the unresisting parent in the direction of Bourke Street and their hotel. By this time Sal had recovered her breath, and turned in fury upon Smudgee, asking—

" Wot yer think yer doin'? Who d'yer think yer are? Who d'yer think *I* am?"

" I think I'm tryin' to make yer be'ave yerself, an' I think I'm yer daughter, and I think you're my mother. And I'll tell yer somethink else I think. That is, I wish I weren't—for yer ain't nothin' to be proud of. Some o' these days, if yer ain't careful, I shall 'ook it, and yer'll never see me agin. I'm full up o' this kind o' thing."

There was no threat or argument that could have influenced Sal more than this happily-hit-on one of Smudgee's disappearance. Sal knew that without Smudgee there would be much less chance of the Landale estates falling into her hands. She had no authority over Smudgee—not a scrap of influence. She did not understand the child, was mentally and morally her inferior. Smudgee would only yield to reason and kindness. Ignorance and brutality disgusted her. For what she thought was right she would suffer anything; and she would be cut to pieces before she would do what she considered wrong. Smudgee was of the stuff that martyrs are made of.

They reached their hotel to find Nat full of his new plans—and whisky. The average, low-class Australian can scarcely be said to be lacking in self-esteem. Whatever he does, he does better than any one else in the universe. If there is any man doing something, somewhere, that he cannot, it is because he has never troubled himself to try. Nat had his full share of the blatant conceit of his class. Give him a few glasses of whisky, lend him your ears, and he would talk on steadily about himself and his achievements for hours without ceasing. He had been wanting somebody to brag to, and he was out of temper.

"Oh! 'Ere yer are, at last!" he grumbled. "I thought I'd lost yer. Where in kingdom come 'ave yer bin?"

Smudgee was looking out of the window at the wonders of Bourke Street. Sal had sat herself down, and, with folded arms, was glaring at the empty fireplace.

"Well, don't 'urry yourselves to answer. It might injer yer 'ealths," Nat continued. "When yer *can* find time, p'raps you'll tell me where you've bin."

Smudgee surveyed him quietly from head to foot, and answered—

"Well, p'raps we've bin to Government 'Ouse to see his Lord and Ladyship—an' p'raps we bin ter call on the Bishop—an' p'raps we bin ter arsk the Lord 'Igh Chief-Justice ter renew his acquaintance with your noble self—an' p'raps——"

"'Old 'ard! 'Old 'ard!" cried Nat. "Wot's yer givin' us? Not so much chin, Miss Loocy Landon." Turning from Smudgee to his wife, he asked, "Wher' yer bin, Sal?"

"Collins Street, to tea," morosely answered Sal.

"Tea! Seems to 'ave upset yer, don't it?" he asked.

"Yus, it 'ave." And Sal helped herself to a strong dose of whisky and soda, as an antidote.

"Well," said Nat, "I got somethin' ter tell yer as'll do yer good. The best spec I was ever in. We're bound ter pull it orf; leastways, if they'll only do as I tell 'em. Yer see, these blokes as I'm in wiv are all very well, but they ain't got my 'ead—see? They ain't got my 'ead. When they're told wot ter do, they can do it; but if they 'adn't got me ter show 'em wot's wot, they wouldn't be nowheres."

" Lucky they've got you, then, ain't it?" Smudgee said satirically.

" You bet it is! Well, wot I'm goin' ter do is this. Just keep yer eyes open, an' I'll astonish yer."

" Well," interjected Smudgee, " as I don't feel up ter bein' more 'stonished than I 'ave bin to-day already, p'raps you'll excoose me if I go to my own room. Yer see, ye're *so* clever, that listenin' to yer too often 'urts me 'ead. Yer give us too much—me 'ead won't 'old it. I ain't just trained up to it. I'd rather take yer in smaller doses, if it's all the same." So saying, Smudgee went to her room.

" Bly me! I never can understand when that kid is in earnest and when she's chaffin'. Well, as I was agoin' ter say—jist listen to this, Sal."

Sal didn't listen, although he continued to talk, brag, and drink whisky and soda for fully an hour. Nor need we listen, either. It was a very commonplace swindle that he had planned. A thing that happens every day on these outside racecourses; a cunning design to fool the credulous dupes whose mission in life seems to be to help to fill the pockets of the scoundrels who thrive on race-course knavery, as maggots do on dunghills.

Sal had a thinking-spell on her. She was sensible enough to know that her afternoon had been a failure. Her fine, new clothes had not quite created the impression she had expected. True, men had followed and stared at her, but they were not the kind of men she had hoped to attract. She knew exactly their wishes and intentions, and valued them to a nicety. But it was not men of their stamp she wanted to fascinate. Compared with Jack, they were contemptible, and it was Jack she had in her mind's eye when she sallied forth to do battle with Collins Street. She could not flatter herself that she had succeeded. Would she fail with Jack as she had failed this afternoon? Then, there was Smudgee. Each day she felt her daughter more and more of a stumbling-block. Every hour she fell more and more under her influence, grew more afraid of her. Things she would not hesitate to do in her absence, she was ashamed to do in her presence. As Smudgee grew older, so, gradually, were their positions reversed. The child became the monitor and guide; the mother, the scholar. The good that was in the daughter perplexed and angered the parent. Sal had no wish to lead anything but a life of selfish pleasure, and her idea of pleasure was not Smudgee's.

As she sat in silent thought, Nat rambled on about his schemes, blustering, bragging, and drinking, until Sal, weary of him, herself, and all the world, helped herself freely to the whisky, went to her room, and, throwing herself upon the bed, was soon steeped in heavy, alcoholic slumber.

Nat sought the congenial atmosphere of the bar, where he "shouted" and was "shouted" for, until he and his companions were led, staggering and half senseless, to their rooms.

It must be admitted that if, under such conditions and with such surroundings, Smudgee retained her natural rectitude and goodness, they were based upon very firm foundations indeed. Smudgee did not go to sleep. She locked herself in her room, went to her box, and, taking out Jack's letter, read and re-read it. She had not yet answered it. She had tried again and again to do so, but she wrote so badly, there were so many words she wanted to use that she could not spell, that, in disgust, she tore up what she had written, and diligently stuck to her copybooks. Now she must make another attempt to put her thoughts upon paper. Jack had given her no clue to his whereabouts—only his address at Martin & Martin's, Sydney, to be forwarded. There her letter must go. It was hard, slow work, but she persevered, and the first letter she ever wrote was eventually finished. Thus it ran :—

" My own derest Night,—I receeve your lovely presents quite safe. It made your lovin princess feel quite ashamed having done nothing to deserve such lovely presents. I wish you could see me in some. I do love you derest night not for the presents but I alwys love you befor you sent presents i wish you could see me so different with my hair dresed there is plenty water in Sydney and Melbourne and i have Two bath every day but derest night your lovin princess is very lonely now she have not her night. She was not so dresed and washd at Woolloogolonga but her derest night made it not so lonely as in Sydney and Melbourne. I have a new uncle Nat, i don't know where he cum from but I wish he wuld go bak me and mother wented to Collins Street—you would not now your lovin princess if you was to see her in collins Street which is were all the people which is high society go to show their new frocks and stare at each others frocks. i went there in your new presents. I was sory them women at anthonys stores was rude when you buy my presents. I went to see what they was like. I know I did see them, because one larfed and sed why that's the hat and dress that handsome man bought for them two women in the back blox. Derest night they is cats! I sed to myself they is *dam* cats. That was the first swear I sweared since you went away but I miss my swear about uncle Nat, he make me want to so bad sometimes—but I said it three times in the shop, twice going home and three times when I undress your lovely presents because they sold them to my derest night which is a better night than Lanclot which was Elanes night. Oh derest night Jack I wish you wos here. I always wish you wos here. It is so hard I do not know were you are derest Jack—is it in Australia or were is it derest Jack, I do wish I knew were it is. Why do I not now—that I could see you. i don't hev no one to speak to. Mother is full of frocks and hats, and uncle Nat is always full of whisky—I wos going to sware—but i wont derest night because you do not like me to sware. Besides in your lovely presents it is different to my old close. Derest night i wish i culd speak to you dere Jack i wish i new were you was so i culd think i see you—wot you got on and wot all round you wos like. but i carn't i don't now wot you wear now nor were you are derest night. i kiss this place just here. please kiss it to. Do write your lovin princess which is lonly without her derest Jack do write quick at once your lovin princess.   SMUDGEE.

"*P.S.*—I do love—love—*love*—*love*—*love* my derest night. *P.S.S.*—I am so lonly without my derest Jack."

Many, many hours had Smudgee spent over this letter, which had to be copied out several times before it satisfied her. Then she kissed it over and over again, and talked to it, telling it many things she did not like to write, begging it to go quickly and bring back an answer at once. Putting it into an envelope, she took it herself to the General Post-Office; she would not trust it to a pillar-box. She had it sealed and registered, asking the clerk to let her look " if the address was quite right"—really, to hold it once more and charge it with some other sweet messages to her friend.

" You're sure it'll go all right?" she asked the clerk.

" Quite sure, miss," he replied gravely.

With the receipt for her letter thrust into the bosom of her dress, she made her way past the brilliantly-lit shops back to her hotel, to find her mother too tipsy to talk intelligently, and her Uncle Nat snoring, with his head on the table beside an empty whisky-bottle, half-a-dozen empty soda-water bottles, and the stumps of many bad cigars. Bidding her mother good night, she went to her room, re-read Jack's letter, said a little prayer to God to " look specially after her derest night," then, with her locket, her note, and the receipt for her registered letter hugged tightly to her bosom, she softly cried herself to sleep.

CHAPTER XVI

A DAY AT FLEMINGTON RACES

NAT and his precious syndicate " did the trick" at Fitz-roy pretty well, and made a very fair haul comparatively. Still, on the course where a " favourite can be stiffened for a fiver," the plunder is necessarily not large. There were some races to come off at Flemington in a week, and to these the knot of scoundrels next turned their attention. The horse they owned was a really good steeplechaser. He had won some money up country and at Sydney in previous races. They changed his name, altered his appearance as much as they could, and entered him for several of the coming events. They had to work very cautiously, as little was known of them, and that little was not to their credit. Their jockey had orders to come in among the tail of the runners in all the races but one in which he took part. These orders were faithfully carried out. In the one race for which he was " meant to try," there was but one other horse that could beat him. This was the " Star-Gazer," a fine galloper, and a splendid jumper. He had but one vice—a bad one—he was an inveterate shyer. His vision was defective. A leaf, a stone, a piece of paper in his path would make him jump yards aside—this the syndicate knew, and laid their plans accordingly. The betting was heavy on the favourite; their own horse, the " Trundler," was at fifty to one. Quietly they went to work, and backed him to win whenever they could find takers. They attracted little attention at first, but some of the bookies looked askance at the long odds, and presently the " Trundler" went down twenty to one. Still there was no real suspicion of what was going on.

The day came, and Nat was in a particularly excited

frame of mind. The scheme, which was entirely his own, was to let the horses take their first round unmolested, their jockey having orders to watch the "Star-Gazer," and keep him within distance. On the last round, while all were intent on watching the horses, Nat went across to the far end of the course, close to a nasty stone fence which the horses had to take, got his back to the wind, and as the field came along, with "Star-Gazer" next to the rails, he let the wind blow a newspaper he was holding out of his hand right under that horse's nose. With a start, the nervous animal swerved on one side, refused the jump, letting the "Trundler" and another horse, the "Magpie," pass him. "Star-Gazer's" jockey put him at the fence again, but in vain. The newspaper was still fluttering in the wind against the fence, and nothing would induce the horse to take the leap. A man ran out and caught up the paper. Instantly "Star-Gazer" took the fence flying, but his chance seemed hopeless. The "Trundler" and the "Magpie" were lengths ahead. As if aware of his fault, "Star-Gazer" augmented his speed, but to all appearance he was out of the race. There were only two other obstacles to negotiate, and then the clear run in home. Over the last but one hurdle, the two first horses went neck and neck. "Star-Gazer's" jockey bent to his work and plied both whip and spur. "'Magpie' wins!" "No, the 'Trundler'!" "The 'Trundler' has it!" "No, the 'Magpie'!" roared the excited throng. "Ten to one on 'Trundler'!" shouted Nat's friends. The "Trundler" was gaining between the two fences. "The 'Trundler'—a pony." "Twenty to one on the 'Trundler'!" "'Star-Gazer's' beaten!" yelled the crowd. Now for the last fence. The "Trundler" was a full length ahead of the "Magpie." The "Star-Gazer" was just taking the last fence but one. "Beaten, hopelessly beaten —a hundred to one against the favourite!" screamed the bookies. The "Trundler" went at his last fence like a bull at a gate. His jockey, too excited to take matters quietly, plunged in his spurs, the animal swerved a little in his take off, caught his hoofs on the stone coping, and, turning a somersault right in the path of the "Magpie," brought him down, too. Midst a swirl of struggling hoofs and scrambling, injured jockeys, the "Star-Gazer" cleared the last fence and cantered in an easy winner—the rest of the field being nowhere. Never were heard such shouts and cheers. The crowd seemed frantic. Nat and his pals slunk away. They had ventured every cent they owned—they had lost. Their horse had broken his back, and they were all hopelessly ruined.

Sal and Smudgee watched the calamity from the Grand Stand with varied feelings. Smudgee, full of grief for the gallant animal lying there, groaning in its death-agonies; Sal inwardly cursing the jockey who had, in her estimation, lost the race by his want of skill, thus bringing about their temporary ruin.

The death of a horse at a steeplechase does not excite too much sympathy. There are some "Oh! Oh! Oh's!" from the fair sex, a few exclamations of pity from the men, the course is cleared, the next item on the race-card claims attention, and the dead animal is forgotten.

Nat waved a signal to Sal, who, with her daughter, left the stand and followed him to the gate. He called a cab, and they drove back to their hotel, Nat cursing the jockey and bewailing his ill-luck at being "associated with a set of shysters and duffers, who were totally unworthy of being bossed by such a Napoleon in trickery as himself."

Sal did not know how heavily Nat had plunged, but she guessed by his manner that he was badly hit. He was. About five pounds was all that was left of the hundred Jack had placed to her credit, and there were their hotel bills and their fares back to Sydney to pay.

After much discussion, it was decided by Nat that Sal should, with the better portion of her newly-acquired wardrobe, and the best of Jack's presents to Smudgee, pay a visit to an adjoining "Mont de piété," or pawn-shop, and raise as much money as she could. Sal was in a fury.

She raged and stormed at her husband for speculating with and losing her money (she had not objected when he had won), and called him several kinds of thieves and all sorts of fools, until Nat, giving her a heavy slap on the face, sent her whimpering to the whisky-decanter for consolation. Smudgee, who saw this, promptly threw a tumbler at Nat's head, and hit it, raising a bump as large as a pigeon's egg over his right eye.

"Yer big, ugly brute! You dare to lay a finger on my muvver, and I'll smash yer!" Smudgee blazed out.

Nat, enraged, sprang towards her, but now Smudgee had a whisky bottle by the neck, poised ready for flight, and Nat contented himself with a volley of oaths and half a tumbler of raw whisky, grunting—

"Wot in 'ell did she want ter tork to me like that for?"

"'Cos yer spent her money—and mine. Mine—you 'ear me! Mine. Pawn my things, will you? Pawn my lovely presents from my Knight! Not much yer don't! Not a button, nor a 'ook, nor a eye! They wos give ter me by a better man than you could ever think of, an' if you put a finger on 'em, I'm off ter the perlice. Yer my uncle Nat—or yer sez yer is—and no uncle Nat is goin' ter touch Jack's presents while Smudgee is about. And Smudgee is about now, and likely ter be about where Jack's presents is concerned. Put as much as a finger on 'em, I'll jail yer. Now, go and git yer hotel-bill paid outer somethin' else. Yer don't git it out o' Jack's presents, not much yer don't! I know yer!"

Smudgee burst out of the door, slamming it behind her, and, retiring to her own room, locked herself in, as usual, and sat down to think.

"She's a beauty, she is!" said Nat, after Smudgee had gone. "I'd like to——"

"Let 'er alone. It'll pay you better," retorted Sal. "Mowbray said he'd provide for me while I was good ter Smudgee, don't you forget it. Let 'er alone, if yer don't want ter spile everything."

A DAY AT FLEMINGTON RACES

"Well, wot the blazes is we goin' ter do for money?" growled Nat; "we're dead broke."

"You're dead broke, you mean," she retorted. "Not me. Wot did yer go and speculate for? Why couldn't yer let well alone?"

"Yer didn't say that when I pulled it off at Randwick, did yer? Yer thought it was good enough then, didn't yer? Jist like you women—all smiles and shirt-collar wen a man's in luck, an' all grumps and grumbles wen he's broke."

"You ain't bin in much luck lately," Sal answered. "'Cept the luck of droppin' in on us when we tumbled into a good thing, and then doing yer best to spile it. Luck! There ain't much luck about you, and I'm beginnin' ter think not too much sense either!"

Nat's affronted vanity prompted him to rise and give his wife another personal reminder that he was her lord and master, but he bethought himself of Smudgee's threat, and refrained.

Thus, all unconsciously, did Smudgee begin to get the whip hand of her unscrupulous parents, and guide them, all unwillingly, into better behaviour and more decent ways. In the end, Smudgee had her wish. Not a thing of hers was taken to be sold or to the pawn-shop. Upon Sal's wardrobe sufficient was realised to clear their liabilities and pay their fares to Sydney, where, in a cheap boarding-house at Redfern, they concocted plans for the future and awaited another remittance from Jack.

In this unwholesome and evil-smelling place, Smudgee drooped and grew pale. She missed the free life and the fresh air of the bush. She packed away all her fine clothes, wearing the plainest she possessed, Jack's locket and chain being the only handsome or expensive thing she excepted. Day by day she grew more quiet and pensive. She had not even the spirit to reply to the vulgar chaff of the young "larrikins" of the neighbourhood. It was a very pale princess and a very peaky Smudgee who sat at her copy-books—in the wretched little bedroom which she shared with her mother; she never sang, seldom smiled, and felt so sad and wretched that she began to wonder whether she was not going to die for her knight and never see his handsome face or hear his kind voice again. She took no interest in anything; did not care to go out, either in Sydney or the country. She would wander down to the Australia Hotel sometimes, where she knew he had stayed, and, gazing up at its many windows, wonder which one he had looked out of. Every day, wet or fine, she would go to the General Post-Office, ask if there was any letter for Miss Lucy Landon, turning away, looking a little more pale, as the inevitable answer came: "No, nothing for that name, miss," and walking back to the dingy boarding-house with heavier feet and more saddened spirits.

Never once in her own mind did she reproach her knight. She knew he would keep his promise and write to her again, but oh! it was such a weary time to wait and wonder. If she only knew where he was—whether he was well! But no news came. There had not been time, she told herself. Perhaps all the mail was not in. He would write as soon as he could. Perhaps he had written and some one had stolen the letter. Every morning she went for her letter, and every evening she said her little prayer for her "own dearest knight," hugged his locket and his letter, and passed most of the dark hours before morning staring into the blackness of the night, wondering—wondering—wondering.

CHAPTER XVII

IN SAN FRANCISCO

ON the arrival of the *Alameda* at San Francisco, Jack found a cablegram awaiting him. Opening it eagerly, he saw it was from Sybil. It was as follows:—

" Hope all is well with you. Mother so much better at prospect of your coming. Make haste. Letter at Post-Office. Dearest love from both.—SYBIL."

Jack handed the message to Tom without a word.

" Doing good already for her, Jack," Tom said cheerily.

" I hope so," Jack sighed gloomily. " I feel like a thief."

" Nonsense! You mustn't look at it in that way."

" I can't look at it in any other way," answered Jack. " Let us drive to the Post-Office and get the letter."

Giving Wong instructions to follow to the hotel with the baggage, the two friends drove straight to the Post-Office. Jack felt a thrill of sadness pass over him as he drove along the well-remembered streets. Recollections of his old lonely life came back to him—his struggles, his poverty, and, he said to himself, his *" honesty."* He had never wronged a man of a penny-piece at that time. And now!

Seeing his friend's depression, Tom chatted gaily as they drove along, pretending to take more interest than he really did in what he saw, and he was interested deeply, too. One could scarcely fail to be so in a first visit to San Francisco. There is so much that is distinctly American in the city, yet much that is not. The types of character are exceedingly varied. Few nationalities are unrepresented. Many of the Chinese wear their national costume, the better class dressing in very bright colours, handsomely embroidered, the women often being very richly and tastefully clothed. Mexican, Italian, German, French, Irish, English, Polish, Russian, and Spanish names appear over the shops, offices, and stores. Their representatives throng the streets.

Arriving at the Post-Office, Jack got Sybil's letter, which was registered. He put it unopened into his pocket, and covered the pocket with his hand. On reaching the hotel and securing his rooms, he asked Tom to excuse him, shut himself in, and, with trembling fingers, opened Sybil's letter and eagerly read it. How he remembered that firm, strong handwriting!

" DEAR JACK," it ran,—" When you receive this letter, you will be only two weeks away from us. Think, dear, what that means to darling mother who has been waiting for you for twenty years. Ever since we received your cablegram saying you were sailing that day from Sydney, I have kept a large almanac in front of my desk, and, like Robinson Crusoe, I have notched off each day as it passed, saying to myself, ' One day nearer to Jack.' Each day the little mother has grown brighter and stronger. You cannot imagine the change the thought of your coming home has made in her. She grows every hour younger, every hour more beautiful. We have already prepared your rooms. You are to have papa's bedroom (you remember, it is the one with the oriel windows, looking over the park), and his study is to be your ' den.' Sir James never cared to occupy those two rooms; indeed, scarcely ever entered them. They have been kept expressly for the master's home-coming. My dear, dear brother, you cannot imagine how glad everybody will be to see you. You are a Landale, and, after all, the dear old place is Landale, and no one who does not bear that name could ever be quite the same to the old people, the servants, and the dependants. Sir James was never looked up to as you will be. There was always the feeling that somehow he was a usurper. But with you, dear Jack, how different it will all be! Two weeks—fourteen days—and you will be with us, in our arms, being hugged, kissed, and spoiled by both of us. I am going to do a sum in arithmetic when I have finished this letter: divide the weeks into days, the days into hours, the hours into minutes, the minutes into seconds, and tick off every second that brings us one second nearer to seeing you, and sum up the total in kisses when we get you! We shall spoil you, you big, handsome Jack, for ever going away again. You will never want to leave us for a day—*never! never! never!* That's my prophecy—a prophecy that will come true. Kisses from little mother and from me. Do not delay, dear. Remember, mother's life is in your hands. Do not disappoint her in any way. If you have faults, hide them away. If your whole heart is not bound up in us and the dear old home, do not let her see it. If you have learned to love anything or anybody better than you do us, do not let her know it. She could not bear it, dear. Do not think me unreasonable; only remember you, her only son, have been absent from her for twenty years—from me the whole of my life. God bless and guard you, brother of mine, and bring you safely to us.—Your loving sister, SYBIL.

"*P.S.*—Lorna Mannerly is so excited about your coming. Indeed, so is everybody. *Make haste.*"

Jack's eyes were dimmed when he had finished reading the letter. For a long time he sat still and silent, holding it in his hand, gazing at it, thinking deeply. The beautiful nature of the girl, her goodness, sweetness, tenderness, and love for her mother permeated every line she had written, and sank deep into his very soul. And he was to see her and her mother, and live a life of fraud and hypocrisy with them! The thought was horrible to him, and yet what could he do? He should never have yielded to Landon's prayer. Having given way, having made these two women believe the brother and son was returning, he could never break their hearts by disappointing them.

How long he would have remained staring at the letter it is impossible to say. Tom's rattle at the door startled him into action. He rose, and, letting Tom enter, put the letter in his breast pocket. He could not show that to Tom as he did the cablegram. It seemed too sacred for that. To him it was almost an outrage that even he had read what was intended for his poor friend, Landale, lying dead and alone in Woolloogolonga Gully.

Tom had come to announce Wong's arrival with the baggage, and to ask Jack to convoy him round San Francisco and show him the sights.

As usual, Wong had done everything exactly as it should have been done. He was proving a perfect treasure of a servant.

Jack despatched a cablegram to Miss Sybil Landale, and another to Lady Walgrove, telling them that he had arrived safely, thanking Sybil for her sweet letter, and promising to try to be all she wished and hoped he would be.

After arranging everything necessary for Jack's comfort, Wong asked permission to visit some friends in Chinatown.

"Got a Mrs. Wong there?" Tom asked laughingly.

Wong smiled, and shook his head, answering—

"Wong no mlarried—no lookee for tlubble. Tlubble come allee klick enough."

"Well, trot along, Wong. We may see you by-and-by. We are coming that way. If we have time, we can drive out and see the seals at Seal Rock, but we had better make sure of the city."

"For old Wong's sake, take me to Chinatown," said Tom.

And to Chinatown they went. It is a curious place—China in America. People, houses, shops, wares, customers, costumes, language—all Chinese; the narrow streets, shops, opium-dens, and houses, all giving forth an indescribable Oriental, Mongolian odour; the provision-stores and eating-houses, with horrible fleshy-looking articles gone rusty black, blue, and brown with age and apparent putrefaction, hung in and outside the shop windows. Little Chinese urchins dabbled dirtily and apathetically in the running gutters. At the corners of streets, small groups of men collected to read the announcements of various meetings, events, and tradesmen's sales, printed in Chinese characters upon dirty white, yellow, and red bills. Flaring oil and naphtha lamps lit up insufficiently the narrow passages and alley ways. Sounds of strumming on unmusical instruments, and the curious, cat-like chanting of native voices came from the tea-houses.

Diving down some narrow, unprotected steps, Jack led the way to a cellar, where, in semi-darkness, the opium victims were lying in various stages of narcotic oblivion. Yellow and emaciated figures looked more like dried mummies than living, breathing beings. Up and out into the streets again went the friends, where there was a great gong beating, calling audiences to the Chinese Theatre, with its strangely-protracted drama, its never-ending plot, and its wonderfully patient audience.

Up dark, narrow, winding passages, men were shuffling, knocking at doors with their knuckles, knocks that were evidently pre-arranged signals. A door would be gently opened but a little way, a few sounds would be exchanged, and the new-comer would enter to join the gambling mob which already crammed the rooms to evil-smelling completion. Through streets with small houses in long rows, with windows scarcely breast-high from the side-walk, from which, behind lattices and jalousies, leered painted Jezebels, whose names were boldly engraved upon brass plates on these doors. Louise, Fernando, Clotilde, announced the presence of ladies of La Belle France; Violet, Lily, Rose, Annie, the English; Maggie, Norah, Biddy, the Irish; Jean, Elspeth, Mary, the Scotch; Fredrica, Gretchen, the German, &c. No other sign was necessary

—no need for announcements. The women at the windows spoke for themselves and their horrible trade.

As the night wore on, the streets became more and more crowded; progression was difficult. Up a narrow flight of steps they went, and through a curtained door. This was the Joss-house, or house of prayer. The Joss, a hideously ugly idol, sat cross-legged, staring at vacancy with exaggerated glass eyes. The air was heavy with the smell of burning sandal-wood. Little praying-sticks were stuck in vases all round the Joss's altar. These the worshippers took haphazard, after praying, and read the Joss's answers to their prayers. As they were all printed and ready in hundreds, it required more faith than the two friends possessed to accept them as direct replies to the solicitations of the worshippers; but, to the native mind, they were the decrees of the gods themselves. Most of the replies were favourable, few were the reverse. The Joss-house keepers know their business too well to ruin it by prophesying bad luck to their customers. Numbers of Chinese filled the room, prostrating themselves before the idol, some beating their foreheads on the floor.

Out of this, into the streets again went the friends; but these streets were now well-nigh impassable, and they were glad to leave Chinatown for the cleaner, safer, and more sweet-savoured streets of civilisation.

After a visit to a so-called gymnastic arena, where two gladiators were contesting for the heavy-weight championship of the world, surrounded by hundreds and hundreds of the roughest and toughest men of the West; and some supper at Madame François', a well-known café in Montgomery Street, the two friends retired to their beds—Tom to sleep the dreamless sleep of the unworried; Jack to lie awake thinking for hours of Sybil, and eventually to fall asleep only to dream of her.

Next day Jack, all impatience to be on the way to Sybil, hurried Tom away, and soon they were bidding farewell to curious, contradictory, but splendidly hospitable San Francisco.

IN SAN FRANCISCO

"Good-bye, you strange anomaly," said Jack, "where goodness, kindness, rapacity, and rascality jostle each other cheek by jowl; where the mornings are glorious summers, the afternoons foggy autumns; where you can only wear muslin or linen at twelve, and wools or furs at four. Farewell to you, San Francisco, queen city of California, glory and pride of the West; city of brave men and beautiful women, gentlemen and rascals; noble wives and brazen wantons! Fascinating, fearsome, handsome San Francisco, fare you well! Your like does not exist anywhere else on this planet!"

The two friends were soon on the car of the express, dashing on the way to the East. Over that wondrous ferry, which takes the whole of a vast train across the bay as easily as though it were a string of orange-boxes; away into the country, through mile after mile of flat, marshy land; then a plunge into luxuriant plains, rich with grapes, fruits, and flowers—two crops of each being garnered yearly—dashing past villages where houses and even trees were overgrown with masses of large roses. Giant oleanders in full blossom, all glistening and smiling in glorious sunshine, make these Californian valleys look like Gardens of Eden.

Out of the valleys and up into the mountains the train sped on its way. The atmosphere became clearer, the air more crisp and cold. Higher and still higher the engines toiled, panting and groaning like living things. Windows were closed, and wraps and overcoats donned. Still up and up they climbed, passing roaring torrents and frozen tarns. In places the snow lay twenty feet deep. Monster pines reared their giant tops, green and brown, against the dazzling white of the snow. Still up they went, skirting round precipices, getting glorious views of crags and lofty peaks, over which the foot of man had never trod. Hundreds of feet beneath them they could see the ice-cutters gleaning their harvest of huge frozen blocks to cool the food and drinks of the heated toilers in the cities of the plains. Still upward and onward they rushed.

With a roar and a whistle, the engine plunged into the sulphurous tunnels of the snow-sheds—the great timber passages made to save the trains from being buried beneath the sliding avalanches, or hurled by the force of the winds over the precipices into the depths below.

Scores of miles of these tunnels did they plough through. At intervals, through the interstices of the sides, glimpses, and glimpses only, could be caught of the most ravishing scenery—tantalising, appetising, and fleeting.

Out into the air again, with all the glory of clear blue sky, dazzling ice, snow, and towering trees. On and on they travelled, in daylight and in darkness. Out of California, through Utah, and the parching alkali plains of Nevada. At a little wayside station on the borders of Nevada, a pale-faced man stood waiting for the train. His coat was buttoned tight round his throat; his hat pulled down over his forehead; his right hand thrust deep into his coat pocket, in his left he carried a small handbag. On his face were stamped deep grief and grim determination. As he boarded the train and took a seat opposite to the two friends, Jack's heart was strangely drawn to him. For hours they travelled without speaking to him. He spoke to no one. Jack yearned to be of use or comfort to the man, yet hesitated to intrude upon his obvious sorrow. Seeking the conductor of the car, he asked—

"Do you know who that man is who sits opposite me?"

"Ya-as," drawled the conductor. "The Depot Superintendent told me. His name is Needham."

"He seems in trouble," said Jack.

"Yes, sir—guess he is," replied the conductor, "and pretty bad trouble, too."

"Can I help him in any way?" Jack asked sympathetically.

"Well, I guess you ca-an't. His daughter skipped with a blamed scoundrel on the morning train. The skunk's a married man, tu. He's off with her tu Mexico, he reckons. He's following them. If he catches them, there'll be a muss."

"Can he catch them?"

"I guess not! if we can't make time to make connection with the Sunset mail at Pueblo, they'll be away before we can reach them. I reckon he's not too flush with dollars, neither, and the President of this line ain't givin' passes to distressed fathers just at present."

Jack thought earnestly for a few minutes, and then asked—

"How much are we late now?"

"An hour, I guess, but a lot may happen between here and Pueblo."

Not an hour after this they came upon a snow-slide. A small avalanche had descended from the side of a mountain, and the line was blocked. Setting the train back, and uncoupling it, the driver ran the engine into the mass, butting at it again and again, to force a passage for his cars. Willing hands plied shovels and picks, and eventually a passage was cleared. But another hour had been lost. Needham worked with the energy of twenty men, taking out his watch every few minutes to see what time had been wasted. When again under weigh, he stood on the back of the car, alternately looking anxiously ahead and eagerly watching the mile-posts as the train sped past them.

The man's grief made Jack feel heart-sick, but there was nothing to be done—at least, not yet. They were now descending. The traces of snow began to disappear; it was getting warmer. They were nearing Montrose, where engines and drivers had to be changed to make the ascent of the precipitous Marshall's Pass. This splendid piece of engineering winds round and round, in corkscrew curves, up the side of the mountain. Slowly the train crawled up the steep incline, Needham counting every mile, his face white—his lips drawn tightly over his teeth, his eyes strained upward, looking for the curves of the railway track. At last the snow-shed on the summit of the pass was reached. The train was now two hours late. Unless time could be gained, the Southern train would have left Pueblo long before Needham's arrival.

During the pause necessary for the readjustment of the engines, Needham walked nervously and rapidly up and down in the gloomy recesses of the shed. Jack went to the engine-driver.

" We are over two hours late, driver."

The driver did not even look round. He was oiling his engine. He answered curtly—

" Ya-as."

" Can you make time going down?" Jack asked.

The man looked round, surveyed Jack leisurely, and replied—

" Make time goin' daown Marshall's Pass! No, sir!"

" I think you can. It's a matter of life or death."

" No, *sir!*"

" I think you can." Jack held out a roll of dollar bills.

" No-o, *sir.*"

" I think you can."

The notes were in the driver's hand. He pocketed them, saying—

" Wa-al, it will be hell ter split, but we'll let her rip."

And he did.

The descent of Marshall's Pass is like the ascent—a series of sharp curves round rocks and hills, hovering at times over gullies and precipices, not pleasant to contemplate from a rocking, swerving train running on a narrow ledge hundreds of feet above them. The train jolted, jumped, and swayed as it flew down the pass. Parcels, hat-bags, and rugs were shaken from the racks, and flew all over the carriages. Women screamed, and men looked askance. But still the train tore on. Only three men among the passengers were content that the dangerous speed should be continued—Needham, and Jack and Tom. Down the train plunged and rattled, mile after mile, without a pause, until the plain was reached, and the driver drew up at Salida, having gained thirty minutes of his lost time.

The conductor went to the driver and asked a question or two. The driver drew Jack's roll of bills from his pocket and handed some to the conductor, and made what the latter called " a squar' divvy."

One hour and a half of lost time still to recover!

Drivers and engines were again changed. Jack strolled up and interviewed driver Number 2.

" An hour and a half behind time, driver," he said.

" That's so," was the laconic response.

" Can you make time between here and Leadville?" he queried.

The driver spat experimentally at a fly buzzing in front of him, and missed.

" Ever bin to Leadville?" he queried.

" Yes; twice."

" At night, maybe. Asleep, I guess?"

" Once at night, and once in the day."

" Walked, maybe?"

" No, went by train."

" Nuthin' at all to say about the *ascent and* the curves?"

" I know all about them. But it's a matter of life and death. See here," and Jack held out another wad of dollar notes.

" Wa-al, ef it's a matter of life and de-ath, guess we'll put her at it." And he did.

Never was the ascent to Leadville made in less time. The line runs for miles by the side of a rushing, roaring torrent, which bounds along in a deep gorge, dashing over huge boulders, swirling round corners in miniature whirlpools, falling over rocks in broad, deep, brown masses, to be churned into snowy foam as they dash into the rapids below. Again the train was bumping and banging along the track—again passengers were holding on to their seats, and their belongings were careering through the air. Many of the passengers were complaining loudly, but Needham, Jack, and Tom were not among the number. The conductor listened with stolid indifference. He had heard passengers complain before. It was a habit passengers had as a race. He simply said, "Tickets," which, as he received, he examined most earnestly, looking with the gravest suspicion at that handed him by a man who had complained the loudest. First he turned the ticket over in his hand and frowned at it, then fixed his eyes on the unhappy passenger, with a "How-did-you-come-by-this" sort of expression, under which the passenger quailed visibly. Then he held on to the straps of the carriage to avoid falling over the passenger; then meditatively scratched the side of his cheek, and gazed again at his victim. At last, with a deep sigh, as though pardoning some almost unforgivable sin, he slowly punched the ticket, handed it back to its owner over his shoulder, and passed on to the next.

The man had come by his ticket in a strictly honourable way by paying the full price for it, but, by the time the conductor had examined and returned it, he was wondering if, after all, he had not in a fit of mental aberration unconsciously purloined it. No other passenger complained after that, and the train glided into Leadville, having saved another twenty minutes.

One hour and ten minutes late still. The conductor told Mr. Needham of Jack's interest in him, and what he had done. He went to Jack, and, holding out his hand, said simply in tremulous tones—

"You air a white man, sir."

Jack gripped the man's hand in answer, and stood watching the passengers go in and out of the cars and dining-room, while the fresh arrivals got their luggage and themselves into their places in the several carriages.

The driver and conductor, acting in concert, did not lose or waste a moment, and started the train as soon as possible. It was calculated that the Sunset mail would wait half-an-hour. It was doubtful if the difference in the time could be made up. It was not, but, when the train drew into Pueblo, the Southern train had not left.

Jack heard an exclamation from Needham, who was on the rear end of the carriage, before the engine stopped. Needham had leaped out on to the platform, and was running swiftly towards the dining-room, at the door of which were standing a man and a young girl. Jack quickly followed. As Needham approached the two people, the girl saw him, and, with a scream, cried out, " Father !"

The man saw the enraged parent coming towards him, and thrust his hand into his right side coat pocket. Jack guessed what the action meant. The brute intended to shoot through the pocket. He struck the hand back. A revolver in the pocket exploded, and the bullet struck the ground. Before the man could recover his hold of the trigger, Jack hit him square on the jaw, and he dropped like a log to the platform. Putting his hand into the man's pocket, Jack drew out the revolver and handed it to the station-master.

A large crowd gathered immediately. Jack slipped away, unnoticed in the rush, and hid himself until the train moved off. He had no desire to be detained as a witness. The police searched for him in vain. There was no one who knew him, or where he had come from; and he went bowling along, unmolested, through glorious Colorado, through the magnificent cañons with their sky-reaching crags, suggesting cathedrals, minarets, castle-turrets, steeples, palaces, fortresses. It was as though Nature had been amusing herself constructing gigantic edifices which should laugh to scorn the puny efforts of man.

Through day and night the train sped on—through the Royal Gorge, beautiful Colorado Springs, wonderful Denver; down into the vast Kansas plains, into wheat-fields, stretching farther than the eye could reach, ploughed and ready for the seed; through Kansas City, the city of the hills and bluffs, away into Missouri; through St. Louis, with its busy life, its handsome streets and beautiful suburbs, its warm-hearted and generous people. On and on, by sunlight and moonlight, through Indiana into Pennsylvania, stopping at the American Sheffield, Pittsburg, with its Carnegie Steel and Iron foundries—one of the wonders of the world. Through miles and miles of oil districts, with their hideous pumps, and flaming natural gas jets, flaring up like so many witch-fires in the darkness of the night.

It was growing bitterly cold. The wind whistled round the cars, penetrated under the doors, through the frames of closed windows and ventilators. The conductor turned up the pressure on the hot pipes, but the cold still conquered. The outsides of the windows were frozen and opaque. Fine snow began to sift through cracks and openings. Jack went to the rear of the car, opened the door, stepped out, but only for a moment. He was glad to return.

"Looks rather bad, doesn't it?" he said to the conductor.

"You bet!" the man replied. "We're in for a blizzard, and a tough one at that."

They stood watching the snow through the side windows of the door of the vestibule passage. It was coming down in masses of fine powder, swished and swirled about by the fierce wind, which shook the cars, making them oscillate, vibrate, and sway as though they were to be blown from the track.

"Guess this means mischief. Git it as fine as that, you'll git it deep," said the conductor.

The wind howled and shrieked round the train like myriads of demons let loose. The engine was already fighting deep snow upon the rails, and was slackening speed. They were now in a vast plain. The wind swept the snow against and over the fence on to the track, building up high masses of white on the sides and tops of the cars and engine, wheels, axles, steps—wherever there was a projection, the snow heaped itself up in little mounds of whiteness. The driver and stoker had constantly to clear the glass of the weather-house to look for the signals. The wind howled and whistled, the snow still poured from the sky in thick, powdered clouds. It was impossible to see more than a few yards ahead, and the driver slowed down to about ten miles an hour. Harder and harder had the engine to work to force itself through the snow. Into a cutting they went, where it had drifted and was getting seriously deep. Still it was, as yet, light, and the engine drove slowly on, over trestle bridges, spanning wide streams that were lost in the clouds of snow that was now falling in dense sheets; slower and slower the wheels of the engine turned, struggled convulsively, then stopped entirely. They were in a drift, and snow-bound.

The conductor descended and fought his way to the driver, who confessed himself beaten. He could get no farther. It was useless to try. Turning off steam, he left the engine with his mate. Taking a red lamp with them, the men fought their way to a telegraph pole from which the wires had been torn by the weight of the snow, and, after tremendous exertions, lashed it securely, and struggled back to the train and waited for the dawn.

The snow still fell, until not a vestige of the train could be seen, save around the funnel and boiler of the engine, where the warmth melted it.

CHAPTER XVIII

JACK MEETS MAMIE D'OLAN

AT the time the engine came to a standstill, several of the passengers had retired to their sleeping-berths for the night. At first, the delay did not attract much attention, but soon the news ran through the cars that the blizzard had stopped and buried the train, and then there was a general hustling, various exclamations from behind the curtains, and calls for the conductor. That much-sought individual, who was doing his best to be everywhere at once, said—

" You'd better get up and dress, I guess. There ain't no telling what may happen."

" Where are we?" asked an excited female voice.

" About fifty miles from nowhere, ma'am, near's I can figger it out, and we're here to stop."

" Hully Gee!" said the voice. " Then what's the matter car. " That gets me! Say, conductor, d'ye mean ter tell me I can't send a despatch to New York to say we're stuck?"

" I guess not."

" I'm not limiting the cost to a few dollars."

" That ain't the trouble. The wires are down."

" Hully Gee!" said the voice. " Then what's the matter with gettin' up and havin' a circus among ourselves? Poker, or a song, if the ladies don't object. It's goin' ter be purty slow lyin' here, I reckon. See here, conductor, switch on some more light, and let us fix things up a bit. Ef we got ter stop, may as well stop comfortable as uncomfortable."

There was a general chorus of assent to this, and soon most of those who had retired were dressed, sleeping-berths turned up, and the Pullman put on its all-day garb once more.

"Guess we'd better make believe it's breakfast-time. What's the matter with having some hot coffee, and something along with it?"

"Guess the cook's asleep," replied the conductor.

"Well, guess he can wake up same as other folks. Just go and tell him to get a move on him. If we *are* buried, it's our funeral, anyway, and we'll hev the fixing of it."

There was a general laugh at this sally, and the conductor, taking the thing in good part, went through the vestibule passage to rouse up the cook. That individual, however, was already awake, and had begun, at the solicitations of some passengers in another car, to prepare refreshments for them. Soon the grateful aroma of steaming hot coffee greeted the nostrils of the imprisoned travellers, and the waiters were busy handing it to them.

"Well, this is *great!*" said the owner of the voice, who was a Mr. Hiram A. Flinders, as he stepped out of the lavatory, fixing a large pair of diamond-studs in his shirt-cuffs. "Say, gentlemen, this is out of sight; this is *the* limit! Haven't been stuck up like this since '88, when I was drumming for Marshall A. Field. I was in the New York express, and we got buried six hours after we left Chicago in the biggest blizzard you ever saw. My! Here's the coffee. It makes me feel good ter smell it. Say, ma'am, ain't it worth while to strike a blizzard once in a way, when coffee smells as good as this?" And he handed the cup to a rather frightened dame who sat opposite.

The men turned to with a will, making the ladies comfortable before thinking of themselves. Jack and Tom, not having retired, were busy handing round tea which Wong, at Jack's orders, had prepared with his own special tea and teapot. Rolls and butter were brought in, and soon the bulk of the passengers were making themselves fairly comfortable.

" Say, conductor, bring me a gla-ass of ice-water," cried a female voice from a still-curtained berth.

" Ice-water in a blizzard like this?" whispered Tom, with a suppressed giggle. " What's the woman made of?"

" I believe if you woke an American out of his sleep at the North Pole the first thing he'd ask for, out of sheer habit, would be ' ice-water,' " Jack whispered back.

" Ain't there nary a banjo in the crowd?" asked Mr. Hiram A. Flinders. " Can't we extemporise a bit of a concert? Things'll get pesky dull. Ef we air snowed up, guess we ain't corpses yet."

" Did any one ask for a banjo?" a sweet female voice inquired.

The door of the private saloon at the end of the car opened, and a very beautiful girl of nineteen or twenty entered.

All the men rose and bowed, and Mr. Hiram A. Flinders answered—

" Yes, Miss D'Olan, I guess that war so. My card, Miss D'Olan—Hiram A. Flinders. Miss Mary D'Olan, ladies and gentlemen, daughter of Colonel Nathaniel D'Olan, President of the Longleash and Chickapoo Railroad. I know your poppa well, Miss D'Olan. Say, is your momma along?"

" Yes, mother's in there, Mr. Flinders. I'll get my banjo. We seem to be in a bad fix, but I quite agree with you that we must make the best of it," smiled Miss Mary D'Olan—or, as her friends called her, Mamie—as she went back to her room.

" Whew!" whistled Tom; " what a lovely girl!"

Tom was right. Mamie was really lovely. Tall, lithe, yet well-rounded in figure, golden-brown hair, a pure, classical face—dimpled chin, delightful mouth, filled with even, pearly teeth, long lashes, fringing large grey eyes, which could look sympathetic and tender one moment and dance with fun the next; a wonderfully well-modulated voice, especially for an American. Exquisitely dressed in a tailor-made travelling suit of grey, she did indeed look beautiful; and, be it said, she was as good as she was beautiful.

"That gal's worth four millions," sighed Mr. Hiram A. Flinders. "Hully Gee! I wish I war a British duke, and free; guess I'd call on her poppa to-morrow. We Americans don't get no show with our heiresses these days."

"Here's the banjo, Mr. Flinders," said Mamie, as she entered with a handsomely-decorated, silver-mounted instrument. "Do you play?"

"No, Miss D'Olan; not on such a banjo as that. Hully Gee! that must have cost two hundred dollars, if it cost a cent. Guess the company would be glad to hear *you*. Yes, ma'am, go ahead. Our ears are just thirsty for it. Go ahead, Miss D'Olan, go ahead."

Mamie smilingly complied, and struck into an American medley of "rag-time" song-and-dance tunes, played with such perfect time and expression that soon most of the men were clapping time to the music, and all were excited with it.

"Wa-al! Say!" said the delighted Hiram. "Ain't this *the* limit? I'm just tickled to death!" And the good-natured fellow, who would possibly be two or three thousand dollars out of pocket by the disaster to the train, stamped and clapped to the music, as happy and careless and jolly as a boy of ten.

When Miss Mamie had finished her medley, there was a general cry for more.

"Just one more, please, Miss D'Olan!" the men pleaded.

Mamie yielded, and sang the old-time, never-to-be-worn-out "Suwanee River," with such tenderness and tunefulness that more than one eye was moist when she had finished. Hiram A. Flinders yelled with delight.

"Ain't this real elegant?" he queried of the entire car. "Guess this concert's goin' ter cost me two thousand dollars, if it costs a cent, but I wouldn't have missed it for five thousand. Say, gentlemen, it's great! Guess it's my number. Just vamp in G, please, Miss D'Olan." And he rollicked into a jolly negro-ditty with a gusto that delighted himself to such an extent that all the others were delighted with him. Never was a buried party more alive than this. The sound of the music had brought in some of the passengers from the other cars and two or three nigger porters, who stood with grinning approbation, clapping and stamping to the time as heartily as though they were in a plantation barn rather than, as they were, buried beneath fifteen feet of snow on a railway track.

When Hiram had finished his song and responded to an encore, he looked round at Jack, who had retired into a corner, an amused and interested spectator of the scene, and said—

" Say, mister, you've a singing face. Won't you oblige the company? Guess we're a whole troupe here—all stars and no back rows or dummies. *No*, sir! you can't refuse, after Miss D'Olan started the show. Say, ain't that so?"

It would have been churlish to decline, under the circumstances, so Jack rose and, addressing Mamie, said—

" If Miss D'Olan will be good enough to vamp for me, I'll do my best. Do you know ' The Devout Lover,' Miss D'Olan?"

" Yes, sir," Mamie replied, with a little start, as she looked at Jack, whom she had not seen before. " This is it, is it not?" And she played a bar or two of the song.

" That will do splendidly, thanks."

Jack sang delightfully. His ear was as true as the needle to the pole. He had a rich baritone voice, sang naturally, yet with great taste and cultivation. He held his hearers under a spell. Mamie's sweet mouth opened with surprise and pleasure. She loved music, and knew a singer when she heard one. And Jack was a born singer. Moreover, in that, as in all things, his natural, unaffected manliness and his strong magnetism affected all who heard him. Mamie once or twice forgot the accompaniment, so interested was she.

JACK MEETS MAMIE D'OLAN

When Jack had finished, there was silence for a moment, then a burst of applause and calls for an encore. But Jack turned to the passengers, saying—

" I think we have tired Miss D'Olan sufficiently. My friend here, Mr. Hewley, will, I am sure, sing us something without accompaniment, and give Miss D'Olan a rest."

Tom, nothing loth, burst into a humorous patter song, and soon had the company roaring with laughter.

" Say, isn't this *co*-lossal?" roared Hiram. " Hully Gee! but ain't it great? *Ain't* we a combination? The only Mammoth Concert Combination performing under snow, or earth. Gee-whizz! but it's out of sight! It's *the* limit!"

They were making the best of it, as Mamie said, but after six hours, even their spirits began to flag, and there was no sign of relief or rescue.

The heat of the cars melted the snow around them for an inch or so, and the water began to penetrate in to them. The atmosphere was getting foul and unwholesome. Packed in as the carriages were by snow, no fresh air could enter. Jack suggested to Tom and Hiram that they should make an effort to dig up through the snow, and get, if possible, some ventilation into the cars. This was readily agreed to. Putting on overcoats, the men got some sticks and a spade, and, bursting open the side doors of the platform, they began to make the effort to reach the outer air. The task was not an easy one, but in time an opening was made. The men got on to the roof of the car, and looked out. As far as the eye could reach, there was nothing but snow. They were in a cutting, and could only see forward and backward through it. The sides were above them. Not a sound was to be heard; nothing to be seen.

" Hully Gee!" said Hiram, " but this is a hippodrome on a particularly large scale. We're in this for another twelve hours, I guess. We men'll be as right as rain, but I reckon the women will have a bad time."

"Let's get in some air, anyhow," said Jack.

The snow had ceased to fall; the air was crisp and sunny, but the sun was not powerful enough to melt that which had already fallen.. The three men struggled on. After two hours' hard work, the roof of the car was cleared, the ventilators opened, and a rush of pure, cold air filled the interior of the carriages, bringing a shiver to the passengers, but, at the same time, reviving their drooping spirits.

Another eight hours passed before a welcome engine bell and whistle announced the arrival of the steam plough, which had been sent with a gang of men to their rescue. After another tedious delay, the train was cleared, and, sixteen hours late, was hurrying on towards New York.

Mrs. D'Olan had joined her daughter, and was chatting, with American freedom and absence of restraint, with Jack and Tom. Mr. Hiram A. Flinders was in the smoking-car, with three fellow-passengers, deep in the toils of poker, as intent on turning a few dollars at that game as he would be in gaining thousands by trade.

"You're English, I guess?" said Mrs. D'Olan, whose accent was much more distinctly American than her daughter's. Mamie's was delicious in its quaint intonation.

"Yes," replied Jack.

"Proud of the fact, no doubt?" queried Mrs. D'Olan.

"Well, yes. I would sooner be an Englishman, if I had to choose, than any other nationality—unless it were American."

"It was real nice of you to say that, especially as you did not mean it," said Mrs. D'Olan.

"Well, perhaps I did not mean it, Mrs. D'Olan. But I can tell you what I do mean, and that is, I think America is going to be the greatest country in the world. I have only been away from it ten years, and the strides it has made, even as I have seen it from the windows of the cars, have amazed me. Such wonderful improvements—everywhere, and in everything. Where, ten years ago, I saw a few cabins on untouched prairie ground, I now see magnificent granite and marble buildings, in broad, paved streets. Villages have become towns, and towns vast cities. You are a great people, great in enterprise, invention, endurance, and ambition. Your future is a glorious one, and we, your elder cousins, are proud, even if a little envious of your greatness."

" Well, every day we get closer united, I guess. We are intermarrying pretty freely for cousins, don't you think ?"

" So I believe," replied Jack. " As I have been away from home so long, I cannot pretend to be intimately acquainted with our progress in that respect."

Mamie was watching Jack very closely the while she was chatting away gaily enough with Tom, who was, as he afterwards remarked, having " a beanfeast and a birthday all in one" with such a delightful companion. Mamie had shrewdly got a considerable amount of information out of Tom during the three hours' ride to Philadelphia, where they left the train, Mrs. D'Olan volunteering the information that they were going to England by the White Star steamer, the *Majestic,* on the following Wednesday.

Tom looked at Jack, and said—

" Well, as we've missed the Cunarder through this delay, and as we are going to England too, it is probable we may sail with you."

Tom felt sure he saw a distinct flush of pleasure on Mamie's face, although she only said, in a formal way—

" We shall be very glad if that is so." And she bade the friends good-bye.

" Well, that's the most charming thing I've seen for many a year," said Tom, as they steamed out of the Quaker city. " She's divine, Jack. Think of it! This lovely being, and four millions! If I had your infernal good looks, and confounded taking ways, I'd have a cut in there, if I lost my stake. Did you ever see a more delightful being?"

"She's certainly a very charming girl," answered Jack.

"Charming! You cold-blooded old fish! Charming! That divine creature charming! What a word for such a goddess! If they grow many of that kind over here, carry me home before I'm a lost orphan. And the simple naturalness of it all! Did you ever see anything more sweet than the way in which she plunkety-plunked that banjo of hers to amuse us? No affectation—no bounce. She simply did it."

"As to that, Tom, the whole thing was wonderful. Where else in the wide world would you have found people behave so well under the circumstances? All taking the trouble as an incident in the journey to be met, dealt with, and made the best of. They are a marvellous race. The more I know them, the more I respect and like them. Look at what we've seen on this journey alone! Think of the cities we've passed through. Then think of the youth of most of them. They are the most self-reliant, resourceful people on this earth. If they want a thing, they get it. If it doesn't exist, they make it. We're going to be beaten if we don't wake up. Perhaps even if we do. They have all our pluck and bulldoggedness with a snap and a go all their own. Mrs. D'Olan asked me if I was proud of being an Englishman. I am, and for many reasons, one of which will serve—I am kinsman to the Americans."

"Well, we shall have Mrs. and Miss D'Olan on the *Majestic* for a whole week. Go in and show your appreciation of America by winning one of her daughters."

"No, no," said Jack seriously. "Miss D'Olan is not for me." And his hand wandered to an inner breast-pocket, where rested the letters and photograph of Miss Sybil Landale.

"Well, how did you finish?" asked Tom of Mr. Hiram A. Flinders, who came into the car at that moment.

"Came out on top—carried off three Jack-pots in succession. Say, wasn't that concert great? Say, isn't Mamie D'Olan a peach? There ought to be a special Act of Congress to prevent a girl like that ever growing old. She's just a great hunk of sunshine after a thunderstorm—something the eye must turn to. Isn't she *the* limit?"

"She's lovely—just lovely," said Tom. "Have you many like that over here?"

"Many! Say, they're just like huckleberries on bushes—they are there in their tens of thousands. See here! American women have *got* to be like that, or what have we American men to live and work for? Yes, *sir!* That's our mission in life—just to go ahead, warm up this old planet, beautify it, and sweeten it, so our American women can sit around on it in comfort, and have fun. Yes, *sir!* that's our mission; and Hully Gee! we're going to fill the bill every time, sir—ev-er-y time." And Hiram rubbed his hands with vigorous and sustained satisfaction.

"Well, the man who is lucky enough to fill the bill for Miss D'Olan will have an attractive programme, anyway," said Tom.

"She's a nectarine with the bloom on. And there isn't a whiter man on earth than her father. Knew him in Chicago, when I was drumming for Marshall Field. Great man that, sir! Don't drum no more. No, sir! Here's my card—Hiram A. Flinders, of Twenty-Storey Block, Soft Goods store, 5021 Madison. I'm on my own—turn over a million dollars a year. How's that? Ten years ago I hadn't a nickel. Peddled five-cent notions on Madison Avenue, right there where my store now stands. They call me Five-cent Flinders to this day, and I'm proud of it. Yes, *sir!* The old tray that hung round my neck in all weathers now hangs in a glass case, framed in five-cent pieces—five thousand of 'em, all welded together—and a hundred incandescent lamps round 'em, always alight, night and day. Yes, *sir!* Know Chicago?"

"Never been there, I am sorry to say," said Tom.

"That so? Hully Gee! You're never going back to U-rope without seein' the greatest city on earth!"

"Fear I must," replied Tom.

"Sir, no man's lived until he's seen Chicago. No, sir!

173

It's no use *talking*—there's nothing like her. She's just the biggest thing on earth, is old Chicago."

" Not so old, neither," said Tom.

" That's so," acquiesced Hiram. " Why, sir, there's men living there now who remember Chicago when she was a baby of a place, with half-a-dozen wood cabins, and the only amusement the inhabitants had was an old fiddle played by a little Frenchman on the lake shore. That's so. See it now in the Calumet Club. Then she ran along until that blamed old cow kicked over the kerosene lamp, and burned her down. We just had to begin her all over again. *And* we did. And now—Gee-whizz! Next census, she'll tot up to six millions. Yes, *sir!* Chicago scoops the confectionery."

" Sorry I cannot see her," said Tom.

" See here—I go back Monday. Come right along. I'll fix you up at my house, 2041 Calumet. Built it myself. Call it Five-cent Flinderana. Makes folk talk and be funny about me. Let 'em. More they talk, more business for me."

" Married?"

" Some."

" I beg your pardon?"

" Some; *I'm* married. *Yes,* sir! And she fills the bill, does Mrs. Flinders. Every time, sir; ev-er-y time. You should see Mrs. Hiram A. Flinders! Say, will you come along, Monday? Now, do! It'll be just *lovely* if you will. You'll have the best time you ever struck. Bring your friend along. Mrs. H. A. Flinders will be glad to see you, sir; an' I'll take half a day off, and tot you round. Show you *my* store, Armour's Pork-packing Establishment, Pullman City, the Auditorium, Marshall Field's—and the tallest blocks in the world—thirty-two storey sky-scrapers. Eh? It's no use *talking*—Chicago swallers the bun. Say, you'll both come along Monday?"

" You're very kind, Mr. Flinders," answered Jack, " but we've missed the Cunarder and must sail on the *Majestic* on Wednesday."

" That's so? Well, I'm *real* sorry. I'm hurt that you haven't seen Chicago. She's an education, sir."

" I have seen her—ten years ago," Jack answered.

" You don't say! My! But ten years ago—and now! You'd never know her, sir. She's grown out of sight."

" I thought she was a great city then."

" Not a circumstance to what she is now, sir. Didn't amount to a row o' beans. She's *co*-lossal, sir; she's just *co*-lossal!" And so the bright fellow rattled on—proud of his native city, never tired of sounding its praises.

It must be granted he had much to eulogise. He was right. Chicago *is* co-lossal.

They were running into the Jersey City depôt. The conductor had dusted them all carefully with his swish brush, as though they were so many articles for sale in a shop window. Their baggage was checked through to the Waldorf Hotel, New York, so, without worry or delay, they were soon on the ferryboat, crossing the river for Cortlandt Street. Arriving there, Mr. Hiram A. Flinders said—

" Now, say, is there anything I can do for you fellows? Say *right* here. You can *own* Hiram A. Flinders, if there's anything you want."

" No, thanks, you've been very kind already. Again, thanks," replied Jack.

Mr. Flinders shook hands warmly, ran after a car, caught it, stood with some other dozen busy men, packed like sardines on the steps of the over-crowded vehicle, and was soon rattling along in a discussion on the relative merits of New York and Chicago with a New York friend who was on the car.

" There goes a man typical of his class. Keen, bright, proud of his city, his country, and his business. No shame for his humble beginning—indeed, glorying in it. And there are millions more like him. Men who think no toil too great, no personal sacrifice too heavy that helps to build up their trade, and who, in building up that, help to build up their nation."

" By Jove ! what a clatter !" exclaimed Tom, putting his hands to his ears as they turned into Broadway. " What a row !"

And indeed, to the two men lately from the great Bush and the ocean, the roar of the streets was almost deafening. There had been in New York a sudden thaw. The snow was just disappearing under the combined attacks of the sun and the army of snow-sweepers. It still lingered in side streets, and much was left, built up by the side-walks, but the centre of Broadway was clear. The rattle of the wheels of the different vehicles, the constant clang-clang-clang of the bells of the cars, the clash of the iron hoofs of the horses on the stones, the whistle and rush of the elevated railway, all combined to make up an ear-splitting, nerve-destroying noise, from which there was no escape.

Jack had a call to make in Broadway. The office was the twenty-second storey of a twenty-six storey block. Entering the passage he saw four electric elevators or lifts. " Express !" shouted the conductor of one. " Slow !" the other. The express went up to the sixteenth floor without a stop. The slow paused at each landing. Jack and Tom entered the express. It was at once thronged with passengers. The iron gates were slammed to with a clash, and, without warning, the passengers were shot up like a stone from a catapult. Sixteen storeys without a pause ! Jack and Tom felt the breath leave their bodies. Up and up they went to the twenty-second.

" Where is Hooper & Co.'s office ?" Jack asked of the conductor.

" Sixth door, passage to right." And almost before they were out of the lift, it was on its way to floor twenty-five.

" Phew !" gasped Tom. " Where am I ? Am I a Mauser bullet or an electric current ? Gee-whizz ! as Hiram says, I was never so catapulted in my life."

Hooper's office was found, and Jack's business transacted.

JACK MEETS MAMIE D'OLAN

" What a wonderful view you have here, Mr. Hooper."

" Ya-as, so I suppose. Not much time for looking round for 'views' in this office, though, 'cept Sundays, and then we're not here." And he turned to the next client.

Jack and Tom left the office and studied the view from the window on the landing. From this they could see nearly the whole of Manhattan Island, the river encircling it like a broad band of blue and white. On the roofs of the houses the snow was still lying, dirty and black. Huge buildings of sixteen storeys looked dwarfed in the streets below them, the vehicles like toys, the human beings like mice. Long lines of pigmy traffic crawled along the thoroughfares. The elevated railway trains rushed in and out, threading the streets, turning abrupt corners so close to the houses that the passengers could see right into the rooms and almost shake hands with the occupants. The river was crowded with all sorts of shipping, the steamers and ferryboats gliding about, sounding their moaning, mournful steam-whistles. Ocean-going vessels moved solemnly and majestically along; white-sailed yachts skimmed lightly over the waters. Life everywhere—busy, bustling, struggling, striving, over-driven, over-strained life! A ceaseless stream of toilers, looking ever ahead, heeding no obstacles, stopping for nothing and no man. " Come with me, or stay behind. I'm going on!" is the cry of the average American. No time for fooling in business hours. Minutes are dollars. Hours and days, hundreds or thousands of dollars. The word is everywhere in New York. On the hoardings, in the store-windows, in the newspapers, in the mouths of the pushing men, on the lips of the lovely women. Dollars! dollars! dollars! It is the tick of the American pendulum—dollars! dollars! dollars! Swing to, swing fro, tick, tick, tick—dollars! dollars! dollars! Listen to it on 'Change, in Wall Street! Hearken to it in the cars! Hear it in the stores! the side-walk! the clubs! the homes!— dollars! dollars! dollars! Incentive, spur, reward, bane,

12   177

antidote, life and death—all flow to and from dollars! dollars! dollars! With them are to be purchased place, power, fame, office, luxuries, necessities. The best work and the heart's blood of men, consciences, wives, and husbands. Only life and health are unbuyable, as the many-times millionaire who lay gasping out his greedy life in his palace on Fifth Avenue knew all too well.

Entering the elevator, Jack and his friend were shot down as rapidly as they were shot up the building, and, with a queer thrill through their spinal-cords, they found themselves once more on the pavement of Broadway.

Crossing the road at the peril of their lives, dodging lorries, cabs, waggons, and the ever-rushing-up-and-down lines of the cars, Jack entered the office of the Commercial Cable Company, and despatched messages to Lady Walgrove and Sybil, telling them that they had missed the Cunard liner, and intended sailing on the *Majestic* on the following Wednesday. Getting into their cab again, they were bumped and jolted up Broadway, through Union and Madison Squares, turning off into Fifth Avenue to the magnificent Waldorf Hotel.

Having two days and a half, they had ample time to get a good general idea of New York and its surroundings. Jack dearly wished to take a run down to classical and beautiful Boston, which he had visited ten years before, but time would not admit of it. Tom was simply amazed, as most Englishmen are, at the greatness of New York, the immense business quarters, the palatial dwellings of Fifth Avenue and the upper portions of the city, the splendid Central Park, Brooklyn Bridge, and, above all, the enormous rush and energy of the people themselves. As a Southerner once remarked, "Every one in the city seems to be hurrying to a fire." At night there is a queer suggestion of Paris in certain quarters of New York. The women are exquisitely dressed, extremely beautiful, and their horses and equipages not to be beaten anywhere except in London during the full season. Wealth in profusion is in evidence everywhere in the fashionable part of the city; poverty, in its most hideous and squalid form, in the lower portion. In the tenement-houses vice, disease, dirt, and hunger are rampant. Men, women, and children are huddled together like rats in a sewer, starving, festering, dying. The Bowery, with its dirt and blackguardism; the pestiferous Tenderloin district, where vice is winked at, even fostered by those whose duty it is to suppress it, stand out in strange contrast to the wealth, luxury, and refinement of the other world a little higher up the town. It is all very wonderful, very fascinating, and, in some things, very horrible. The very air is intoxicating, and seduces the stranger into New York ways and New York rush in an incredibly brief space of time. So accustomed is the New Yorker to the lightning rapidity of his native city that he will tell you placidly " the grass grows in the principal streets" of a neighbouring town, and " whiskers on its side-walks."

There is much to admire and much to learn in New York. It is the centre of the fashion of America, the corner-stone of its commerce. From its offices, the affairs of the whole world are influenced, in many ways regulated and dictated to. Daily its power is growing. Its Companies, Trusts, and Corporations increase and multiply almost hourly. Its daily and weekly press are unequalled anywhere. No price is too large for the New York journals to pay for news, local and universal. Its power is marvellous, its influence unbounded. It is absolutely fearless. It attacks men, systems, parties, governments, with equal vigour. If it cannot be said that it is always just, it must be admitted that it is never dull. To Tom, who had never seen New York before, the time between his arrival and departure by the steamer passed like some wild dream, leaving in his memory a whirling kaleidoscope of huge buildings, brilliant sunshine, rushing people, luxury and poverty, splendour and squalor, never to be forgotten.

On the Wednesday, a little after noon, Jack and Tom went on board the *Majestic*, inspected their cabins, and came on deck to watch the dense throngs that filled every available corner of the promenade and saloons: friends and relations of the passengers, journalists, curiosity-mongers, business men, having a last chat over matters and giving final instructions to their agents, and the passengers themselves so crowded the boat that progression was almost impossible, except by using actual force. For a time, Jack did not see a face he knew, but Tom, who had been on the look-out for Miss D'Olan and her mother, suddenly nudged his elbow as they leant over the ship's rail, and whispered—

" There she is, Jack !"

As it happened, Jack was thinking of Sybil, and he gave a start at Tom's remark, asking hurriedly—

" Whom do you mean ?"

Tom noticed Jack's movement at his remark, and mis-construed it, thinking, after all, Jack was more interested in Mamie than he had assumed to be. So he watched him narrowly as he replied—

" Miss D'Olan, of course."

Jack turned in the direction in which Tom was looking, and saw Mamie, surrounded by a whole lot of friends, male and female. Some of the former wore a worried, anxious look as they watched Mamie, that betokened a warmer interest in her than that of a friend or a brother. They were all gentlemanly, clever-looking men, but to no one did Mamie show any particular favour. Indeed, her eyes had wandered often from them all to where Jack was standing. She had seen him from the time he crossed the gangway, long before Tom saw her, and her cheek had flushed with pleasure, which one of her admirers at-tributed, all wrongly, to a remark he had made to her.

" Miss D'Olan, you look like a streak of sunshine," said a white-headed, white-moustached, military-looking man.

He was not far out. She was, as always, delightfully dressed, in a tailor-cut, tight-fitting travelling dress of navy blue soft cloth, which clung tightly to all the curves of her lovely figure, a Tam o' Shanter hat of the same material, with a black cock's feather fastened by a small gold buckle, and a narrow rim of sable fur round the brim. Small gold buttons and a narrow gold belt were all the trimmings on the dress, while a large bunch of forget-me-nots, given by a girl-friend, were thrust into her waistband. Her face was fresh and radiant. Her hair shone in the bright spring sunshine. Her hands were thrust into a small sable muff, on which another girl-friend was just pinning a small bunch of purple and orange pansies. She wore no visible jewellery or ornaments of any kind, but looked what she was—every inch a lady and a sweet, good woman.

A very distinguished-looking man of about forty-five was standing by her side, looking at her with loving solicitude, and to whom she turned every now and then, giving a little affectionate squeeze of his arm and nestling up to him with an unaffected look of love in her sweet eyes, that some of the men near her would have given half their fortune to be the recipient of. This was her father, Colonel Nathaniel D'Olan, a Southerner, who had served as a mere boy in the last days of the struggle with the North, and had seen his father and only brother fall fighting by his side. When the war was ended, he went north, and by his brilliant talents soon won a position that a man ten years his senior might have been proud of. He married at twenty-four the daughter of a wealthy railway magnate. She was about his own age. It was a pure love-match, and their lives had passed in unclouded happiness. Mamie was their only child, and their love and care were lavished upon her in a manner that would have spoiled nine girls out of ten. Mamie was not of the kind to be ruined or spoiled by love or attention. It made her more tender and loving, not only to her parents, but to all she came in contact with.

"Are you sure you have got all you want, girlie?" her father asked tenderly.

"Quite sure, dear. More than I want—more than I shall know what to do with." And she placed her hand on his and pressed it. "And you're not to worry," she continued. "I'll take care of Mamsey, and you'll come right along in three weeks, won't you?"

"Right along, if the old Longleash and Chickapoo Railway has to bust for it," he replied, half smiling and half in earnest. "This is the first time we've been parted —that is, by more distance than a ten hours' trip by rail —and I'm not quite sure I like it," he said rather ruefully. "All my family going—a lonely and unprotected old bachelor—and all these lovely girls around! How do I know what's going to happen?"

"Old bachelor, indeed! At the opera the other night, I heard some one say, as we were walking around during the intermission, 'Those two seem mighty spooney together. Just married, I reckon.'" And Mamie laughed, to make her father smile too, for she could not bear to see his dear face sad.

The warning to go ashore was given, and, with many a hearty hand-shake, many a kiss and embrace, the passengers and their friends parted. The great vessel left her moorings, and slowly moved from the dock into the river. Mamie, with her mother, stood at the extreme end of the promenade, watching her father until completely out of sight, then, taking her mother tenderly in her arms, she led her to her room.

The harbour and the bay of New York are exceedingly beautiful, and as the sun set, the views were most picturesque and delightful. For various reasons, the decks were gradually deserted, and, drawing their deck chairs into a corner, the two friends dropped into a quiet talk.

Jack's mind had been running on Sybil all the day. Now that he had started for England, now that but a week's journey stood between him and Landale Abbey, it seemed as if the final step had been taken, and he was alternately glad and remorseful.

"Didn't that girl look a picture?" said Tom, whose thoughts were still running on Mamie.

"Do you mean Miss D'Olan?" asked Jack.

"Of course I mean Miss D'Olan. That was evidently her father who kissed her good-bye. What a handsome fellow! How young he looked!"

"Perhaps it was not her father. Why not her be-trothed?"

"I'll bet a hundred to one that it was her father, and that she's not betrothed at all."

"Why should you think she's not?"

"Because she's a girl who would never betroth herself to a man she did not love, and she's never been in love yet." Tom rather emphasised the word " yet."

"How do you know that?"

"Because—well—" Tom did not like to say what his suspicions were, nor tell Jack with what interest Mamie had regarded him, so he juggled with his answer, saying—

"Well, all her real regret at leaving New York was at parting with her father. A fool could see that. With that one drawback, her heart was light at the prospect of this voyage."

"Perhaps she's going to meet ' Mr. Him' on the other side."

"No, indeed, she isn't, because there's no ' Mr. Him' for her on the other side." Tom was speaking with much more seriousness than was usual with him, and Jack turned and looked at him in some surprise, saying, half in earnest, half in jest—

"Tom, I believe you're in love with that girl!"

"Me!" almost screamed Tom. "Me in love with her! No, Jack, drop that out of your calculations. I know too well what is good for my peace of mind to fall in love with Mamie D'Olan. If she wants a man to die for her some day, or do any other little service, Tom Hewley can be had for the asking. But not for love—at least, not that kind of love. I'm not the sort of little boy who cries for the moon. My head's got to look out for my heart. Can't afford to let my heart run away with my head, to the detriment of my whole corporation. The Mamie D'Olans

of this life don't fall in love with the Tom Hewleys. I'm
that girl's friend or brother for life, if she wants me, but
there the line is drawn. Confound it, man! Can't you
see what a dear woman she is?"

"Yes, I can, Tom. I think she's all that you think her
and a bit over—the sort of woman who sweetens the air
about her—and I think I could, and would, play the friend
and brother as readily as yourself."

Somehow Tom was disappointed with this answer. In
his own mind he had been building up a nice little
romance, in which Jack and Mamie played the hero and
heroine. Jack's speech was hardly as fervent as he desired his hero's to be. After a short silence, Jack asked—

"Tom, do you realise what this voyage is bringing
us to?"

"Rather! I realise what it *may* bring us to. Portland or Wormwood Scrubs. But that is not what you
were thinking of, is it?"

"No, it is not. I was thinking of the fraud, not of
the punishment. Thinking, as I watched Miss D'Olan
and her mother, of another mother and daughter I was
soon to meet. Oh, Tom, lad! there's a weight at my
heart whenever the thought of Sybil enters my mind—
and that's nearly every moment. How will she meet me?
How will she look? What will she say? Wormwood
Scrubs! Portland! They would be heaven compared
with the hell of her scorn and contempt!"

"You will not get her scorn and contempt, or any
other woman's, if it comes to that. You're not built that
way."

As they wandered down the deck they met Wong, who
said—

"Clabin allee leady."

He had unpacked, and everything was in order for the
two men when they went to dress for dinner. The vessel
had begun to tumble about a little as she passed Long
Island, and the dinner tables were only moderately well
attended. Jack found, to his surprise and pleasure, that

he had been placed at the captain's table, next to Miss D'Olan. How this was arranged perhaps the astute and most obliging Mr. Hustle, the purser, and the fair Mamie, could explain. At all events, it was after a little chat between the two that some slight alteration had been made in the table plans. Can it be possible it was through Mamie's suggestion?

Tom sat opposite, next to Mrs. D'Olan, whom he kept in a constant ripple of laughter by his humour and good spirits. Jack greeted Mamie with real friendliness, and expressed his unfeigned delight at having her next to him.

"I am glad, too," said Mamie quietly, with a glance towards Mr. Hustle. Perhaps, after all, it was to keep some other less agreeable person away from her that she spoke to that amiable gentleman. Who can tell? The ways of women are devious and strange. Weak men can only conjecture the motives which prompt them.

"Quite a lucky accident for me, at least," said Jack. "I wonder how it happened."

"It's a handsome saloon, is it not, Mr. Landale?" asked Mamie, who seemed rather anxious to change the subject.

"*Mr. Landale!*" Jack felt the hot flush of shame rise to his cheek as Mamie pronounced the name. It was the first time she had done so. He looked at her honest eyes, her truthful, clear, noble face, and wondered what expression would cross them if she knew what little claim he had to that name. Fortunately, some one else spoke to her just then, and she had to answer.

The other seats at the table were filled up by the captain at the head, an elderly gentleman—a Mr. Eriksson, a Norwegian by birth, now a banker in New York—at the foot. Mamie sat next to the captain on one side, her mother on the other. Next to Jack, on his left hand, was a Mr. Philip Blecker, a New York judge; and next to Tom was a Philadelphia railway man, named Arthur Marriner—both clever, companionable fellows, as indeed most American gentlemen are. They had crossed in the

Majestic before, and knew the captain well. They also knew each other, and Mrs. D'Olan and Mamie. Eriksson they knew by name and reputation. The only strangers were the two Englishmen, Jack and Tom—of them they knew nothing.

"Glad to be off, Captain Campbell?" asked Mr. Marriner.

"Yes, and no," replied the captain. "I am always sorry to leave New York, but always glad to arrive in Liverpool."

"How happy could I be with either!" said Tom.

"Well, yes. I have many friends in New York, and a wife and family in Liverpool, so I am pulled both ways."

"Full passenger-list, I see," said the judge. "Sorry your father's not along, Miss D'Olan."

"You know my father?" asked Mamie.

"Indeed I do, and am proud of it. Who does not know and respect Colonel D'Olan?"

"Thank you, sir," said Mrs. D'Olan. "My husband joins us in London in three weeks. Some urgent railway business that he could not leave to others happened along at the last moment. As we had made several important engagements in England, we could not wait for him. So here we are, alone."

"Not alone, ma'am. You've every American gentleman on board this boat with you."

"And every Britisher too, I hope," said Jack. "If Mrs. D'Olan will permit them to consider themselves attendants."

"Why not?" asked Mamie.

"Why not, indeed?" retorted the judge. "A real Anglo-American Alliance for the protection and defence of our joint queen—for this trip at least, Miss D'Olan," and he lifted his glass of champagne, saluting Mamie—an act of old-fashioned courtesy which every one at the table followed.

"I am honoured, I am sure, Judge Blecker," replied Mamie, blushing deliciously. "But I shall make but a poor queen, I fear. I have had little experience as a ruler."

" My dear Miss D'Olan, you began to rule on the hour you first breathed. You were just born for that purpose, and no other; and, unlike any other monarch, your kingdom extends all over the world; wherever men are not blind and women not hateful, you are———"

" Please talk about the moon."

" If I knew her ladyship as well as I do you, Miss D'Olan, I would. Unfortunately, I have only a bowing-acquaintance with her, and that, usually, after a prolonged sitting at the clubs. I am afraid I have not seen enough of her—or, perhaps, at times too many of her—to be a good judge———"

" You're always that," said Mr. Marriner.

" Of the moon, I was going to say," continued Mr. Blecker.

The steamer was now feeling the effect of a rather lively head sea, and Mrs. D'Olan, looking a little white and a little depressed, asked to be excused, and left the table, taking Mamie with her.

Jack did not see Mamie until noon next day, when she came on deck looking as lovely as ever, if a little paler. Her maid was following her, carrying her wraps. Half-a-dozen men rushed forward, but she politely declined their assistance, and walked alone, with quiet composure, to her chair. Mamie hated the fussy attention so many women seem to find such delight in. She was grateful for any real service rendered her, and liked to be admired. She would not have been a woman if she did not. But the good opinion of an intellectual man or woman pleased her far more than the fulsome adulation of a score of so-called admirers. While quite conscious of her beauty, she would at all times be more grateful for a little love and affection given to herself. Some called her cold. They knew nothing of her. She did not gush, or flatter men or women; neither did she wear her heart upon her sleeve. She would sooner do a kind thing than talk of it. She seldom received an affront, because, perhaps, she was never on the look-out for one, so that she seemed comparatively calm and cool, but a warmer heart never beat in a human body for those she knew and cared for. So the would-be attendant swains made their ineffectual efforts to make an impression upon the beautiful creature all in vain.

A quiet, dignified smile, and " Thank you," meant for their dismissal, secured it, and Mamie was left to arrange the rugs and herself to her own liking and satisfaction. Jack, who had watched the little scene at a distance, with some amusement, felt now more respect and liking for her than ever.

The sea was sufficiently rough to make walking on the deck disagreeable, and when, as he bade her good morning, Mamie asked him if he would not bring up his chair and talk to her, Jack very gladly complied.

" You're a good sailor, Mr. Landale."

" I don't suffer from sea-sickness," Jack answered. " I hope you have not been troubled that way?"

" Well, I have felt more comfortable than I did last night, but I am going to battle it out with the waves this morning. And now, tell me about England. I have never crossed before. Shall I like it, or shall I not?"

" I hope you will, but you must expect to find it very different from America."

" Tell me in what way."

" In everything that is distinctly American. We are of the same race, the same blood, speak the same language, are ruled—broadly speaking—by the same laws, but we are older, more sedate, slower, more conservative, and slaves to our own traditions. The Englishman is too apt to say, ' What was good enough for my father is good enough for me.' The American asks himself, ' How can I go one better than my father?' An English manufacturer, if he sets up a plant of machinery, as a rule uses it until it is worn out. The American only until something better is invented. He is not going to let another man get ahead with better machinery. Out goes the old, and in comes the newest and best that is to be got for money. The man who does not move in America does not stand still—he goes back, as they say, 'way back—way off.' Climate has much to do with the resistless push and go of the Americans. The climate north, east, and west won't let a man sit still; he must keep moving. In the South, as you know, it is different. A man can sit still there, and too often does. All the same, I love the South."

"I am glad of that. I'm half Southern. My father is a Virginian, my mother a New Englander."

"Is D'Olan a Southern name?"

Mamie's eyes twinkled as she replied—

"Not exactly, Mr. Landale. It's Irish."

"Irish? Surely not?"

"Oh, but it is. It's simply Doolan, with an *o* knocked out and a hiatus and an apostrophe put in. It's simply D-o-o-l-a-n." And Mamie laughed merrily.

"Why was it changed? Wasn't Doolan good enough?"

"Well, it was for papa, but mamma's mother said she would never give her consent to her daughter marrying an Irish name. Papa said he would call himself 'Mud' or 'Dennis' rather than lose mamma. Grandmamma said she would compromise the matter, so we became big D, apostrophe, one O, lan—D'Olan."

"Why did your grandmother dislike the Irish?"

"That's the joke. Because she was Irish herself. Her maiden name was Flannagan. Better than that, it was Bridget Flannagan! And better even than that, everybody called her Biddy till her dying day!"

"So, really, you are Mary Doolan?"

"I guess so. But my friends call me Mamie."

"Amongst which thrice-blessed company I dare not consider myself included."

"Dare you not? You don't look like a coward either, Mr. Landale. I don't like cowards."

"I am sure you could not dislike a coward even, Miss D'Olan."

"How?" she queried. This was an American "How" of Mamie's, equivalent to "What did you say?" not "What did you mean?" Not to have heard Mamie say "How?" is to have missed one of the most musical intonations known in our—nay, pardon!—in the American language.

"I said I did not think you were capable of disliking anything very much."

"Don't you bet on that. There's a man over there whom I dislike very much indeed. No, don't look round yet; he's watching us."

"Let me go and kill him before lunch, Miss D'Olan," said Jack, with mock ferocity.

"No, let him live until dinner, and see how he behaves. But you don't seem to understand what I mean, Mr. Landale."

"About what?"

"Well, what were we talking about?"

"About your name."

"Well?"

"Well?"

"Don't you see I'm just crazy to hear you call me Mamie?"

"Good gracious! May I?"

"Guess I'll try to bear it if you do."

"Well then, I think the name of Mary D'Olan very pretty—but I think Mamie Doolan too lovely for words."

"How? Do you mean the name?"

"I mean both."

Mamie looked at him with mischief and fun just bubbling out from her eyes, and said—

"No, Mr. Landale. I guess you're not a coward. I never thought you were."

This must all read very dreadful and improper in cold print, and I can even hear some of her own sex call dear Mamie "a forward minx," which she certainly was not. Mamie allowed very few people indeed to address her by that name. It was a privilege confined to her own immediate kin, some girl-friends, and one or two of her father's intimates who had known her from childhood. When she said she wanted to hear Jack call her Mamie, she meant it.

Jack was thoughtful for a moment. He was wondering whether he was a coward or not, in going on with his imposture; whether it would not be braver to confess all to Lady Walgrove and her daughter, and——

"Have I shocked you, Mr. Landale?" asked Mamie apprehensively.

"No, no! Please do not think that," answered Jack earnestly.

"If I have, forgive me, and remember I am an American girl. I would like you to be my friend. We have only five or six days in which to get acquainted. After this week we may never see each other again." Mamie's voice was not quite so firm as she could wish as she said this. "You are English. Had I not expressed a desire to know you better, you would have thought it presumption on your part to do more than bow to me, or say 'good morning,' and I should have lost a friendship I should like to gain. We should have stood or sat staring at each other, like two figures in a waxwork museum. Do you forgive me?"

"Miss Doo——I mean, Miss Mamie, I am flattered by your good opinion, and I honour your frankness. Believe me that both are understood, and shall be respected."

Mamie knew this perfectly well. Her quick woman's instinct had told her that, else had she never confided in him.

When Mamie went to her mother's cabin, she looked so radiantly happy that her mother said—

"Why, Mamie, whatever is the matter? You're looking so bright! What's come along since you left me an hour ago?"

"You won't scold me if I tell you, will you?"

"Why, no, honey. Why should I?"

"Well," blushed Mamie, with her arms round her

mother's neck. "Let me whisper it in your ear. There's a man on that deck whom I would sooner have for a— friend—than any one I have ever met before."

Jack and Mamie had many opportunities for becoming better acquainted during the voyage, and the more they knew of each other the stronger became their mutual regard. As Mamie's nature unfolded itself, Jack became deeply interested in her. But he had never forgotten Sybil for a moment. A hundred times a day his hand went, with a caressing little pressure, to her portrait, nestling in his breast-pocket. He had been encouraged by Mamie to tell her something of his past life, and Tom had told her a great deal of his character and good qualities, all of which, although it came as no news, Mamie was delighted to hear. Mrs. D'Olan was much alarmed, at first, at Mamie's confession, but, after watching Jack very closely, and learning that he was the head of so good an old English family as the Landales, she grew to view the situation with more calmness, with no less care for her daughter's happiness. She had every confidence in Mamie's discretion and goodness; still, the possibility of her falling in love, and her love not being returned, haunted and, at times, terrified her. She devoutly wished that her husband had accompanied them. He would have known so much better how to deal with the situation. Jack was a gentleman—she did not doubt that.

Meantime, how was it with Mamie? The girl had questioned herself often and anxiously. Certain she was that she felt for Jack a deeper feeling than any other man had yet inspired her with. Was it love? She was afraid it was. She could not quite confirm it yet. But she was destined to be quite sure within a very few hours.

That night, after dinner and the usual promenade on deck, they were standing leaning over the rails, watching the path of light the moon was making on the waters, and Mamie had been coaxing Jack to talk of himself. She had aroused his feelings strongly, and under this influence he had spoken so tenderly of his anxiety to be all that his mother and sister desired to find him, that, when he said in all sincerity that he could " never be worthy of the love that they were prepared to lavish upon him," Mamie said—

" But why do you say that, Mr. Landale?"

Jack started as if he had been stung. The name struck him like the lash of a whip.

" For pity's sake!" he exclaimed, " don't call me by that name!"

" How?" asked Mamie, in surprise.

" I mean—that—" He could not tell her it was remorse that hurt him, and he said—

" Well, you wished me to call you Mamie. Will you not call me Jack?"

" Isn't that a little different?" she asked.

" How can it be different?"

" I don't know—but—" Mamie paused. She was gazing into the water.

" Please let it be Jack!"

" Jack!" Mamie murmured. Her heart fluttered. She knew it now. She loved the man into whose face she looked with a long, searching, earnest gaze. Offering her hand, she said, " Good night, Jack."

He replied, " Good night, Miss Mamie," and they parted.

As Mamie went away, Tom strolled up. He had seen the parting between the two, and the expression on Mamie's face as she passed under the electric light on her way to the saloon stairs, and it had startled him.

Jack was looking over into the sea as Tom placed his hand on his shoulder, saying—

" Well, Jack, old man, how goes it?"

" I don't know, Tom. All seems so different, so strange. I seem to have drifted into a new world. Everything that was hard and bitter seems to have vanished, and all that is beautiful and sweet has come about me."

" Have you anything else to tell me?"

" What do you mean?"

" What do *you* mean, if it comes to that?" retorted Tom.

" Where and how?"

" Jack, don't jump down my throat if I say something, will you?"

" I won't jump down your throat, anyway. What's the trouble?"

" Mamie!"

" Mamie? What on earth do you mean?"

" Jack, if I didn't know you were as straight as a die, I should say you were acting on the crooked. As I am aware of your general moral rectitude, I am constrained to ask you, are you a benighted ass, or are you not?"

" Explain, Tom. Don't wobble in circles. Come to the point."

" Are you in love with Mamie?"

" Good heavens, no! What put that into your head?"

" Your conduct."

" My conduct! How?"

" Oh, come! Jack. Do you know that you have monopolised that lovely girl's company the whole of this voyage?"

" I have been with her a great deal, certainly. What then?"

" What then! That's exactly it. What then? That is for you to answer. What then?"

" We are the best of friends, and I hope we ever shall be."

" Is that all?"

" Of course! What else?"

" Is that what Mamie says?"

" Not in so many words, but that's what she means."

" Has it ever entered into your handsome, but, at times, damned thick head that it is within the bounds of possibility that that dear girl might—I only say *might*— fall in love with you?"

" God forbid!" said Jack, so earnestly that Tom felt a

cold thrill pass over him. He remembered Mamie's look
of rapt happiness as she passed him. If ever the love-
light shone in a woman's face, it shone in hers. He
shuddered for her.

"Then I wish you'd never met her!"

Jack stared, in astonishment. The idea of Mamie's
falling in love with him had never entered his head. Nor
did he believe it now. Her friendship was most precious
to him, but no other thought of her had suggested itself.
He had asked her to call him Jack. He could not explain
that he had no right to the name of Landale, and for that
reason could not bear her to address him so. A moment
ago, all looked so bright—he felt so happy—and now!
Truly, the deception he was practising seemed destined to
bring even with its success a great deal of grief. He
would not hurt this beautiful girl for the world, if he
could avoid it. Even if he loved, he could never marry
with this fraud blackening his future. He did not love
her—nor did she love him. Tom was mistaken. He
must be!

"Tom, old fellow, you are worrying without a cause.
Mamie likes me as a friend. She has been too frank and
free to be in love. We are just two good pals—nothing
more. I am sure of it."

"Let us hope so," said Tom mournfully. "I wouldn't
have that dear girl unhappy for the world."

"No, nor I, old man," Jack exclaimed heartily. "God
bless her! She should know nothing but happiness."

Some time next day they were to sight the coast of
Ireland. About seven o'clock in the evening was the time
anticipated; but some would-be clever person had circu-
lated the report in the steerage, where many returning
Irish emigrants had taken passage, that it would be seen
at five in the morning. It was a stupid, cruel joke. At
daybreak all the Irish were on deck, straining their eyes
to catch the first glimpse of their own dear native land.
Hour after hour passed, and yet no sight of it.

"Maybe it's missin' it we'll be afthur," moaned a poor

old woman, who, with her white head enveloped in a plaid shawl, had been looking for it since daybreak.

"Missin', is it, mother darlint?" answered her daughter; "and the captain, glory be his bed, knowin' the path across the wather like his walk up yondher on the bridge! Och! it's nonsense you do be puttin' out at us."

"Glory be! but it 'ud break me heart to give ould Oireland the go-by, afthur the weary years since I saw the green turf uv her," whimpered the old woman.

"Ah, mother dear, is it the captain ye'd be doubtin'? Or maybe ye think Father Moriarty, the good man standin' there watchin' for her green cliffs, 'ud be loikely to let us pass her unbeknowned?"

"But they tould me five in the mornin' I'd be seein' her, and it's now twelve, if it's a minute. Will ye be afthur askin' his riverence, ef yer plaise, sir," she said, turning to a sailor just mounting the stairs to the promenade deck, "when we'll be seein' Queenstown?"

"I needn't ask him, mother. He'll not know more than we do. It may be any time this afternoon. We can't say."

"Musha! but me heart's weary for the sight of her," cried the poor old soul.

And so, hour after hour they waited, watching for the first sight of the bank of clouds lying low on the horizon, out of which would presently loom the dim outline of the hills, and the first glimpse of the green that mantled them; then the full, close view of rock and turf, which the poor exiles had never once forgotten in all the whirl and excitement of their struggle for bread in the Empire of the West.

It was near five o'clock before the call came—"Land ahead!" Men sprang into the rigging, women crowded to the bulwarks, some holding up children to get a view of the land where their parents were born, but which they had never seen. The sun was setting over the west coast when they came within easy distance of seeing their own native land, and over and over again Jack heard them say,

"God bless her! the ould counthry—the ould mother—God bless her! Oh! glory to the sowl of the good ship as has brought us!" And, with many a lifting-up of hands and choking sobs, the wanderers greeted the dear little Island where stood the poor mud cabins that saw their births, and on whose green bosom they were cradled.

Jack looked at Father Moriarty and saw the tears streaming down his kindly face.

"Have you been long away, Father?" he asked.

"Ten long years, Mr. Landale. God save me! but she's as beautiful as I always thought her," he said, waving his hands towards the cliffs and the emerald sheen of the grass beyond. "You're beautiful, mavourneen! God be praised! Erin, acushla machree, but you're beautiful! and God's been very good to me to let my ould eyes behold your loveliness once more."

Jack had passed the greater part of the night in thinking over what Tom had said. He was the least vain of men, and the thought that every one who spoke to him in friendliness was of necessity in love with him was not possible to his nature. He still believed Tom to be mistaken. Anyway, he would not render the thing more possible by being so much in Mamie's company as heretofore, and, after a little chat in the morning, he had kept out of her way.

Calling Tom to him, he said—

"Tom, old man, I shall get off at Queenstown, and go by Holyhead to Landale. They will not look for me until Thursday. We can be there on Wednesday, have a look round, and see how the land lies. We may in a few hours learn many things of the old place and the people that may be of infinite service. What do you say?"

"Great idea!" Tom answered; "but——"

"But what?"

"Have you told Mamie?"

"No; but if in what you said last night there lies the least possible grain of fact, it is for her good that I go."

" Yes, I suppose so ; but——" Tom hesitated.

" But what ?"

" Oh, damn !—that's all. I'll go down and tell Wong to get our small baggage ready to land, and you go and tell Mamie you leave the boat at Queenstown."

Mamie had not understood Jack's absence from her side all day, and had, in fact, been a little pained by it ; but she had attached no serious meaning to it. She had been pestered all day with the crowd who habitually tried to press themselves upon her notice, and she attributed Jack's non-attendance to a desire not to unduly thrust himself upon her. She was little prepared to hear him say, when he strolled to her side—

" I am getting off at Queenstown, Miss Mamie, and so shall have to say good-bye."

Mamie's heart stood still for a moment. She could not speak, and Jack continued—

" You see, the mother" (he could not bring himself yet to say " my mother") " and sister will be waiting—will be anxious. We shall save a day by going to Holyhead, and —and so I thought it would be better. You see that, don't you ?"

Mamie was not a coward, and though she winced within herself she said bravely enough—

" Yes, of course, it is only natural. You must be terribly anxious to see your mother and sister. Every minute must seem hours to you. I hope you will find them well. When do they expect to reach Queenstown ?"

" About ten o'clock, they tell me."

" Well, I shall be up to see you off, Mr. Lan—I mean, Jack," said Mamie. " And—now—now—I'll just run along and tell mother that—that—we are to lose you—to-day." And Mamie, with a smiling face, but with a sinking at the heart such as she had never felt until this moment, hurried to her mother's cabin.

At ten o'clock the *Majestic* was at anchor in Queenstown harbour. The tender, looking small and insignificant beside the monster liner, was alongside. Jack's baggage was aboard it, and he turned to find Mamie to take his leave of her.

"We shall meet again, Miss Mamie?"

"Of course," she answered; "I shall—that is, we shall —be only too pleased. We are to stay at the Carlton Hotel until papa comes over."

"You'll call when in London, I hope, Mr. Landale?" asked Mrs. D'Olan. "We shall always be delighted to see you."

"I will call with the greatest of pleasure," replied Jack. "Of course I shall not leave Landale for some little time, unless the mother and sister want to come to London, when I hope I may be allowed to introduce them to you."

"Do—please do," pleaded Mamie. "I shall so much like to meet them."

The tug whistle sounded for the last time, and, with a hurried "Good-bye," Jack and Tom went down the gang-way to her, and were soon lost in the darkness.

The *Majestic* steamed out of the harbour, and Mamie, with a strange, unaccustomed sense of loneliness, stood at the spot where she had talked with Jack the night before, staring down into the sea.

CHAPTER XIX

AT LANDALE ABBEY

THERE are many larger, but few more beautiful ancestral homes in England than Landale Abbey. It was built in Queen Elizabeth's time, on the brow of a hill, overlooking half a county. Its quaint gables and porches were covered with creepers, now in full flower. In front of the house was a long terrace-garden, rich with early spring blossoms. The roses were just bursting into bloom, and there were roses everywhere. There had been a heavy fall of dew in the night, followed by brilliant sunshine in the morning, which had drawn out the perfume of the flowers, and the air was filled with it. The sky was bright blue, decked in the distance with snowy, fleecy clouds. Larks soaring upwards filled the vault above with their music. The bees buzzed in contented toil around and in the myriads of blossoms. A flock of rooks sailed lazily out of the plantation at the back of the house, cawing and calling to each other the orders and plans for the day. Some doves were strutting and cooing, with sleek, well-kept plumage, round the margin of the fish-ponds on the terrace below. A noble, rough-coated St. Bernard dog paced, with slow dignity, along the upper terrace, sniffing the air, looking with grave eyes around him, as if he owned the property and was seeing that it was well cared for. Catching sight of a figure delving in one of the flower-beds, he paused for a moment, watching it, then, with head erect, as if satisfied with the scrutiny, turned his eyes in the direction of one of the upper windows farther along the mansion, and walked in that direction. On arriving under the window, he faced it, and, looking up at it, gave out a sound which was more a summons than a bark—" Woof! woof! woof!"—then awaited with anxious expectancy an answer. None came. With a little growl of dissatisfaction, he gazed up and down the terrace. Seeing no one but the old gardener, he looked up once more to the window and, in rather a deeper and more aggrieved tone, he repeated his call—" Woof! woof! woof!"

A large white Persian cat, running out from under a rose-bush, with bushy tail erect and stiff, scampered off to where the dog stood, and standing by his side, turned her eyes upwards to the window and mewed plaintively. The dog looked at her with quiet contempt, as though her interference were unnecessary and uncalled for, and once again called, " Woof! woof!"

A leaded window, bearing in its centre, in stained glass, the crest and motto of the house, was opened, and the lovely face of a young girl appeared.

"What is it, you impatient old thing? What's the matter, Barry? Eh? eh?" she asked.

The dog gave a little romp of pleasure, and lashed his tail in delight.

"Come down? Well, I am coming down, but I'm quite sure you're before your time, sir. Take that!" And she pelted him with a large piece of sugar, which he crunched and swallowed. The cat mewed. "Ah! you too, Toosens! Nice pair of tyrants you are! Well, there's some for you too. I'm coming. Wait a minute."

The girl disappeared from the window, and the dog and the cat scampered along the terrace to the porch to meet her. It was Sybil—the original of the portrait Jack had so carefully guarded since the night he took it from the breast of his dead friend in Woolloogolonga Gully. She soon appeared, a vision of radiant loveliness, on the steps of the porch. She was dressed in a soft, creamy white crêpe; the body of the dress was cut with a clever compromise between modern dress and Grecian peplum. All delicately simple; not a touch of colour anywhere, save in the peach bloom of her healthy cheeks and the ruby-red of her full lips. Her dark hair was, like her gown, arranged in semi-Greek fashion. She looked, in face, form, and gracefulness, like a young Greek goddess, endeavouring to conform to the exigencies of modern fashion.

"Now, come along, you two," she said, patting the dog and rubbing up the fur round the cat's neck, until it stood out like an exaggerated Elizabethan ruff. "Come on! A race to the end of the terrace, and back! One—two—three—go!" And off she scampered, the dog on the one side, the cat on the other. She ran swiftly and easily, the animals having to gallop to keep up with her. To the end of the terrace she sped, touched the balustrade lightly with her fingers, then turned, calling—

"Now, off again! Whoever is in first gets the sugar!"

And back she tore to the starting-point, all breathless, to sit down upon the steps of the porch, laughing and tumbling her two friends away from her to avoid their too effusive embraces.

"I was in first. I get the sugar," she laughed, munching up a piece between her strong white teeth.

The dog "woofed" and the cat "mewed."

"Ask for it," she said, drawing out two more lumps from her pocket, and the dog put up one huge paw, and "woofed," while the cat sat up on its hind legs, and "mewed."

Laughingly she stuffed a piece of sugar into the mouth of each. "Ha! ha!" she laughed, "I beat you! I beat you!" And she tousled the dog's fur in affectionate fun, until he seemed to laugh too, in full enjoyment of the romp.

A sedate, portly, elderly man appeared in the porch, and said, in grave tones more befitting the delivery of a message of the King to his Parliament than of a butler addressing his young mistress—

"The morning papers, Miss Sybil."

Sybil started up lightly, and stretched out her hand for the journals, saying—

"Oh, give them to me, Spurdy! Quick!"

Swiftly unfolding the *Times*, and scanning the pages rapidly, she found the "Shipping Intelligence." Giving a little scream of joy, she ran into the house, followed by the dog and cat, calling—

"Mother! mother! He's at Queenstown! The *Majestic* arrived off Queenstown at 10 P.M. yesterday!"

Sybil's mother, Lady Walgrove, rose from her seat as she entered the room. Lady Walgrove was a woman of fifty-five. She must have been exceedingly beautiful when younger—indeed, she was so still. Her figure was slim and youthful; her face, although thin and grief-worn, was almost free from wrinkles; her large, luminous eyes still retained their fire, but the face was pale, the lips thin and drawn, the hair snowy white. She was dressed entirely in black, and wore over her head a black mantilla of lace. There was something strangely pathetic in the whole figure. As Sybil read the news of the *Majestic's* arrival at Queenstown, her lips were parted, her eyes strained, and her long, delicate fingers were clasped and unclasped in feverish excitement.

"How long will the vessel take to reach Liverpool?" she asked, in a sweet, sad voice.

"About twelve hours from the time of leaving Queenstown," answered her daughter. "But she may be delayed. All depends upon the amount of her mails and the number of passengers who may land there. Stand down, Barry!" This to the dog, who, sharing his mistress's excitement, had thought it necessary to place his forepaw on her shoulder and look over the paper, as if to share in the news.

"Is there no telegram?"

"Not yet, mother dear, but they explained that the tug would have to bring it off the *Majestic*, and it might be hours before it was despatched."

Sybil's arms were around her mother. She gently placed her back in her seat and kissed her lovingly. Barry lumbered down, and, stretching his great head upon his paws, watched them both with the most tender solicitude and sympathy. How much do intelligent dogs know of the human language? Surely the best of them not only understand but sympathise with all the sorrows and troubles of those they love!

"Then he will be here to-morrow night?" the mother asked.

"Yes, dear—or Friday morning, early. He may not be able to get a train in time to arrive here until very late, and he would not like to do that. However, we shall see by his telegram, when it comes."

The mother's eyes were gazing out of the window in the direction of the lodge-gates as though they were expecting her son even now.

"How hot your hands are, mother dear! And your dear head, too. Come out on to the terrace until breakfast is ready."

"No, dear child, let me stop here. Where's Lorna?"

"Here I am," answered a clear, musical voice. "Have I kept you waiting?" And Lorna Mannerly, a beautiful girl of nineteen, entered the room.

"No, Lorna. The *Majestic* is in," cried Sybil.

"In?" asked Lorna.

"Well, that is, she is reported at Queenstown."

"Oh! Isn't that good, Lady Walgrove! Then he'll be here to-morrow?"

"Or Friday morning, early. It doesn't seem possible. But we've had no telegram yet."

After breakfast Lady Walgrove went to her son's bedroom to add some extra touches to it, and the girls strolled out on to the terrace to chat over the brother's homecoming.

Meantime, Jack had travelled to Dublin, crossed the Channel to Holyhead, and was now speeding on his way to Landale Abbey.

Sybil and Lorna had been friends from childhood. They had been educated and had grown up together. Lorna was an orphan, and a ward of the late Sir James

Walgrove. When he died, Lady Walgrove took her entirely into her home, where she was treated in every way as one of her daughters. She was a bright, clever, lovable girl, and the mother felt that no better companion for her daughter could possibly be found. The girls were great cronies, had no secrets from each other; they were both of strong, healthy bodies, and pure, innocent minds. Though, as was but natural, Sybil held the first place in the affections of the Landale people, Lorna was but little less esteemed and loved.

"Will it not be delightful to have Jack here?" said Lorna.

"Yes," answered Sybil. "Every hour now is torture to dear mother. She is in a burning fever. She has not slept nor eaten for days. She is fretting because we have no telegram from Queenstown. She does not think it can be possible to have her boy with us again after all these years, and fears that something may happen at the last moment to rob her of him. But Jack will come. I know it. I feel sure of it."

"Of course he will come! If he had not left on the *Majestic* he would have cabled. Besides, his name was on the passenger-list. He will come."

"And you must love him. You *must!* And he will love you. Then we can all live together, and be happier than ever. Is it not a blessing he has never married? He might have brought home some awful person whom we could not possibly love, and with whom we could not live. Ugh! It would have been dreadful!" Sybil shuddered.

The day wore on, and still no telegram came. It was pitiable to see the anxiety upon the mother's face as she watched the path that led to the lodge, waiting for the few words flashed by the wires from her son.

In the afternoon, two visitors called. One was Lord Thorland, a man of forty-five, of very distinguished appearance. He was tall, well-built, had dark brown hair and beard, aquiline nose, high forehead, firm mouth and chin—an English nobleman of the better school, not one of the rowdy, dissolute, brainless beings who have nothing in common with nobility except the name they bear. He had known Sybil from her childhood, and had loved her since her girlhood. He was very wealthy; his estates joined those of the Landales. He was in every way an eligible match for Sybil. Lady Walgrove dearly desired the marriage, and although Lord Thorland had never actually proposed for Sybil, her mother knew it was but a question in his mind as to whether as yet she was old enough to know her own heart. He knew he loved her. He wanted to be perfectly sure Sybil loved him.

The other visitor was of a very different type. He was a distant relative of Sir James Walgrove—a Mr. Caerwohn Moody—a small, weedy man of eight-and-twenty. He had published a book of poems—at his own expense—called "Decay," which a very small cult pronounced "majestically mystic"—whatever that might mean. Nowadays, to be admired, poetry must be, like Dogberry, "too cunning to be understood." "How supremely unintelligible!" "How divinely unfathomable!"—these are the highest forms of praise possible; at least, so thought Mr. Caerwohn Moody—the author of "Decay"—and his little band of followers.

Mr. Caerwohn Moody had an income as small in proportion as his brains and poetic powers. Lorna's inheritance was an exceedingly good one, and to compass this and the fair Lorna was Mr. Moody's ambition and intention. He sent her sonnets and songs of love which, to her vigorous and healthy mind, seemed sickly and unwholesome. She seldom read them, usually put them in the fire or the waste-paper basket, and forgot them as soon as she could. She cared even less for Mr. Moody than she did for his poetry, and she often devoutly wished that there was a waste-basket into which she could thrust him. He was one of those awful people whom it is impossible to snub. Enveloped in the impenetrable armour of their own self-conceit, they are unassailable.

Lorna's open dislike he attributed to maiden coyness. When she felt that she would dearly love to box his ears, he fondly persuaded himself she was dying to throw herself into his arms. The Moodies of this world are difficult people to handle—even with tongs.

Mr. Caerwohn Moody never seemed quite clean. He had that nameless look that makes men feel creepy when they see it, and long to kick the object that possesses it. His hand was flabby and wet. One always wanted to wash after coming in contact with it. Lady Walgrove felt in duty bound to receive him, for her late husband's sake. She did not know what the man really was.

The afternoon was pleasantly warm. Lady Walgrove had ordered tea to be served on the terrace, and Mr. Spurdy, her butler, was arranging the table under a rich crimson silk tent-umbrella, near to which Bruds, the gardener, was planting some pansies and primroses.

Mr. Bruds had been in the service of the Landales for three generations. He was nearly eighty years of age, but had all the strength and energy of fifty. He was a little, rosy, apple-faced man, who had a perpetual smile of contentment upon his dear old face and a twinkle of mirth in his blue eyes. His scant hair was white, his face clean-shaven. He was a little bent with age and rheumatism, and his voice had " turned again to childish treble "—but he was still hale and hearty.

" I am much concerned, Mr. Bruds," said Spurdy, " to know what our new principal, Mr. John Landale, will be like."

" Aye, aye, so is most on us, I reckon," answered Bruds, prodding at the mould with his trowel.

" As to what difference he will make to us," continued Spurdy, emphasising the pronoun.

" Aye; likely he'll shake the whole lot on us up a bit," chuckled Bruds.

" Shake *us* up! Not me, Mr. Bruds! I'm past the shaking-up age," indignantly retorted Spurdy.

" That's what the butcher said to the bull, but the bull

h'isted him over the fence for all that," drily replied Bruds.

"Your comparisons are inappropriate, Mr. Bruds. I'm neither a butcher nor a fit subject for h'isting. I've managed this family for twelve years, and——"

"Aye! and I have gardened it for fifty, but I may be h'isted, for all that. When's he due?"

"In the next two or three days. You remember him as a boy?"

"Aye! I knew him in the seed, so to speak," said Bruds, patting the mould round a root.

"What was he like?" asked Spurdy, a little anxiously.

"Well," replied Bruds, pausing in his work and sitting on his heels, "in the first stage, as much like a prize tomater as anythink—as most babies is, 'cept to their mammies. Second stage, a forked red-and-white radish, wi' a dark-brown broccoli top. Next——"

"Excuse me, Mr. Bruds, his external appearance at that early period does not interest me."

"What was you wantin' to know, then?"

"I mean, his mental attributes—his temperament."

"Temperament! Well, it were quiet enough if you treated him fair, but if you put upon him, a red pepper-pod were cool to him, and when he said he'd do a thing, he'd do it, in spite o' man and Beelzebub. He fowt old Sir James hisself once—swore he'd never come back while Sir James lived, and 'ooked it to furrin parts."

"Australia is not a foreign part," said Spurdy didactically. "It is an integral and important part of the British Empire."

"Well, it's furrin enough for me. I don't hold wi' such places. Nawthin' but a lot o' blacks and bummerangs, kangaroos and cannibuls. I read all about it in Captain Cook when I were a young 'un, so don't you try to teach *me*, Mr. Spurdy. 'Sides, I 'ad an uncle who went out there once, and never comed back. 'Ow do I know they didn't eat him?"

Mr. Caerwohn Moody came along the terrace. He

was dressed in black, and wore a Byronic collar and a red tie.

"Is Lady Walgrove in the house, Spurdy?" he asked.

"No, Mr. Moody, she's somewhere in the grounds."

"Where are the other ladies?"

"In the tennis-court, I believe, sir."

"Tennis! So unpoetically energetic! So crudely vigorous! Is Miss Mannerly playing too?"

"I believe so, sir."

"I'll wend my way thitherwards," he sighed, and, turning suddenly, he nearly stumbled over Bruds. "Planting, gardener?" he asked, recovering himself.

"Aye, sir, plantin'."

"A foolish, futile proceeding! What is the gardener but a fool? What is his work but folly? He plants, he fertilises, he rakes, he waters—and to what end?" He asked this of the air, with eyes upturned.

"'Pends on what he plants, sir," answered the practical Bruds.

"Plant what he may, the end is the same."

"No, I'm danged if it be. If I plants roses, the end ain't ingons."

"Gardener, you misconceive me. Whate'er you plant, the end is the same—decay. Decay and death.

> "'A little seed, a little earth,—and then,
> A little life, and back to earth again.'"

And, sighing heavily, the poet wandered down the steps of the terrace.

"That's a lively party for a wet Sunday! Who's he?"

"A distant connection of Lady Walgrove. A minor poet, Mr. Bruds."

"Thought he was a undertaker. If that's the sort o' stuff he gits with his minin' and poetin', 'e'd better take off his funeral-clothes and dig a bit in my garden. Tell 'ee what, Mr. Spurdy, some o' these nowadays youngsters ain't no more life in 'em than a year-old plucked peony.

Blest if they don't seem to be born dyin'. Is yon the chap they say is sneakin' after Miss Mannerly?"

"He is paying his court to that lady," replied Spurdy, with dignity.

"He'll pay a lot afore he gits her, I reckon. A healthy plant like she ain't to be gobbled up by a cankerworm like 'e. Ah! here's Miss Sybil, bless her!" he said, as Sybil came from the house.

"Ah! Spurdy—tea ready?"

"When you are, miss."

"I think you might bring it now."

"How many, miss?"

"Let me see. Mamma, Miss Mannerly, Lord Thorland, I—Four!"

"Excuse me, miss, Mr. Moody has called."

"Oh!" pouted Sybil. "Where is he?"

"Gone to find Miss Mannerly, miss."

"Oh, poor Lorna!" laughed Sybil. "Bring a cup for him too."

"Yes, miss." And Spurdy went along the terrace to the servants' door.

"Now, Bruds, where's my greeting?" asked Sybil of Bruds.

"Bless 'ee, missie! give a old man time," he answered, rising slowly and painfully. "Rheumatiz, missie,—rheumatiz! The 'eart is willin' but the jints is stiff." He cut a red rose from the bush. "There, missie! 'Ow's that?"

"Beautiful! Now, my dearest old Bruds, listen! Brother Jack's arrived at Queenstown."

"Lor'! is he, missie?" asked the delighted old man.

"And we're expecting a telegram, telling us when he will be home. Bruds, put your dear old hand here." She put his hand on her heart. "Tell me, what do you feel?"

"Why, missie, your dear heart is goin' pittiti-pattiti, like a frightened dove's!"

"And it will never stop going pittiti-pattiti until I get my arms round brother Jack, and hug and kiss him within an inch of his life. Think, Bruds—twenty years of arrears of kissing and hugging to be made up on the first day he comes home! What do you say to that, Bruds?"

"Well, I sez this, missie. I wishes as 'ow I was Master Jack the first day 'e comes 'ome."

"Oh! you dear, gallant old Bruds," laughed Sybil. " I fear you were a gay young rascal once!"

" A gay young rascal once, missie! Why, lor' love 'ee? I wur a gay young rascal 'unnerds an' 'unnerds o' times!" And he gave a playful little kick. " Not that you need say owt about it to Mrs. Bruds. She don't take much stock in my gay-young-rascal days and rakishness. Strange 'ow easy wimen-folk du get jellers," he added seriously.

" That's their way of showing their love."

" Is it, missie? Well, all I can say is, they might just as well 'ide their love, for all the comfort it du bring when they du show it that way. But 'ow's your mamma, missie? Is she bearin' up pratty well?"

" She's very restless. She cannot stay in the house, or out of it. She's been in his room twenty times already to-day, smoothing and kissing his pillow, altering this and arranging that. She won't let me touch his bedroom. But I'm to have his den, and I'm going to smother it with flowers. You must let me have bushels and bushels of your very best—and, perhaps, I'll give you a kiss, if there are any left after brother Jack has had his share. But, Bruds, we won't tell Mrs. Bruds, will we?"

" Not much we won't, missie! Us knows better'n that, don't us?"

Here they both laughed merrily, and Sybil took Brud's gnarled and twisted hands in her own soft, warm fingers, and danced him round until he was almost giddy.

Lorna came up, and with mock astonishment asked—

" Mr. Bruds! Mr. Bruds! what does this mean? Sybil! I'm ashamed of you both, flirting in that outrageous way!"

" There! that's exactly what you said, Mr. Bruds! It *is* strange how easily some women-folk do get jealous!"

" Ah, missie! you will have your little joke."

" Any telegram yet, Sib?"

" No. Oh! how I wish it would come! Will he come to-morrow, I wonder, or the next day! Now, Lorna, re-member, if you don't fall in love with him, and make him fall in love with you, I'll never forgive you."

" Falling in love with him will be easy enough, but to make him fall in love with me is another matter."

" But it must be. I have quite decided. You're to be Jack's wife. I won't let any other woman touch him."

" I expect Master Jack will choose for himself, Sybil. Where's my flower, Bruds? Am I to be left all forlorn?"

" Lor' bless 'ee, no, Miss Mannerly! How'll this do?" asked Bruds, giving her a sprig of lilac.

" Lovely! Now, you darling old pincushion, where's that pin?" And she turned him round, taking a pin from his vest. " Now, how's that?" And she put the flower in her dress, and swished herself round for inspection.

" Two as pretty flowers as there's in my garden, Miss Mannerly."

Lady Walgrove strolled up, and asked—

" No telegram yet, Sybil?"

" Not yet, dear."

" I hope nothing has happened!"

" No, dear, no. Do not get nervous."

" Strange we have not heard yet!"

" Telegrams are so uncertain. He will be here to-morrow, dear."

" Yes, to-morrow. He must be here to-morrow! I can't wait longer—I have waited so long! Twenty years —a lifetime! Will he remember, I wonder? Will he love us, Sybil?"

" Yes, I feel that he will. I am sure that he is a good, noble fellow whom we shall both be proud of. Think of his portrait. I never saw a kinder face."

" Yes, it is a kind face—a good face. So like, and yet so unlike what he was as a boy."

" Not more unlike than I as a girl to what I am now.

Oh! that portrait of me at the age of ten! Was there ever such a little frump? Can't see myself in it a bit. And boys change ever so much more than girls."

The two girls rattled on rapidly, trying to divert the mother's thoughts.

"Where's Lord Thorland?" asked Lady Walgrove.

"We left him talking to Bradford," replied Sybil.

"Lord Thorland is a very noble fellow, Sybil."

"Indeed he is!" said Sybil enthusiastically. "Jack will like him, I am sure."

"Very rich, and very fond of my little girl, and——"

"Hush!" whispered Sybil, putting her hand over her mother's mouth. "Hush, mammy, hush! He's here."

Lord Thorland crossed the garden, went to Lady Walgrove and, lifting his hat, said, "Lady Walgrove—Ladies!"

Lady Walgrove gave him her hand affectionately.

Spurdy, with a footman, was preparing the tea at the table under the tent-umbrella.

"Just in time, Lord Thorland. Shall I help you?"

"If you will be so kind."

They grouped themselves around the table, the two girls helping to serve the tea. Lord Thorland was watching Sybil tenderly.

"Have you heard from your son yet, Lady Walgrove?" he asked.

"Not yet. I am getting anxious."

"Don't, dear friend. Telegrams are often delayed when sent from steamers."

Lorna had tried to avoid Moody, in vain. He had followed and cornered her. Sighing heavily, he simpered—

"Miss Mannerly! Oh, that we were alone!"

"Dear me! Why, Mr. Moody?"

"My soul shrivels always in a crowd."

"Dear me!"

"Inspiration fails me. I love solitude."

"Drink your tea, and go into the jungle, Mr. Moody."

" The jungle, Miss Mannerly!"

" Yes. Bruds will show you the way. It's at the end of the plantation. That's solitary enough. Nobody ever goes there except we two girls—and the cats. Wild cats, too."

" Wild cats, Miss Mannerly! I cannot commune with wild cats! Wild cats would not understand me. I cannot pour out my soul to wild cats!"

" You didn't say you wanted to ' pour out your soul.' You said you wanted to be alone."

" Oh!—Ah! yes!—alone with a kindred spirit—with an affinity, Miss Mannerly."

" Ah! yes. Well, why not go and get an affinity?"

" Really, Miss Mannerly! You speak of affinities as if they were marketable articles, to be bought at so much the dozen."

" Well, what is an affinity?"

" You are one, Miss Mannerly."

" Really, Mr. Moody! Am I really? I never felt like it. How do you know that?"

" I feel it. My soul is attuned to yours—doomed to be linked through all eternity, fluttering, sailing—so to speak—for ever through the endless, boundless, multitudinous worlds."

" Oh! don't, Mr. Moody! Please don't. I don't wish to be linked and flutter and sail through anything!"

" Let me rouse the wish! You must hear my last poem. I *must* read it."

" *Must* you?" asked Lorna, with mock earnestness.

" I *must*."

Looking round at the rest of the party, Lorna said—

" But it is rude."

" Rude! It is divine! Hearken! Hush!" And the poet chanted, in a monotone—

" Give me the drear, dark days and deep dank death
    Of Autumn's brooding, life-destroying breath;
    The dear, dead leaves—the sweet of dread decay—
    The rotting leaves that choke the swampy way!"

He paused and looked up for admiration.

Lorna screwed up her nose, and rising, said—

"Go away, Mr. Moody! Go away, please!"

"Miss Mannerly!"

"Go away! Oh, do! You've spoilt my tea." And she got up and went to the table with her cup.

"Crude—unformed—protoplastic!" said the poet to himself. "If it were not for her superabundant income, I'd cut the embryonic nonentity for ever."

Spurdy came along the terrace, holding a telegram.

"A telegram for my lady."

Starting up, Lady Walgrove cried—

"Ah! give it to me!" And he did so.

She tore it open eagerly. Sybil ran to her mother, and led her to a seat, and looked over her shoulder. Having read the telegram, Lady Walgrove softly sobbed, "Thank God!"

"Good news, dear?" asked Lorna.

"Yes, yes!" Sybil replied. And she read, "All well, hope to be with you at latest by Friday—earlier, if possible. God bless you both! May my coming home bring happiness and peace to you. I bring with me a friend who acts as my secretary—Mr. Hewley. He will stay with us for the present.—JACK."

"Oh, how good! Isn't that lovely?" cried Lorna.

"Excuse me, please," said Lady Walgrove faintly. "Sybil, stay with your guests. I will see you all again presently."

"Let me come with you, dear Lady Walgrove," pleaded Lorna, taking her arm and helping her into the house.

Lord Thorland turned to Sybil, and said earnestly—

"I congratulate you, Miss Landale."

"Thanks. It seems too good to be true."

"The good is always true. You will be very glad to see your brother?"

"I cannot tell you how glad. I have longed for him all my life. Then, my mother's deep sorrow for him, and her patience—her sweetness! Oh, Lord Thorland, you don't know how good my mother is." Sybil's eyes were moist. She looked exquisitely tender and loving.

Lord Thorland was moved by her beauty and earnestness, and replied—

" I think I do, Miss Landale."

" Jack must be a good man with such a mother."

" And, may I add, with such a sister, Miss Landale."

" Oh! I shall never be as good and patient as dear mother."

" I think you will."

" No, there's no one like her in all the world."

" I have every reason to admire and love your dear mother, too. She has been very good and generous to me."

" She is that to all, Lord Thorland."

" Yes—but especially so to me. Shall I tell you how?"

" Yes, please."

Lord Thorland paused for a moment; then, in a voice that trembled, in spite of his efforts to control it, he said—

" She has given me permission to speak to you."

Sybil's manner and voice were hushed and quiet as she asked—

" What about?"

" Yourself," he replied, almost in a whisper.

" Myself?"

Lord Thorland hesitated, looked at the fair young face, and said—

" I am twice your age; to you, must seem almost old."

" Indeed, no!" answered Sybil quickly. " I never looked upon you as old."

Lord Thorland looked relieved. He smiled, saying—

" I am glad of that, for age seems the only barrier between us. I cannot make romantic speeches, Miss Landale—I feel too deeply for that. I can honestly say I love you with all my mind, soul, and heart."

There was no doubt of the truth of what he uttered. Sybil was startled and distressed. She felt deeply, for the man's love was so evident and so sincere.

"Lord Thorland, I wish—I wish——" She stammered and stopped.

"Yes?"

"I wish you had not spoken of this to me."

"Why?" he asked, in alarm.

"Well, I mean, just now. I—well, you see, I am thinking of nothing but Jack and his coming home."

"Do you care for me a little?"

"Indeed, I care for you very much."

"There is no one else?"

"Oh dear, no! No one—except Jack, of course."

"Then I may hope you will be my wife?"

"Lord Thorland, I cannot say you may hope."

He looked so pained that Sybil added hastily—

"Ah! don't let that pain you. I don't mean that there may not be a time when I may care more. I—don't know. I am not sure that I know what love means. I do care for you. I do like—I do admire you. Whether—Ah! please, Lord Thorland, don't ask me more at present. Jack is coming, and his coming may change everything. Who knows? Let us be the same good friends we have always been. You will not let this make any difference, will you? Please!" she pleaded earnestly.

"No, I will not. Why should it? I am flattered and honoured by what you have told me, and I will wait patiently and hopefully."

There was a painful pause, and then Sybil asked, turning towards the house, "Won't you come in?"

"No, not now. I—I—Well, I have something to think over, have I not?" he said, taking her hand and looking thoughtfully at it. "Remember, my whole life and happiness hang upon your answer. I will not distress you further. I will wait your own time and wish. Let me know as soon as your brother arrives. And—and—believe——" His voice broke. He could not continue. He kissed her hand, respectfully lifted his hat, and went quietly away, leaving Sybil deep in thought.

Sybil was puzzled at her own feelings. She had never

thought deeply of marriage, but, somehow, had grown to accept it as a possibility that she would one day become Lady Thorland. She knew of his love for her, and she felt a deeper regard for him than for any other man; yet, at his avowal, there came a chill of absolute fear. The features of Jack, which she had studied so lovingly in the photograph, seemed to come between her and Lord Thorland, pleading dumbly for her to pause, to wait before giving her answer. So real did Jack's presence seem that it became a little uncanny. She almost expected that he must be near her. Never to her dying day did she forget the strange reality of the impression made upon her mind at that moment. When they talked this over long after, and compared notes, Jack remembered that he must have been at that moment about to enter the lodge-gates—that he felt a sudden dread—a thrill of apprehension, as though some unseen danger were at hand, and he had hurried on, as though by hastening he might avert it. The moment he entered the gates he felt relieved, as though the peril had passed.

"How glad I am," thought Sybil, "that I told Lord Thorland I would wait until Jack came!" She felt a sensation of intense relief at the thought that she had not accepted his offer, but she was utterly unable to find the cause.

Lorna came from the porch, saying—

"Sib dear, I've disposed of the minor poet for the present. He's gone to gain inspiration from the fish, I fancy. He's making his way to the pond. It is too much to hope that he is going to throw himself into it."

Sybil did not answer. Lorna took her two hands, and, drawing her from the chair, peered into her face, asking—

"What's the matter, dear? You have been startled. You are quite pale, and there are tears in your eyes." Then suddenly she looked round for Lord Thorland, and, not seeing him, said, "Where's Lord Thorland?"

"Gone."

"Has he—Oh! tell me quick! has he—has he——"

"Has he what?"

"Has he—proposed?"

"Please don't ask me, Lorna."

"Then he has! He has! And you've accepted him, of course?"

"No, I have not."

"Wha-at!"

"I have not."

"But why not? What did he say? What did he do? What did you do? What did you say?"

"I said Jack was coming home, and I could think of nothing else."

"Then it isn't all off?"

"I don't know. Don't ask me any more, please. Let us go in to mother."

Perplexed, and a little angry at Sybil's conduct, Lorna went with her friend, and left her with her mother.

Meantime Mr. Spurdy and Judson were removing the tea-things from the table. It was known that a telegram had been received by Lady Walgrove, and the servants' hall was alive with curiosity to know the contents. Judson had thrown out several hints to Mr. Spurdy to this effect. Mr. Spurdy declined to be drawn. There was nothing for it but to put the question direct. Not without some trepidation did he do it. He asked—

"Was the telegram from the young master to say 'e was comin' 'ome, Mr. Spurdy?"

Mr. Spurdy looked at Judson as a Prime Minister might have looked at a cabman who asked to be informed as to the probable outcome of the next Cabinet meeting. Judson shrank visibly. Then, with a dignity wonderful to behold, Spurdy replied—

"Young man, when the private affairs of this family become public property, you will learn something about them. Until then, be good enough to convey these things to the kitchen, and cease asking impertinent questions."

Judson " conveyed" the things, and " ceased" with so much alacrity and confusion that Spurdy puffed himself out somewhat after the manner of a mammoth pouter-pigeon, and rubbed his hands slowly over each other in supreme satisfaction. Spurdy dearly loved to exercise his authority. He had done so on this occasion, and was comforted accordingly.

Jack and Tom were coming up the avenue leading from the lodge to the house. It was a footpath, shorter than the carriage drive, and more secluded. Jack's feelings were complex to a degree. He was in a fever of expectation and excitement, yet was intensely apprehensive. He wished earnestly for the meeting with the mother and daughter, yet felt that he wanted to postpone it till the last moment.

The place enraptured him. Who but a lover of his country, returning after an absence of many years, can imagine the feelings that well-remembered scenes or characteristics evoke? He looked round with intense delight at the exquisite landscapes, the beautiful gardens, the old trees, the stately homes. And of all that he was to become master, by a fraud—a conspiracy.

"Tom," he said, "how good all this is! How peaceful! How well kept!"

"It's immense. As Hiram would say, it's co-lossal."

"It's no use, Tom—there's nothing like it. We've seen almost everything, but the dear old land stands alone."

"Good old mother, eh, Jack?"

"Good old mother!—yes. A bit feminine and changeable in disposition, but kind, loving, and faithful, even in her fickleness. Ready to take you to her bosom, and croon and lull you to sleep. Look at it, Tom. Doesn't it spell peace and rest? And, Tom, doesn't it spell 'Welcome home'?"

"That's it. Welcome home! And what a home!"

"And what a home! You can't make these homes, Tom, they've got to grow."

"And it's yours, Jack."

"No, Tom. It's poor old Jack Landale's, whose bones

lie mouldering in that Never-Never Land by Woolloogolonga Gully. Dear old Jack—dead and buried!"

"Yes, kindly remember that! He *is* dead and buried."

"I never was a real live liar, Tom, and here, in this frank, open-hearted, truthful old place, I've got to live a lie, morning, noon, and night—day in, day out! It's a cheerful kind of life to look forward to! But I suppose the gift of lying, like one's chest, expands with exercise."

"If it does, some men I know must do a fair bit of exercising. All men are liars, Jack."

"Except women, Tom."

"Yes, of course. You can't call a woman a liar, can you? First place, it isn't polite; second place, the epithet doesn't seem to surround the fact. It's like calling Mont Blanc a snowball. It doesn't fill the bill."

"How am I to meet the dear old mother and the sweet sister?"

"With your eyes shut and your arms open. If the sister is as pretty as the picture, that part of the business needn't fret you. It wouldn't trouble me."

"How am I to do it?" asked Jack, half to himself.

"Don't you think it was a bad move to drop in unexpectedly like this?"

"No, it gives me time to look round a bit—time to learn. Taking them by surprise, I take them off their guard. They'll be too excited and startled to be critical, and it's the first plunge that takes the breath away."

"You'll be all right."

"If the mother should detect the fraud, I shall blow the roof of my head off. I wish I'd never undertaken it. I've been in jail, but never felt a thief before. I'm a fraud, Tom—a contemptible, knock-kneed fraud! A fraud of sawdust legs that can't even stand upright! I, who never knowingly wronged a human being in my life—never touched anything that did not belong to me!"

"No, but Landon did. He was in at the sticking-up of the Wurramurra Bank."

"He was dragged into it when he was drunk. He didn't know what he was doing."

"The law doesn't take cognisance of bad whisky in such cases. He was in it. They hunted for him, and caught you. You answered exactly to his description, were arrested for him, sentenced and punished for him. To save him and his wife and child you kept your mouth shut. Put that against what you're doing now—and doing at his request, remember that!—then strike the balance. You'll find yourself on the right side."

"Ah! you're a better juggler than I am, Tom."

"Well, at least, you promised Landon to do it, didn't you?"

"Worse luck! I did."

"Then go ahead and do it."

When Mr. Moody left Lorna, he wandered out into the garden, and into the avenue. Jack and Tom saw him coming towards them, and Jack, wondering who he was, felt a little nervous as he neared them.

"Who's this, I wonder?" he said to Tom.

They bowed to each other as they met, and Jack said, "Fine day, sir." The poet was evidently depressed. He sighed, and answered—

"Fine now, but behind those clouds is rain; beyond that cumulus lurks thunder."

"Do you think so?" asked Jack.

"Women are like that sky. They smile, and all is blue."

"I should have thought that it would be the other way round—that all would be blue if they didn't smile."

"Excuse me a moment," said the rapt poet, taking out a note-book and writing. Jack was going to speak. "Hush! hush!" implored Mr. Moody.

"She smiled, and blue was all the vast Empyrean round;
But thund'rous black the cumulus whene'er she frown'd."

"Was it?" queried Tom. "That must have been bad for him. The lady seems a little changeable."

Ignoring Tom, Moody turned to Jack, and said—

"Thank you for that thought. It is often so!"

"What is?" asked Jack.

"The poet's greatest thoughts are often suggested by others," replied Moody. "Some chance word gives the cue for the mighty line."

"Indeed?"

"It is the prosaic chalk egg, so to speak," he continued, "that induces the poetic hen to lay. Good day."

Jack was going to speak, but Mr. Moody said, "Hush! hush!" and, continuing to write, walked slowly down the path.

"What a cheerful companion! Who the deuce is he?" asked Tom. "He called you a chalk egg, Jack."

"Not a very provocative one," answered Jack. "The poetic hen did not lay much, did it? We haven't got much information up to now."

They walked on until they met Spurdy, who waited for them to announce their names and business. Jack stopped, and, turning to Tom, said, "One of the servants. I wonder whether he is one of the old ones. We must risk it. Are the family at home?" he asked of Spurdy.

Spurdy, curiously regarding them, replied—

"Lady Walgrove and Miss Landale are, sir."

"Oh! Nobody else?" asked Jack, with affected carelessness.

"Not at present. Mr. John Landale is expected to-morrow."

"Yes—to-morrow, of course! To-morrow. You will all be very glad to see him, no doubt?"

"Of course, sir, naturally."

Jack wondered who the man was, and whether he had known Landale as a boy. To test him, he asked—

"Were you—I mean—have you been here long?"

"Twelve years, sir."

Jack sighed with relief, and said to Tom, "That's all right. He will not remember Landale. I suppose you're quite the oldest servant on the estate?" he asked of Spurdy.

"Oh, no, there are some who have been here much longer. The gardener, for instance—he's been on the estate fifty years. Shall I take in your cards, gentlemen?"

"No, no, not yet," Jack answered hastily. "We are a little in advance of our appointment. Lady Walgrove does not expect us so soon. We would rather not disturb her just yet. Will you oblige me by saying nothing about us till I ring the door-bell? You can announce us then."

"Certainly, sir, but——"

"We'll not do any harm."

"Of course not—but——"

Jack interrupted him, saying, "By the way, what is your name?"

"Spurdy, sir."

"The butler, of course?"

"Yes, sir."

"Thank you."

"Thank you, sir," and Spurdy, wondering who the two men could be, turned and left them.

"So much for the butler!" Tom laughed. "He's all right. He will not bowl you out."

"But there are others who may. This gardener, for instance. It's a terribly risky game, Tom."

"But worth the playing. What a glorious place! Spiffin'! Great! Immense! *Co*-lossal!"

Bruds looked up from his work as Jack and Tom came towards him, and Tom said, "Fine day."

"Yes, good for the roses," answered Bruds. "But peas wants rain."

Tom whispered aside to Jack, "The gardener. Your work does you credit, Mr.——" He tried to induce Bruds to give his name, but Bruds did not understand him. He replied—

"So people du say."

" You know a bit about flowers, Mr.——"

" So I ought—so I ought. I've been gardenin' for fifty years, an' more."

" Time well spent, Mr.—Mr.—— Why the devil doesn't he tell me his name?" Tom said to himself.

" Hope so, sir ; hope so."

" You must have seen some changes, Mr.—Mr.——"

" Aye, 'ave I—me and my old missus atween us."

" I hope she's well, Mrs.—Mrs.——"

" Oh! ah! she's well enough for her time o' life. She's sixty-eight. We don't get younger at sixty-eight, sir."

" You're expecting a change soon, Mr.——"

Bruds looked skywards, and asked, " What change? Looks set fair to me."

" I mean some one coming home, eh, Mr.——"

" Oh! ah! our young master from furrin parts. You bean't him, be you?"

" No, no!"

" No, I reckon not. You don't favour him a bit."

" You'd know him if you saw him, eh?"

" I reckon I would. Many's the time we've worked in this garden together. He wur fond o' me, he wur—main fond o' me. He'd come to me with his troubles, too. ' Bruds,' he'd say, ' Bruds'——"

" It's ' Bruds,' he'd say——"

Jack came forward, holding out his hand, saying—

" Bruds, old boy, how are you?"

" Eh? Why——" stammered the old man.

Jack took his hand, and, shaking it heartily, answered—

" Of course I came to you with my troubles. Who better? Dear old Bruds! Do you remember the time when Sir James thrashed me, and nearly killed me?" Jack ventured on the only piece of information he possessed of Landale's boyhood.

" You bean't Master Jack! Little Jack!" cried the old man.

" Yes, it's Master Jack—little Jack, altered, grown-up,

15   · 225

lengthened, and squared—but still Jack. Don't you know me, old man? Look again."

" You favour him—yo' du that. You've his nose and chin and hair, and—and——"

" And his old love for his dear old Bruds. Shake hands again, old boy. Shake hands again. And see here, Bruds, let me come to you with my troubles always, as I did in the dear old days. For there are troubles ahead, and plenty of them."

Jack was heartily ashamed of his own deceit. The old fellow looked so guileless and amazed as he answered—

" Troubles? Lor' bless 'ee, there won't be any troubles now you've come home—'cept it be in too much pettin' an' cuddlin'. Your mother and sister be just witherin' to get 'old o' yer."

" My mother! Ah! Yes, yes. And my sister, Bruds? Is she as pretty as her picture, eh? And as good?"

" Miss Sybil pretty! Is them there roses pretty? Good! Is God's own Heaven good? Ah, Master Jack, you don't know—you don't know!"

" No, that's it, Bruds—I don't know." There were tears in Jack's eyes as he spoke. " I don't know. I've got to learn. I shall make some mistakes, I fear; many blunders—but I'll pull through, if I can, for their sakes."

" An' you be Master Jack, bean't you? Really? Sure-lie?"

" Yes, I'm Jack right enough—really and surely. And I mean to try to be a good son and a good brother, Bruds, to the best mother and sweetest sister that any world-worn, dusty, besmirched, unworthy young blackguard ever had."

" Blackguard! You was never that! I won't 'ear you say that! Oh, Master Jack! Welcome home! Welcome home!"

Sybil had come forward, unnoticed. She had seen the two men, and instantly recognised Jack. For a moment, the surprise left her speechless; then, with a little scream of delight, she ran to Jack, calling—

"Jack! Dear Jack! Brother, you've come home! You've come home at last!" She threw her arms round his neck, kissing him and sobbing with very happiness.

Jack was speechless, silenced with shame and confusion. Sybil's warm kisses were on his lips, her palpitating form in his arms. He thought her a thousand times more beautiful than the photograph—as indeed she was. And this lovely creature was clinging to him, whom she believed to be her brother, her protector, with all the confidence and security of a child to its mother! And he, impostor that he was, did not dare to return one kiss—one embrace! He could only stand trembling, silent and ashamed.

"Oh! dear Jack, let me have a good look at you! You dear brother!" She held him at arm's length for a moment, then nestled her head upon his shoulder, and sobbed again for joy. "Jack—brother—dear brother! Thank God you're safe and well! Oh, dear, dear brother"—hugging him—"how we have longed for you —prayed for you! And you've come! You've come!"

"Yes, I've come, Sybil—I've come."

"Kiss me again, Jack."

After a pause, he kissed her on the forehead.

"And now, dear, come to mother."

"No, no, not yet!" Jack cried hastily.

"Why?"

"It may startle her—the suddenness of it all."

"Shall I go and prepare her?"

Jack, seeking to delay her as long as possible, said—

"This is my friend—my old and best friend—Mr. Thomas Hewley."

"Glad to meet you, Miss Landale. Glad to see my old friend's welcome home. Bruds knew him at once—didn't you, Bruds?" And Tom turned appealingly to Bruds, who replied—

"Well, arter a bit I did—arter a bit."

"And how is she?"

"Who?"

"Your dear mother."

"*My* dear mother, Jack! *Our* dear mother."

"Of course—our dear mother." This Jack could only whisper.

"She's been weak, but you will make her strong; ill, but you will make her well; grief-stricken, but you will make her happy."

Lady Walgrove came forward, watching them eagerly.

"Yes, God helping me, I will make you both happy, I trust," replied Jack devoutly.

Lady Walgrove tottered forward.

Sybil, turning to her mother, cried out—

"Mother! dear mother, see! he's come home!"

The terrible moment Jack had so longed for, so dreaded, had arrived. What would the mother do? Would she detect the imposture, and spurn him from her, or would she be deceived, and receive him? Jack trembled as with an ague. He could not speak. He was in an agony of fear, remorse, suspense, and shame.

Sybil was watching her mother, whose eyes were fixed on Jack with a terrible strain, as if bridging over the twenty years of her son's absence, and striving to connect the two beings—the boy who had left her, the man who had returned. Jack felt the blood rush to his heart, to his head, then leave both. He felt faint almost to falling. The mother's eyes were still reading into his very soul.

At last, holding out both arms, she tottered forward, moaning—

"Jack! my boy—my son! You've come home at last! Thank God! Thank God!"

As the poor mother sobbed quietly on his breast, Jack offered up a little petition to the Throne of Grace for pardon and guidance.

CHAPTER XX

IN WHICH JACK TAKES POSSESSION OF LANDALE

WITH the mother and sister on either side of him, Jack entered the house which was henceforth to be his. It was a lovely home. As he crossed the threshold he felt less pain, less shame, less regret. The warm pressure of Sybil's hands on his left arm—she had already taken sisterly possession of him—and the loving clasp of the mother's arms on the right seemed to give him assurance that all would be well. A thrill of joy passed through him as he stood for a moment in the beautiful old hall. It was of oak and brass, with rich tapestry round the walls and over the doors. The gallery, with its fine carving, the wide oak steps and heavy balustrades, the large fireplace of the same wood, brass dogs and fire-irons, the old stained-glass windows, shedding their subdued coloured lights on the dark oak, glinting on the brass—how glorious it all was! The few paintings tilted from the gallery were artistic treasures. At one side, with its pipes reaching to the dome of the hall, was a magnificent organ in carved oak. All these things went to make up such a picture of a home that Jack's eyes were moist with mingled happiness and remorse.

On a large white bearskin mat in front of the fire was Barry, the largest St. Bernard he had ever seen. He was lying with his grand head resting on his two front paws. As the party entered he rose, and, with stately tread, crossed the hall, staring hard at Jack, his large ears and tail erect. Carefully sniffing him from his boots upwards, he seemed to be weighing him in the canine balance. No one spoke. At last he decided Jack was a man to be trusted. The tension of ears and tail relaxed, the mouth opened as with a smile, the tail waved to and fro. Standing up on his hind legs, he placed a huge paw on each of Jack's shoulders and bestowed on him a friendly lick.

"There, mother, I said so! I knew Barry would know who he was and would say 'Welcome home.' The dear old boy!" And Sybil hugged Barry. "You are safely installed now, dear Jack. Barry has decided that you are eminently satisfactory."

Barry inspected Tom, and made no hostile remark; but he did not give him so warm a welcome as he had given Jack. Jack patted the dog and praised him, and took him to his heart with the rest of the family.

"How beautiful it looks!" he said, looking round with admiration.

"Does it all come back to you, dear?" asked the mother.

The evasion of the truth almost choked him, but he had to answer.

"I feel a little strange at first, of course—it is so long——"

"Yes, dear," said the mother, with tears in her voice; "so long—so very long. But we are not going to talk of that. We will forget it all and remember only that you are here, and that you will remain."

"Spurdy," Sybil called to the butler, who was waiting, "this is Mr. Landale—and Mr. Hewley."

"We have met before," said Jack, smiling. "I think Mr. Spurdy was a little doubtful about me."

"Oh, no, sir, not at all! But we did not expect you till to-morrow."

"No, Jack. How did you do it?"

"I left the boat at Queenstown, and crossed *via* Holyhead. I was so anxious to—to—be here as soon as I could."

The mother and sister hugged him a little closer to them as he said this, and Sybil asked—

"Will you go to your room now?"

"Yes, I think so."

"You have papa's old room, as I told you in my letter," said Sybil. "Mamsey has looked after your bedroom and

I after your study. We want you to be very pleased with them. Will you go now?"

It was a bad moment for Jack. He had no idea where the rooms were. To betray his ignorance was to excite suspicion. He breathed hard, and grew a little pale, but his natural readiness came to his rescue. In kind and firm tones, and quite the master-of-the-house manner, he gave his orders to Spurdy.

"Spurdy, take Mr. Hewley to his room. You, dear moth——" he could scarcely pronounce the word. He clasped her a little closer to him, and went on, "You, dear mother, shall take me to my bedroom, and Sybil to my den."

This pleased them both amazingly, and got him out of the difficulty. Tom went to his room, chatting with Spurdy, joking and laughing, getting all sorts of scraps of useful information out of him for Jack's future guidance.

Up the broad staircase, the mother and sister holding on to him and Barry following with great dignity, Jack went. Along the gallery into a broad passage, at the end of which was a mullioned stained-glass window; into a large bedroom, exquisitely furnished in masculine style, with a glorious view from the windows right over the grand old park to the country beyond. Flowers were everywhere over the room: on his pillows, on the dressing-table, in the window recesses, on the mantelpiece. Jack's lips quivered. He almost broke down when the mother, tenderly watching him, asked if he liked the room.

"Do I like it? Oh, how good—how good you both are! How—how can I—thank—I can't! Please forgive me—but——" The tears were in his eyes, tears of gratitude and repentance.

It was all so lovingly, so sweetly done. The two dear women were so evidently painfully anxious that he should be pleased—he, the impostor, the thief!—that his heart ached for them. Almost overcome, he sat down in the cosy chair by the fire, and the mother leaned over the back of it and kissed his head, while the sister knelt at his side and put her beautiful cheek close to his. Not to be outdone in the welcoming home of the wanderer, Barry sat in front of him and placed a paw on his knee. Jack was choking. He held a hand of each of the dear ones in each of his and mentally swore that, if God would let him, he would repay with his life, if need be, some of the love that was so undeservedly lavished upon him now.

The mother and sister were in tears: silent, happy, grateful tears. So they sat for fully ten minutes, full of their own thoughts, each sending up a little prayer of thankfulness that the wanderer had been spared to them, and that he had come home.

"Forgive me, please!" Jack pleaded, "but it all seems so beautiful, so peaceful, so like home—and you are so good—that I am—just—a little off—my guard. I will be better—soon—and not foolishly trouble you in this way again. I will—believe me—try to be worthy of all your love and goodness in the future."

"You are worthy, dear son. I know you are."

"I will try to be. May God grant that you will never repent or regret my entrance under this roof."

"Regret? Oh, Jack!" said Sybil.

"My son! Regret? How can you?"

His manly, simple pathos went straight to their hearts, which were, from that moment, opened to him, enclosing him in their loving shrines for ever and for ever.

"Now to my den, Sybil," he faltered.

They could not bear to let go of him even for a moment. They seemed to fear that if they did so he would vanish, and the old, cold emptiness of his absence would return. So, still hugging him closely to them, they passed to his study.

A dream of a den for a man! Another lovely view across the country; a splendid library; fine old pictures; oak dado and tapestried walls. The writing-desk, tables, chairs, lounge were all old oak, luxuriously upholstered. Flowers again, and yet again flowers. On the desk were a handsome blotting-book, inkstand, and pen in gold and jewels, "From Sybil to Jack." Pipe-racks, ash-tray, a match-box in solid silver, and a hundred and one little nick-nacks, quaint and pretty, the outcome of Sybil's warm, loving solicitude, made up an elysium of comfort and convenience such as Jack had never even dreamed of.

He thanked them again in broken accents, and, very reluctantly, they left him, urging him "not to be long"; they would wait for him in the hall. Kissing the mother reverently on the forehead, and reluctantly receiving a warm, sisterly embrace from Sybil, he went to the door, watched them down the passage, then shut himself in, and, leaning his head on the mantelpiece, sobbed like a child. All that he had been denied all his life—a mother's love, a sister's devotion, a home—were now his. And such a home! Such a mother! Such a sister! "God in heaven forgive me!" he prayed. "Let not my sin come home to these two. Let me atone. Punish me, but not them. Make me worthy. Let me make them happy."

As if in answer to his prayer, the full, rich, sweet tones of an organ struck upon his ears. It was Sybil playing, and the music rang through the old hall, along the oak passages, into Jack's heart, and, let us hope, up to the God in heaven he had so earnestly prayed to for forgiveness and guidance.

When Jack went into the gallery of the hall he paused for a moment, looking over the balcony down upon Sybil, still playing the organ. The mother was sitting gazing into the fire. When Sybil finished, he ran down the stairs, and said—   .

"Shall we go out upon the terrace? It looks so inviting. The landscape is so beautifully English, and it is so long since I saw anything like it. I want to feast my eyes upon it. By-the-bye, some one must go to the station for our bags. We left them there. Our heavy luggage should arrive to-morrow, under the care of my servant. He is a Chinaman whom I have brought over with me. He knew me in San Francisco. I—I—went there for a time. You did not know that, of course."

"No, dear Jack. You never told us you had been in America."

"Oh, yes, I have knocked about a great deal while I have been—away. Wong—that is my Chinaman—is a great character, and so much attached to me. He will be a little strange to you at first, but you are sure to like him. Spurdy, please send to the station for my things."

"Pardon, sir, but Mr. Hewley has already done so. They will be here in less than an hour."

"Thanks. I had forgotten dear old Tom. He always does the right thing."

While they were on the terrace Lorna came out. She had kept away purposely until the meeting between mother, sister, and brother was over. She was introduced to Jack, and she looked curiously at the handsome fellow who had been portioned off to her by the sister as her lot in life. He saluted her with kind gravity, and she felt just a little bit in awe of him. Not so with Tom, who, coming up, was introduced to her. They went off into a rattle of chat as naturally and quickly as though they had been acquainted all their lives.

The panorama outspread before him filled Jack with delight. He felt he could never stare at it enough. The flowers, the exquisite green of the fields, the hedgerows white with hawthorn blossom, the fruit-trees laden with bloom, filled his eyes as they had never filled before with the sense of home and country. They sat and talked until the gong called them to prepare for dinner.

"We will not dress to-night. We will sit down as we are," said the mother.

In the dining-room, pictures of the Landales looked down upon Jack; generations and generations of them. Jack thought the eyes not unfriendly. Signs of luxury, good taste, and wealth were everywhere. The servants were on their best behaviour. The master had come home. The dinner was perfection, the wines good; and if Jack's conscience did not sleep, there was nothing the matter with Tom's, who "let himself out to do himself one better than he had ever done himself before," as he expressed it. Soon all tears and sadness were forgotten. The room rang with a joyous laughter that it had not known for many a long year. Happiness beamed from the eyes of the mother and sister. Lorna was laughing and chatting, and Tom—well! Tom looked at Lorna, and thought thoughts that Lorna must have guessed, for she thought thoughts not altogether unlike his, only put in other words.

"What a devilish fine figure she has! What a pretty face!" he said to himself.

"What a nice fellow! How very bright and comfy he is to get on with!" said Lorna.

When dinner was over, the mother begged the two men to smoke. Sybil lighted Jack's cigar, and Lorna Tom's; and Tom said to himself, "This is certainly good enough."

When they had smoked and laughed and talked, they went into the drawing-room, and the girls played and sang. They both did exceedingly well. Then came the parting for the night. With many a kiss from the mother and sister, the ladies went to their rooms, and Jack, calling Tom, lit another cigar and strolled out on the terrace.

"Tom," he asked, "what do you think of it all?"

"Jack, it's heaven—just a corner of heaven; and a cosy, warm, and happy corner at that. What a lucky chap you are!"

"Poor old Jack Landale!" sighed Jack, and smoked on in silence.

The sun had sunk, the beautiful English twilight was fading. Bidding each other good night, the friends went to their separate rooms.

Jack, on gaining his room, threw open the window, and, sitting on the window-sill, gazed out on the landscape, now being lit up dimly by the young May moon. For more than an hour he sat there, thinking of all that had passed, conjecturing what was still to come. He had never imagined such peace and happiness, much as he had dreamed of home and kindred. He had never even seen anything like this noble house. The little suburban London house where he had been kept before he went to school was plain and clean, and that was all that could be said for it. It was cheerless and comfortless. But this paradise of a place was beyond all that he had conjured up in the long journey from Woolloogolonga Gully. This mother, too, nobler, sweeter, more gracious than he had hoped to find her. And then, Sybil! "How beautiful she is! How beautiful!" he murmured to himself. "How full of young, bright, pulsating life! How supple, graceful, and perfect her figure! And her kisses! O God!" he reproached himself, "that he should let her give her sisterly caresses unwittingly to a stranger!" He flushed with shame. And yet, the joy of it all, the fulness of their love and tenderness!

He went to bed, but not to sleep for hours. When at last he fell into slumber it was to see again Sybil's face in his dreams, to hear her sweet voice, to feel her warm embraces and to watch the face of his friend, Jack Landale, grow slowly into being out of a patch of sunburnt scrub, and to hear his well-remembered voice saying—

"Jack, old man, don't fret. It's God's way out of it!"

CHAPTER XXI

IN WHICH JACK "LEARNS" LANDALE.

AT the first sign of dawn, Jack rose and went quietly downstairs, woke Barry, who was asleep on a mat in the hall, and, letting himself and the dog out, closed the door and walked on to the terrace. There was a faint streak of dusky gold in the sky eastward. Away west, it was still a slaty grey. The air smelt fresh and good; the scent of flowers and dewy grass came gratefully to his nostrils, and he opened his chest and breathed it in freely. Barry looked up inquiringly. "What was he brought out so early for?" Patting the big fellow affectionately, Jack said, "Now, old man, go ahead. Lead me round and show me things." The dog looked at him and, as if understanding, trotted on solemnly towards the end of the terrace, paused under Sybil's window, and looked up at it.

"Oho!" thought Jack. "That is her window, is it?" And he gazed up at it too, for a few minutes; then, giving Barry another friendly pat, he added, "Go on. Show me more."

Barry was more difficult to move this time. He evidently hoped that Sybil would look out, and eventually come down and join in a ramble and romp with them. But Sybil was peacefully dreaming of her handsome brother, wandering with him through a dark forest, where, strive as she would, she could not see him— only feel his hand guiding her, only lean upon his strong arm for support. She strove to pierce the darkness that blinded her, in vain. Not a ray of light could be seen anywhere. Slowly, out of the blackness, away up over the tops of the dark trees, she saw a star, large, brilliant, beautiful. Under it, in nebulous letters, was written "WAIT." Then, she looked again at Jack, and saw his face, indistinctly, wavering, uncertain; but his eyes, too, were fixed upon the star, his lips moved as he read the fleecy, vapoury message, "WAIT." All this had she dreamed in the few moments that Jack had passed under her window. She smiled in her sleep—a smile as innocent as that of a child—and, blushing a little, stretched out her hand, let it fall upon her breast, and was once more at rest.

Barry trotted on, Jack following. He led the way through the plantation into the "Jungle," and stopped under a large old beech-tree which had one long, curved branch so low down that it would serve as a seat for two persons. Here Barry stopped and sat down. Jack followed his example. Seating himself on the branch, he looked about him. It was a beautiful spot. All around, the earth seemed carpeted with blue-bells; around the tree itself were large bunches of primroses, cowslips, and violets. Overhead, the young green leaves showed almost transparent under the bright morning sun. Looking down at the branch, Jack saw carved in its silver-grey bark the name "JACK," enclosed in a heart. Something shining in the green moss under his feet caught his eye. Stooping, he picked it up. It was a lady's penknife, with the large blade open. He wiped it carefully and put it in his pocket. Rising, he started at a sharp walk, and went back into the open, round the back of the house, noting all the doors and windows; away to the stables, making mental plans of them, the barns and coach-houses. All had been built for many years, and, for the most part, were of red brick and stone, with red-tiled roofs. Unlatching one of the doors, he carefully counted the number of stalls. Returning, he went into the kitchen-garden, noted the height and thickness of the walls and the several gates, the tool-houses and doors. Back again to the front of the house; down on to the second terrace; studied the masonry of the walls, the situation of the fountains and ponds, and the views from the various points of the terrace.

By this time he had spent over two hours. It was nearing seven o'clock. Barry began to grow impatient, to give little barks, and " point " towards the upper terrace. Up Jack went. Stopping under Sybil's window, Barry gave his old signal of " Woof! woof!" In a moment the window opened and Sybil's lovely head appeared, and, to her surprise, she saw that Barry was not alone.

" Good morning, Sybil," Jack called.

" Good morning, Jack dear. This is a surprise. I did not expect to see you so early."

" Won't you come down?"

" Of course I will, dear. Wait."

" Wait? Yes, I will wait."

Instantly her dream returned to her, and she wondered at the coincidence. The word " WAIT!" under the star flashed out bright and clear. It was only a coincidence, but it was a strange one. She soon came through the porch, looking as fresh and pure as the rosebuds near her. Putting her hands on Jack's shoulders, she kissed him on the lips, holding him for a moment to her. He gently released himself, put her arm through his, and they walked slowly along the terrace.

" Did you sleep well, Jack?"

" When I went to sleep, yes, but there was too much to think about to tumble off at once. Did you?"

" Not so well as usual. Are you glad you are home?"

" Glad! You cannot think how glad."

" Do you like the old place?"

" I cannot tell you how much I love it."

" Are you going to love us?"

" Love you. I love you already."

" Much?"

" Yes."

" Tell me how much," she said laughingly.

" I can't."

" As much as this?" Measuring the length of her hand.

" As much as this." With his two arms he implied the whole of the universe.

" Really as much as that?"

" More."

" Are we as nice as you thought we should be?"

" I have never even dreamed of anything so nice."

Sybil laughed softly, saying, " You dear old Jack! Shall I tell you a secret?"

" Please."

" Will you give me a kiss if I do?"

" Ye-es."

" Well, mother and I talked you over last night, and we agreed that you are a thousand times nicer than we expected. We were horribly afraid that you—well, you won't be cross, will you? because you are not—we were afraid that you would have grown, perhaps, a wee bit coarse, leading that wretched life, with such rough people. Once, a man who had worked here for a little while told one of the servants that he had met you in Sydney."

" Where is the man?" asked Jack quickly.

" Oh! he went away ages ago—I don't know where. But he said—please don't be angry, dear—he said that you drank horribly! But it was false, was it not?"

" Yes. Do I look like a drunkard?"

" No, dear. That's exactly what we said last night—for mother was watching you at the table. Don't be hurt or angry, Jack. You must make allowance for a mother's anxiety."

" I will not be angry at anything she thinks or does, Sybil. I can never be grateful enough to her or to you."

" But, Jack, how could you stop away from her? Not even to write to us? Please, dear, don't think I'm scolding"—Sybil gave his arm a loving little squeeze—" but it was a little hard and cruel to mother, wasn't it? Tell me why you did it. You see you don't seem a bit like that kind of man. You're so wonderfully tender and considerate in all you do. Oh! we've watched you, Jack, and know all about you now you are here, but when you were away, weren't you odd and—well, a little cruel?"

" Sybil dear," Jack began. It was hard to explain

Landale's conduct and justify himself for what Landale had done. Landale was a drunkard—steeped in dissipation—ashamed of his life, his wife, his associations; not wanting to lead a better life, too sodden with drink to care to live soberly and cleanly. He had told her he was not a drunkard. He could not tell her that her real brother was. He had to temporise.

"You see, dear, I had sworn never to return while Sir James lived—never to touch a penny of his money. Our dear mother had nothing of her own—I could take nothing from her. I did not care to write, because—because—well, perhaps I was ashamed, or—never mind that now. Remember nothing but that I am here—that I am not a drunkard—that I can never be hard to you again as long as I live. If there is anything I can do, no matter what it is, how difficult, how painful to me, if it will please you, let me do it. You can't think what pleasure it will be to me. Only tell me."

"Well, there is one thing you can do for me, Jack." She looked up, smiling at his earnestness.

"What is it? I hope it is something really hard to do. What is it?"

"I'm afraid it is really hard."

"What is it?"

"To give me that kiss you promised for my secret." She held up her sweet lips, and looked so lovely, so bewitching in her innocent pleading that Jack felt his heart give a bound that shook him as a heavy blow might have done.

"Oh! it is hard, isn't it?" she pouted.

He kissed her lightly on the lips. She hugged him to her.

"Yes, it is, Sybil—very hard. If you only knew how very lovely you are, you would—that is—I mean——"

"Well, sir? What do you mean?"

"I mean all sorts of things. Isn't that Bruds over there?"

"Yes."

" Let's go and have a chat with him."

" Bless his dear old heart!   Yes, let's."

As they approached Bruds, Sybil had her two hands
linked over Jack's arm.   She looked so happy, so ineffably
sweet and pure, that the old man's eyes glistened with the
joy of looking upon her.

" Good morning, Bruds," she called.

" Good mornin', missie, good mornin'."   His eyes wandered round, looking at the various flowers.

" Good morning, Bruds," said Jack.

" Good mornin', sir, good mornin'."

" I don't think I quite like that ' sir' from you, Bruds.
Can't it be Master Jack, as in the old days?"

" Aye, aye," the old fellow chuckled.   " Old days, old
manners, I reckon."

" Well, they are good enough for me, Bruds ; please go
back to them."

" Well, Master Jack, if it so please you, Master Jack
let it be."

Bruds had been gathering a large bunch of exquisite
Maréchal Niel roses.   Shaking the dew off them, he
handed them to Sybil, saying—

" For your mammy, missie.   And there's one for you."
And he handed her a beautiful, full blush rose.

" Turn round and let me get a pin," she said, taking
one from his waistcoat.   This was a joke Bruds dearly
loved.   He would have been deeply hurt if he had had to
present the pin for his flower himself.

" Do the old place come back, Master Jack?"

" Pretty well, Bruds.   Is your tool-house in the same
place, under that old apple-tree?"

" Yes! that's right, that's right, Master Jack!"

" And do the peaches still grow on the south wall of
the kitchen garden?"

" Aye du they."

" And those two twisted old pear-trees that hang half-
way over the wall—do they still bear fruit?"

" Why, what a memory you've got, Master Jack!   Aye,

that they du. You remember tumblin' out o' that tree, eh?"

" My memory's pretty good for some things. I wonder whether I could tell you how many stalls there are in the stables?"

" Try, Jack," said Sybil.

He was not looking at her when he answered—

" Fourteen stalls and four loose boxes."

" Right!"

" The coach-houses run along by the west garden wall; the barns are opposite."

" Why, Jack, you're a wonder! You remember everything."

" No, dear; not everything."

" Have a flower, Master Jack?"

" Flowers are too delicate, too sensitive for men. Only women should be allowed that luxury. Thanks, Bruds, but not to wear. We are too hard and coarse to touch them—except as you do, Bruds, to grow and train them."

" How funny that be, now, Master Jack! Why, when you were a little sprig of a chap, you used to ask me if it didn't hurt the flowers to cut 'em. You've much the same ideas now, seemingly."

And so, bit by bit, Jack learned all the others knew about Landale's boyhood, and, by care and observation, earned a reputation for a remembrance of the old things and old times that helped greatly to make him popular with all who knew and loved Landale and its owners.

It was beautiful to see the mother's meeting with Jack when he returned to the house. His scruples were lessening each time he looked upon her—she seemed so supremely happy. After breakfast, he went to his study. There were great piles of letters awaiting him, on all sorts of matters connected with the estate; begging letters of all kinds—nearly all the men who wrote had either been to Australia or professed to have done so, and the others had relations out there whom Jack " must have met." Jack called Tom, and the two went at the correspondence with a will, Tom's quick, practical common sense knocking down the sentimental assumptions and pleas of the applicants like so many skittles.

" Well, the gall and cheek of some of these fellows are beyond words!" he said, after opening a score or so of letters asking for relief. " Listen to this playful joker :—

" ' RESPECTED SIR,—I am sure you have a kind heart and can feel for a brother man. Having come back to your fortune which you have, you will esteem it a duty to your brother man to help him as Providence has helped you. " He who giveth to the poor lendeth to the Lord" (see the Scriptures). A few hundred pounds you would not miss—you would not know they were gone, but they would save me from much persecution, and my little home from being broken up. Respected sir, do not refuse. " Cast your bread upon the waters," saith the Scriptures.—Yours, respected sir,

" ' JOSEPH WIDOUGH.' "

" Joseph Widough, indeed!" said Tom. " A little too WIDO. No, gentle Joseph, not for you, my Widough." And he tore it up, and consigned it, with a score of other similar effusions, to the waste-paper basket. There was a letter from the Landale lawyers, asking for an interview. This Jack arranged for the following week. He wanted to learn more of the property before discussing it with them.

One of the first things he did that morning was to arrange for the payment of an income to Sal and Smudgee. This was, as he had always felt it, a very difficult matter to arrange.

" What do you think I ought to allow them, Tom?" he had asked.

" See that they are both well fed; pay for Smudgee's education, and look after her when she is grown up. Not a cent more. Whatever you do, you run the risk of giving yourself away. Sal is sure to be suspicious, and the more you give, the more she will suspect. It's a deuced pity you have to allow them anything. Better to drop them altogether."

"Ah! that's not to be thought of. They have more right to the money than I."

"But not as much right as the mother and sister."

"I know that. Don't fear that I shall ever forget it. I try to put myself in Landale's place in this, as in all other matters. He would have been liberal with Sal. So must I be."

"You will regret it. But you will do what you consider just, I know. What will you give them?"

"Two thousand a year."

"Two thousand a year! Two thousand Balaam's asses! Five hundred would be more than enough."

"No, Tom, the estates can afford it. I shall make more than double that over the usual income in the first six months; and shall double it yet again in the next half-year. I shall send this in monthly payments."

"Great Crœsus! It's madness, and ten to one it will bowl your over. Sal with one hundred and sixty pounds a month to spend! What *will* she buy? What *will* she look like? What *will* she do?"

"That is her affair, not mine. I shall do my duty. If she chooses to drink herself to death, that is not my fault."

And so it came to pass that, when Sal and Nat were at the lowest ebb in Paddington, Sydney, a message arrived from the bank, informing them that one hundred and sixty pounds had been placed to their credit by the Mr. John Mowbray who had previously paid a hundred to their account. Nat and Sal tried in every available way to extract from the bank Jack's whereabouts, but failed—for the best of all possible reasons. No one at the bank knew.

After two hours' hard work, Jack had mastered the bulk of his correspondence and, calling for Sybil, proposed a visit to the stables, with a view to a prospective gallop. Sybil went with Jack to inspect the horses. The head stableman, Comstock, was crotchety and crabbed, as men in his position are apt to be, but Jack had not come into

ing Jack's visit, and had quite made up his mind how he
would deal with him. " I'll let him see, first go off, what
sort of a man I am. ' Begin as you mean to go on' is my
motter." A very good motto, too, if one can follow it;
but when some one stronger than yourself begins in another way, and is determined to go on as *he* began, what is
one to do? He found very early in his intercourse with
the master that he meant to " go on as he had begun," in
his own way. One after the other, the horses were tried,
Jack astonishing Comstock with his knowledge of horse-
flesh.

" Which is your horse, Sybil?" he asked.

" ' Tarquin'—this one."

Jack went up and carefully inspected the horse.

" Does he ever shy?" he asked, after examining his eyes.

" Sometimes, a little," she answered.

" Put a saddle on him," Jack ordered. " No, not that,"

246

as the groom reached for a lady's saddle. "Put a man's saddle on him."

"He ain't used to it, sir," said Comstock surlily.

"Please be good enough, Mr. Comstock, to obey my orders without remark. If I make a mistake, that is my affair."

Comstock was gradually turning purple. He had caught one of the stable-boys hiding his head in a corn-bin to smother his laughter. He felt his dignity outraged, but he did not dare to hesitate. The horse was saddled, and Jack mounted. Devoutly Comstock hoped he would be thrown and break his neck. But Jack had not broken in buck-jumpers and wild Australian horses on a "back-block" station to be thrown so easily. He set the horse at a canter, at a trot, and then at a gallop—purposely choosing places where the shadows of the waving branches danced across the horse's path. He could feel the animal getting nervous. He gave a sudden sharp bark, as of an angry dog. The horse swerved in a manner that would have jerked many a good rider from the saddle, but Jack was prepared, and sat tight as the horse's skin. When he rode back, he said to Sybil—

" 'Tarquin' is not safe for you to ride. Let me pick you out another."

Women are quick to learn. Jack's manner was kindness itself, but "the master" was in his tone, and she was glad to recognise and bow to it. After a full inspection, he chose a horse for her. Turning to her, he asked if she would ride with him. She was delighted to say "Yes."

"Saddle 'The Bo'sun' for Miss Sybil, and keep the saddle on 'Tarquin' for me, Mr. Comstock. Send them to the door in half-an-hour."

"Well, I'm d——d!" was all Comstock uttered, but he caught the grinning stable-boy by the ear and nearly wrung it off.

"I'll teach you, you young hass, to laugh at your betters! Take that!"

It was well for Mr. Comstock that Jack did not see

this playful little exhibition of feeling, or he might have learned exactly the kind of pain the hand of such a man as Jack could inflict by the wringing of one of his own ears.

" Oh, Jack, I'm so glad you gave it to Mr. Comstock! We've never dared. We're awfully afraid of him!"

" So I saw, Sybil."

" And he's really a bit of a bully, dear."

" I saw that, too."

" Dear Jack, how do you see all these things?"

" Knocking about the world opens the eyes wonderfully."

" I am so glad. And, dear, I think you are right about ' Tarquin.' But Mr. Comstock never would admit he was not safe."

" I suppose Comstock bought him, eh?"

" Yes."

" What did he give for him?"

" I don't know, dear."

" When was he bought?"

" Six months ago."

" Humph!" Jack made a mental note to call for Mr. Comstock's books for the past year, in his first spare half-hour.

That was Jack's way. He had a most uncomfortable knack of seeing through knavery and trickery, and a still more disagreeable habit of making it unpleasant and warm for the knave and trickster. Mr. Comstock had a lesson in store for him that he did not expect. When that ill-advised individual came round with the grooms, leading " Tarquin " and " Bo'sun," Jack asked—

" What did you give for that horse?"

" Which, sir?" asked the astonished Comstock.

" ' Tarquin.' "

" I don't remember, sir, exactly."

" Tell me within ten pounds."

" Well, perhaps a hundred and forty—perhaps a hundred and twenty." Something in Jack's eyes induced

Mr. Comstock to knock off twenty pounds in his estimate of the price.

"What!" asked Jack, in a tone that made Mr. Comstock feel exceedingly like having a nip of whisky as soon as he could get it. "What!"

"Well, sir, I ain't quite certain to a few pounds."

"You keep books, I suppose?"

"Yes, sir." Decidedly, Mr. Comstock was not "going on as he had begun"!

"Let them be given to my secretary, Mr. Hewley, within half-an-hour, please." And, helping Sybil into her saddle, Jack cantered off on "Tarquin."

There was little doubt that Jack was learning his Landale, and already some of his Landale was becoming in some slight measure acquainted with him.

Sybil and Jack both rode well, and they had a most enjoyable gallop, Jack letting Sybil choose the route, suggesting only that she should show him some of the tenants, inquiring rather anxiously if there were any who remembered him as a boy. There were "two very old people still left who knew him," she said, "but the others were either dead or had drifted away. It was difficult to keep the young men and women on the land nowadays. They went to the cities or abroad, and drew their relations after them."

Jack got the names of the two who had known Landale, for future use, but said he "would not see them just yet."

Sybil looked a perfect picture in her riding-costume, and Jack was falling deeper and deeper in love with her every hour. He kept his eyes open, watching and noting everything. He had the true Bushman's instinct and training, and where he had once been he could go again without difficulty. He learned the names of most of the tenants, and a great deal of their characters. It was a usefully and delightfully spent two hours. When he returned to lunch, there was little of the estate and people he did not know something about.

After lunch he sent for Comstock. "Tarquin" had shied several times, with very little provocation. Jack was confirmed in his opinion about the horse. Comstock looked extremely unhappy. Jack found in his book the date of the purchase and the price. The figures had been hastily and lately altered from one hundred and fifty guineas to one hundred and twenty. Jack detected the fraud at once.

"Mr. Comstock," he asked suddenly, "are you married?"

"Yes, sir."

"Any children?"

"Four, sir."

"You are fortunate. For their sakes I shall be lenient with you. You have been guilty in this case of embezzlement. I have not the slightest doubt that, when I have your books carefully audited, I shall find this is by no means an isolated instance of your dishonesty. You are discharged from this moment. On consideration of your restoring at once all that you have robbed Lady Walgrove and Miss Landale of, I shall refrain, for the sake of your family, from handing you over to the police. Mr. Hewley here will arrange with you the details of the repayment. Please move your furniture out at once, and leave the neighbourhood."

The man wanted to bluster, but he had not the courage. He whimpered instead.

"If you'll only look over it, sir!"

"No," sternly replied Jack. "Miss Landale's neck might have been broken through the faults of that horse. You got him cheap in consequence of them, and pocketed the difference between the price you paid and the sum you charged in your accounts. I might have forgiven the fraud—I will never forgive you for putting Miss Landale into such danger. Mr. Hewley, show him out of the house."

Mr. Comstock went, and Landale knew him no more.

In the afternoon, Wong arrived with the baggage, safe

and intact. He had some difficulty in making himself understood along the road, but with his quiet persistence and wonderful patience he had overcome all difficulties, and had come out of them in triumph. His coming caused a great sensation at the little station and through the village. He had looked so unhappy and so out-of-place in his bowler hat and "reach-me-downs," as Tom called them, that Jack had insisted upon his wearing his native costume. He had bought several in San Francisco; some plain black and blue ones for ordinary wear, and some extremely rich ones for indoor service. Jack had decided to include in Wong's work the making and serving up of tea and coffee. He made both to perfection.

Wong was much laughed at in the servants' hall when he first arrived, and was the subject of much chaff, but it was very soon discovered that he had a quiet and most effective habit of retaliating on his persecutors. It was done in such a way that, as Judson said, "You never knowed how you was struck, but you knowed you'd got it."

After Comstock's dismissal, it was quite understood that the master would stand no ill-treatment of a servant he liked so much as Wong. Then, he could be so extremely useful, if well treated, that it became a matter of policy to please him. He knew how to make so many tasty little dishes—curries and soups, sweets with wonderful new combinations, and sauces—that the cook found it well worth her while to be exceedingly polite to him. Even Spurdy condescended from his lofty heights to admit that " the Mongolian knew how to polish plate better than any man who had served under him." The laundress learned more from him in a week than she had ever known in her life before. Never was such wonderfully washed linen, such delicately got-up flounces and other feminine things, since Landale was Landale. In so many ways was Wong useful and clever that in a short time he became almost indispensable to all in the household.

By the end of the week, three others of the head-servants had followed Mr. Comstock, and had departed from Landale. Those who had served Lady Walgrove honestly and faithfully Jack rewarded handsomely, immediately increasing their salaries. Before a month had passed, Jack was not only much liked, but was respected. There was not a soul on the estate who did not admit that he was the right man in the right place. They liked him for his manliness and generosity, and admired him for his justice and firmness.

He went to London to see the solicitors, and, after he had arranged his business with them, he called upon the D'Olans at their hotel.

Although the D'Olans had been little over a week in London, they had employed their time to so much advantage that they had seen a great deal and met many of the best people. Mamie's mantelpiece was covered with invitations. She had already become exceedingly popular. She was young, bright, clever, a great beauty, and an American heiress. What more could London society ask for? There was no scandal attached to her name; her character was irreproachable. Those who took the trouble to find out what she was like, personally, thought her a good and most lovable girl. She was courted and flattered " to the top of her bent," but she was too level-headed to let that disturb her balance. She had not heard from Jack, but thought a great deal of him and of her brief intimacy with him. Absolutely frank and truthful, even to herself, she had admitted to herself that he had made no attempt to make love to or even flirt with her. He had been as clear and straightforward in his manly way as any one could be. Tom had told her that Jack was unmarried and not in love, so that he was free and as much hers as any one's. That she was dissatisfied with his silence was only natural.

She was receiving on the afternoon of his call, and her rooms were thronged.

Jack took Sybil with him. Mamie was flushed with pleasure, and, on being introduced, greeted Sybil warmly.

"I am so glad to meet you, Miss Landale. Your brother talked so much about you that I have been real anxious to meet you. Won't you both sit down?" And she made a place for them near her on the lounge.

There was a mutual liking established between the two girls. Each felt the other to be good and true; both were anxious to please. It would have been difficult to find two more lovely creatures together than Sybil and Mamie. Each distinctively representative of her different nationality, they were perfect types of the two styles of beauty— the English and the American.

"I am sorry there is such a crowd to-day," said Mamie. "But you'll wait until they've gone, and we'll have a real good chat. Won't you?"

"I'm afraid that is impossible," Sybil replied. "We only came up for a few hours, and must catch the five train home."

"Isn't there a later one?" asked Mamie of Jack.

"Not one to get us home in time for dinner," he answered.

"That's really too bad! We'll be leaving as soon as papa comes from Paris, and we shall not see you for ever so long."

"Will not you and your mother come down to Landale on Saturday night and stay over Sunday?" asked Sybil.

"Oh, that would be just too lovely! Can we go, mother?"

Engagements had been made for that day, but Mrs. D'Olan knew how anxious her daughter was to go, and replied—

"Yes, honey, I am sure we can, if Miss Landale wishes us to come."

So it was settled that Mrs. D'Olan and Mamie should spend from Saturday to Monday at Landale. Jack felt sorry when he remembered Tom's warning, but he could not possibly raise any objection to the invitation.

After a little chat with the mother, Jack and Sybil took their leave, and left for home.

It was curious to watch Sybil's face as they drove away.

"Jack," she said, "she's the most perfect girl I ever saw!"

This was said in all sincerity, yet not enthusiastically. The tone was more reflective than gushing. She had looked at Jack when he was shaking hands with Mamie, and thought what a wonderfully handsome pair they made, and, oddly enough, she did not know why, the reflection gave her a strange little pang. Why it should have done so she could not guess. She was not jealous of Mamie's beauty: she frankly admired it, but she wondered whether Jack knew how really exquisite Mamie was. She rather hoped he did not, and asked herself why?

At Landale the night was bright and balmy. There was a full moon, and the scene viewed from the terrace was delightful. Sybil asked Jack to come and talk to her a little, and, leaving Lady Walgrove, Lorna, and Tom together, Jack and she strolled to a seat farther along the terrace, and they sat together talking for some time.

They were both very happy—each with a little reserve. Sybil wanted to know how much Jack cared for Mamie; Jack was, as ever, remorseful at Sybil's abandonment of herself in her sisterly way to him. She was hugging his arm with both of hers, and her head was nestling on his shoulder—a very enviable position to be in, either as an accepted lover or a brother, but for Jack, who was neither, it had its sting as well as its pleasure.

"Don't you think Miss D'Olan is a glorious creature, Jack?" she asked.

"Yes," he replied, "and she is as good as she is beautiful."

Sybil did not know what to make of this answer. It was not enthusiastic enough to excite her alarm, yet sincere enough to make her a little uneasy.

"How lovely the stars are to-night, Jack!" said Sybil, turning up her face to the sky. "I am like the child —'How I wonder what you are!' I heard somebody say once—or I read it somewhere—that it might be that in some star there is a duplicate of ourselves, exactly the same in form and feature, only nobler, better, purer —in other words, ourselves perfected. That these better selves are conscious of all that we think and do. That our good deeds bring them happiness, our misdeeds sorrow. That, when we have passed through this stage of existence and become like them, we shall be fused in them, and become one perfect, glorified being, dwelling in happiness for evermore. If it is true, Jack, I wonder whether we are giving our counterparts pleasure or pain at this moment? What do you think?"

"You can give your other self but little sorrow, Sybil. I wish I could think the same of my own."

"If Mamie has another self more beautiful than she is, how beautiful she must be!"

"I don't think, Sybil, that a duplicate of yourself is possible or necessary. You are perfect already," said Jack, earnestly.

"Oh, you dear old brother! How nice that was! A lover could not have said anything sweeter!" And she kissed him lovingly. "It is not a bit true, but it is awfully good of you to say it is."

Then they relapsed into that sweet, strange silence that often falls upon two beings who are united by ties of love and real fellowship. A silence that speaks from soul to soul of things and thoughts for which speech has no language. Sybil was perfectly happy; Jack as nearly so as he dared to be.

Saturday came, and with it Mamie and her mother. It was a glorious May day, and Landale looked at its best. To the D'Olans, who had never before seen an English country home, it seemed a paradise. Most Americans have great reverence for family and race. The old and beautiful touches them, as a rule. The quaintness, comfort, peace, and quiet of Landale appealed to Mamie with great force.

"The whole place is perfect!" exclaimed the mother; "just perfect!"

"It is a heaven upon earth," said Mamie.

Lady Walgrove and Mrs. D'Olan were soon great friends. Mrs. D'Olan had praised Jack so highly and sincerely that the mother's heart was touched and pleased.

"How proud you must be of such a son!" said Mrs. D'Olan.

"I am indeed," replied Lady Walgrove, "and have every reason to be so."

Quick and clever as Mamie was, she could not fail to be deeply impressed with the good taste and refinement that Landale was famous for. The evening passed away like a beautiful dream to her. The home life was so "perfect," as her mother called it; all the people were so unpretentious, yet dignified; undemonstrative, yet so loving and tender! Her heart was deeply touched. Sybil's unaffected admiration for Jack hurt her a little—she did not understand why. Why should not such a sister love such a brother? she asked herself, yet she did not quite like it. There was something in Jack's manner towards Sybil that puzzled her. She could not account for it; could not define it. She had no brothers of her own, still, she had seen the brothers of other girls often enough—none of whom behaved quite like Jack. Again and again would she catch him looking at Sybil with so unusual an expression on his face that she was startled. What was it? There were, to her keen eyes, so many conflicting emotions passing over him that it was quite impossible for her to follow or comprehend them. His adoration—there was no other word—for his mother she understood, and loved him for. But the sister! She saw him shrink a little when Sybil sat by his side, holding his hand; saw him look at her with intense love, yet avoid touching her. What could it mean? There was certainly something out of the common here. What could it be?

Jack was, to all seeming, honest, manly, and a gentleman. Sybil was as obviously pure as a dewdrop on a hawthorn blosom. They were brother and sister—yet— What was it? Sybil she understood. Jack mystified and angered her. He showed no desire to seek her company. He was kind and attentive as a host should be; but he went as readily to her mother as to herself— to his mother sooner than to either. And wherever he went, and whomever he spoke to, his eyes involuntarily went back to Sybil; and yet he avoided her, never once went to her of his own accord. What was it? Mamie could see no clue—no light. It was all dark and obscure.

Before retiring for the night, the two girls had a long talk in the room assigned to Mamie. Mamie sat in a cosy arm-chair next to the fire. She felt a little chilly, missing the all-pervading heat of the American "regulators"—the hot-air pipes used for warming the rooms. Sybil sat on the bed. Whenever Sybil rose to go, Mamie begged her to stay a little longer. She did so, to Lorna's disappointment, who always had her gossip with Sybil before going to sleep. Mamie wanted somebody to speak to her of Jack. She found a ready talker in Sybil, who never tired of that subject.

"How glad you must be to have him back again!" said Mamie.

"Glad! We have never known happiness until he came."

The two girls chatted on, as girls will chat, on all sorts of seemingly small and unimportant matters, keeping back till the last that which they were burning to speak of first. Mamie wanted to be told of English customs, and Sybil of American fashions; and always, some way or other, the conversation went back to Jack and his doings, till both were weary in body, although by no means tired of the conversation. With many little gapes and yawns, they bade each other good night, and were left to their own thoughts, which were, in both cases, many and varied, but when sleep kindly descended on both, the same name hung upon their lips—and that name was Jack.

Sunday was passed in a thoroughly happy, if quiet way. Service in the quaint old village church in the morning; a walk through the grounds before lunch; tea on the terrace, and a stroll by Sybil and Mamie into the " Jungle " to the seat on the old beech-tree. Here Mamie saw Jack's name carved. Asking who had done it, she learned that it was Sybil herself; and again she felt hurt, and again she asked herself " Why?" Why should a sister not carve the name of her brother, enclosed in a heart, on a favourite tree? There was no answer, and no explanation of her resentment that it should have been done by Sybil. Mamie had too generous a nature to encourage unkind feelings, and she resolutely beat them back, but it was not without an effort.

Tom and Lorna were having a fine time together, and Jack was with the elderly ladies, strolling through the gardens, the mother clinging to him with loving tenderness, he paying her the utmost respect, showing her every possible attention.

The day passed very pleasantly for all save Sybil, Jack, and Mamie. There was a sort of restraint upon them that the girls could not account for. The fact that they had taken a strong liking for each other only added to the mystery. It was so unlike them both to harbour any little annoyance or ill-feeling that they were angry with themselves.

Jack found his admiration for Mamie increasing. She was such a bright creature, so devoid of nonsense or affectation of any kind, that, had she been a plain instead of a very lovely woman, he must still have liked her exceedingly. But he knew he could never go beyond sincere respect and friendship with her. With Sybil it was different. Every hour increased his love for her. It was the first love of his life. He was five-and-thirty, in the full, vigorous prime of early manhood. It was therefore no sentiment to toy with; it was a full, overmastering passion that was growing up within him—a passion dangerous to himself and his peace of mind. It was useless to fight it; it was past the fighting stage. It was becoming a torrent that might sweep away himself, Sybil, and all who were dear to both.

During the afternoon, while Jack and Mamie were left for a time alone on the porch of the house, Mamie said—

" I have many dear girl-friends in America, but not one who has got so deep into my heart—little as I have seen of her—as your sister. A sweeter and more genuine girl I never met. She is as clear as a pure diamond."

" I know it," answered Jack. " She could not think a crooked or false thing, much less do one."

" She must have many admirers amongst her male acquaintances. Is there any special one? I mean, one whom she likes better than any other?"

A chill ran through all Jack's being. Strangely enough, he had never contemplated the possibility of Sybil having a lover. And yet, why should she not? Beautiful, attractive, good, and an heiress—could it be possible that she had not followers by the score, and lovers by the dozen? The thought was torture to him. He was silent so long that Mamie had to ask if he had heard what she had said. Jack's voice was a little hard in tone as he answered—

" Yes, I heard. But I have been at home so short a time that I—well, to be quite candid, I have never thought of the matter."

" It is impossible," continued Mamie, impelled to speak further on the subject by a feeling she could not explain, " quite impossible that such a dear, lovely girl could reach womanhood without inspiring love in some man's heart. If you are not careful, you may lose your sister very soon after finding her. Indeed, if you are careful, you may not have her long. If I were a man, there is no woman I have ever met whom I would look at a second time, after Sybil."

"You have not seen yourself, Miss Mamie."

"It would make no difference if I had," she answered. The compliment did not please her. The tone in which it was uttered destroyed its effect.

Jack was suffering tortures of doubt and suspicion. Why should not Sybil be in love with some one? He must watch and learn.

He did watch, but to no purpose. Lord Thorland had gone abroad on a diplomatic mission. Sybil, for some reason, had never even mentioned his name, and had requested her mother not to do so.

Mamie saw that Jack was distressed, but she could not refrain from saying—

"Brothers should not be selfish, you know. You cannot expect to keep her all your life."

"No," answered poor Jack ruefully. "But, you see, this is the first time in my life that I have seen her—I mean—that is—seen her as a woman," he corrected himself, rather hastily.

He was confused, absent-minded, low-spirited. Mamie felt the effect of his dulness upon herself, and became unaccountably sad and depressed. It was a relief when the rest of the party came up and the talk became more general.

When Mamie left Landale the next morning, it was with a very heavy heart. She loved the place; loved Sybil and her mother—and, alas! she loved Jack too, but it had been borne in upon her mind that there was something—she did not know what—that would make it extremely improbable that her love could ever be returned.

Mamie was not a girl to sit down with folded hands under such circumstances. All her will-power—and she had great force of character—she determined should be exerted to repress the growing passion for the man who had not sought and did not want her love. She was not angry with Jack, did not blame him. It might be that he would care for her even yet, but, until she was sure of his love, hers should not be encouraged.

She flung herself into the vortex and whirl of society with a rush and a swing that carried all before her. She had a crowd of followers wherever she went. She was one of the greatest social successes of an exceptionally brilliant season. Hearts were offered her by the score. She could have had her pick of half-a-dozen coronets. But Mamie, as Tom had said, was not the girl to marry a man she did not love. It was a terrible thing for her. The battle with herself was a fierce one; she did not really conquer. Had Jack been in love with another woman, she told herself, it would have been easier. But there was no one. Universally admired as she was, it was certainly hard that the one man on earth she loved should be utterly indifferent to her. Poor Mamie would clench her pretty hands and grind her lovely teeth, and rage at herself for not being able to forget Jack. Her nature was so strong and true that she had so much more to battle with than an ordinary woman. The very strength of her nature was a stumbling-block. If she was not conquered by her love, she could not defeat it. It was a drawn battle, and as the fight was between Mamie and herself, and her own heart was the battle-ground, it " needs no ghost come from the grave to tell us" that there was a dangerous time ahead for the poor girl. The best thing that could have happened to her at this time would have been for her to have learned the truth, to have discovered the fact that Jack was heart and soul in love with Sybil, who was not his sister, and whom, if Sybil loved him, he could make his wife. Her honour and loyalty under such circumstances would have come to her aid, and helped to save her. But, alas! that knowledge was not hers, and she had to fight, alone and unaided, one of the bitterest contests a woman can engage in—a fight with her own love, wishes, and desires.

Meantime, poor Sybil was having her struggle too; a battle which, if not so fierce, was certainly more puzzling than that waged by Mamie. Mamie at least knew what she was fighting for. Sybil did not. She had a thousand thoughts and wishes, which she could not understand; yearnings for she knew not what; longings for things indefinable. Hour by hour, her love was growing for Jack, and day by day he seemed to be receding from her. He was all that was tender, solicitous, and attentive, and yet she was not satisfied. As she told herself again and again, "no brother could be more affectionate and thoughtful." What more did she want or expect? There was no answer to her questionings. As the weeks wore on, she was growing paler, more quiet, more thoughtful. She was not unhappy. She saw Jack almost every hour, and delighted in his presence. But his caresses grew fewer every day, whilst his solicitude for her desires and wishes was more apparent and deep. It perplexed and tortured her. Her arms longed to embrace him, to hold him for ever close to her heart; and she could only wonder why.

And how was it with Jack—the innocent cause of all this turmoil and mental suffering? He was in an alternate heaven and hell. He loved to the fullest extent of his strong nature a woman he had sworn to look upon as a sister. Sometimes the thought came to him to confess all to Sybil, and beg her to let him try to win her love or leave her. But the gentle, loving, and now happy face of her mother came instantly into his mind, and he knew that to tell her her son was dead, and that he was an impostor, would kill her. He was bound hand and foot, body and soul, by the fraud he had perpetrated; and he knew that, even if he had to die in the struggle, he must continue it.

One evening, after dinner, Jack and Sybil strolled through the grounds into the "Jungle," and he purposely stopped at the seat on the old beech-tree. Motioning Sybil to sit beside him on the bench, he pointed to the name carved upon it, and asked—

"Who did that, Sybil?"

Without apparent reason, and to her own express annoyance, Sybil blushed furiously, but did not answer.

" Was it Lorna?" Jack asked mischievously.

" Lorna! Oh, Jack, why should you think that?"

" Was it your mother?"

" No; certainly not!" laughed Sybil.

" Perhaps dear old Bruds?" teased Jack.

" No, no, donkey!"

" Perhaps Comstock?"

" Worse and worse!"

" Then it was you?"

" Perhaps."

" Why did you put Jack in your heart?"

" I do—not—know."

" There's your knife, Sybil. You dropped it just there."

As he handed her the knife, their hands met, and they both trembled.

For a second he held her hand fast locked in his; and then, without a word, tucked it under his arm and walked back to the house.

CHAPTER XXII

JACK'S STEWARDSHIP

Six months passed over Landale Abbey, bringing to Lady Walgrove a peace and happiness she had not known for thirty years. The last years of her first husband's life had been saddened by his constant losses and the anxiety attendant on them, while the whole of her association with Sir James Walgrove was embittered by his harshness to her son, and the boy's disappearance. She had never cared for her second husband. Her love was centred in her two children. Jack's disappearance and silence were an ever-present sorrow to her. More than for anything else in the world did she pray for his return. Now that he had come home (as she believed), his goodness, kindness, and unselfishness had won all the love her motherly heart had to bestow; while his energy, industry, and cleverness in managing the estate had excited her admiration and intense satisfaction. No better steward could possibly be imagined. Jack's varied experience and natural talents pre-eminently fitted him for the part he had to play—that of master, manager, and steward to the Landale family. To that post he had devoted himself, with the determination to do his utmost to improve the property for the benefit of the mother and daughter. Steadfast in his resolve to appropriate none of the money to his personal use, save what was necessary for upholding the position he had assumed, he had been investing for Sybil all the profits of the estate in such a shrewd way that already they were showing a handsome interest. The property was improving in every direction. Left to the two women, neither of whom had business instincts, it had been deteriorating. The rule of Sir James had been harsh and grinding. Under his widow's guidance, the profits

264

had seriously decreased. She was imposed upon by bad, idle servants, and robbed by those she trusted. Jack soon found this out, and bundled off the black sheep, retaining only those who had done their duty honestly. Among the latter were Bruds and Spurdy. Back debts were called in. If creditors could pay, they were made to do so. Where there was real distress, it was instantly and generously relieved. Jack, who did not care a straw for money himself, grew careful of it for the sake of those he was deceiving. Already they were richer than when he came, and there was every prospect of a continuance of their prosperity.

The knowledge of this eased, to some extent, his tortured conscience.

Jack was a great favourite all over the estate. Although strictly just with the tenants and too sharp to be imposed upon, yet, where kindness was deserved, he was always ready to bestow it. "He be a main just man—upright and down-straight, you may depend," was the verdict of the men. "As kind as he's pra-a-per lookin', you may depend," was the opinion of the women.

Alterations and improvements were being constantly made, which even the conservative agricultural labourer, than whom no more stubborn opponent of what he calls "fingle-fangle dabblements to upset fowk" exists, admitted that "that did brighten things oop a bit, that did. That ain't bad, you may depend."

After the meeting with the mother and daughter, Jack had met with no unpleasant surprise, nor any great difficulty. The mother and Bruds, the only people on the estate who had remembered Landale as a boy, had acknowledged him. Sybil, of course, had received him with delight. There had never been any suspicion or doubt. The portrait sent by Landale was his own, and it was that which the mother had studied and been a little puzzled over. When Jack came, there was no doubt that he was the original of the picture. He had to lie sometimes, to his regret and shame, to avoid the close questionings regarding any topics of which he was ignorant yet expected to be acquainted with. Still, there were so many things new to Sybil and her mother, which he was able by his natural gift of description to make interesting and amusing, that there was always a steady rattle of conversation. If he for a moment flagged, Tom was always ready to fill up the gap in his own cheery style, and a ripple of laughter was constantly heard all over the house.

Tom and Lorna were the best of chums, and were as full of fun and nonsense as a couple of kittens. Never had the old Abbey been so bright and gay. The men and women vied with each other in promoting happiness and amusement. Lady Walgrove looked years younger, and grew more beautiful daily. The youth around her, the high spirits, the happy home-circle in which she lived, filled her loving nature to the utmost. Under this genial sunshine, the bitter frost of Jack's remorse thawed and dwindled. At times he would give way to feelings of shame and depression, but the beaming face of the mother would soon cheer him. "Are you glad I came home?" he would ask again and again. Again and again the mother would answer, "Glad! Dear boy, I thank God for it day and night." Jack had grown to love her with a depth and tenderness Landale could never have been capable of. He reverenced her. A hundred times a day he would give proof of this in little attentions and endearments that never ceased to please the mother's heart, and never failed to bring a smile to her lips.

"Jack dear," she would say, "you are spoiling your old mother. What should I do if you ever left me?"

"Why should I leave you, Mamsey?" for so he would call her. Only when she would insist upon it now and then, as she did, would he call her "Mother," and then it was with a hush in his voice and a reverence in his manner which made her wonder.

"Jack dear, you treat me with such reverence, that I might be some great queen rather than your poor little mother."

And he would reply—

"And you are my queen, dear one, reigning over me in such a regal splendour of love and tenderness that I must ever be at your feet in loyal humbleness."

One of her great delights was to have Jack on a stool at her feet reading to her. He read uncommonly well. She was fond of lace making, at which she was an adept. She would work; he would read. Every now and then she would nestle his head against her knees, twine her fingers through his curls, and, with closed eyes, see him again, in fancy, a merry little tot of three, captivating the whole house with his pretty ways and quaint phrases. Some of these she had told him of, and, when he wanted to please her very much, he would repeat them, mimicking the child's manner and voice in a way that brought tears of joy into her eyes. One of the child Landale's little tricks was to ask for whatever he might want with the preface of "Dear Mamsie, Jacksie wantsie and weally must havsie." So, at times, Jack would, while sitting at her feet, look up and say, "Dear Mamsie, Jacksie wantsie and weally must havsie a smile." And he would get one such as on this earth is never seen, save on the face of a loving mother.

Landale had sent him home to make his mother and sister happy. He had fulfilled his mission to the uttermost.

And what of the sister? She too was happy—very happy. But with it all was a feeling of something lacking, something—she knew not what—that should crown her joy and fill quite full her cup of happiness. She had noticed the growing restraint in Jack's manner towards her. It puzzled and hurt her. While he was kindness and goodness itself to her, while every thought and wish of hers were not only gratified but anticipated, there was something missing which she yearned for but could not define. She would at times get angry with herself at her "wretched ingratitude," as she called it. She never mentioned to Lorna now the subject of

Lorna's marriage with Jack. One day Lorna had said, in fun—

"Well, Sib dear, Jack has not proposed to me yet."

Sybil heard, but started and said nothing.

"Did you hear what I said, Sib? I said Jack has not proposed yet. Our wedding is as far off as ever."

To her own intense surprise, and to Lorna's astonishment, Sybil felt her face grow pale, and she rose, turning upon Lorna a look of anger such as the poor girl had never seen in her friend's eyes before.

"What are you talking about, Lorna?" Sybil flashed out. "I think that remark positively immodest. Leave my brother to make his own choice, please. Do not you undertake to dictate his future for him."

The astonished Lorna positively gasped for breath. When she recovered, she said—

"Why, Sib! Sib dear, whatever is the matter with you? Did you not insist upon it that I was to fall in love with him, and he with me, and we were to be married?"

"Stop, Lorna! I won't have you talk of these things!"

"But you said, before he came home——"

"I said many things before he came home that—that— Oh, Lorna! you make me feel hateful! I—I—oh!" And Sybil left the room to go to her own chamber, lock herself in, stare at herself in the glass and ask of her reflection, "Whatever is the matter with you, you ill-tempered, discontented little beast?"

And the reflection gave no answer. It only stared in a wondering, puzzled way for a few minutes; then the original ran back to her friend, saying—

"Never mind, Lorna, what I said just now. I am a hundred and twenty thousand times sorry, and I beg two hundred and forty thousand pardons. Kiss and make it up." Lorna did so, but at the same time took the lesson to heart. She never again mentioned the subject of her proposed marriage with Jack. As a matter of fact, she had no desire that such a thing should be thought of. "Jack was a very fine fellow, of course, but there were things about Tom that—that—oh, well! what was the use of bothering, anyway? They were all very happy as they were. Why trouble about any change?"

Sybil could not dismiss the subject so readily. Hour after hour she would ruminate over it, and wonder what it meant, but never did she in the least guess the truth.

" Jack," she asked one day, " do you think of getting married?"

Jack's face crimsoned and then went pale. His one fear was Sal. Should any chance reveal the fact that Landale had married, what would be the result? He shuddered whenever he thought of it.

" Why do you ask?" he asked, in a hard, dry tone.

" Because I—well, isn't it natural I should like to know?"

" Yes, Sybil, I suppose it is. But please don't ask. There's plenty of time for that—say, in twenty years from now." And he changed the subject.

Jack had only seen Mamie once since parting from her at Landale. He had called upon her one afternoon, about a month after his arrival, and sent up his card. He was immediately shown into Mrs. D'Olan's reception-room, but, to his relief, there was a crowd of people present, paying court to Mamie, so that he could only, with much difficulty, get a few words with her. She rose when he entered the room, asking him to remain, but he said he " had much business to transact," made his excuses and left. Shortly after Colonel D'Olan arrived in London, and the whole family left for France and Italy. One or two letters had passed between them at this time, of a rather formal character, and since then Jack had not heard of their whereabouts. He quite concluded that he had been right and Tom wrong in his estimate of that young lady's feelings towards him. But he was mistaken, and Tom's idea was correct.

One day Sybil had gone to Jack and, throwing her arms round his neck, had kissed him on the lips, in thanks for some little thing he had done to please her. He had started up, almost thrusting her from him, and, making some excuse, had hurriedly left the room. When they next met, he was as kind and considerate as ever. She was puzzled and hurt, wondering what she could possibly have done to cause him annoyance.

Lord Thorland, who had been absent some months on a diplomatic mission, and had lately returned, was dining at the Abbey one evening, at Jack's invitation. Jack had taken a great liking for him, and he had returned the affection with interest. Mr. Moody, between whom and Tom a deadly feud existed—good-natured on Tom's part, spiteful and mean on that of Mr. Moody—was present too.

Dinner was over, and the party had retired to the drawing-room. Jack was in his usual place, at the feet of Lady Walgrove, reading " Enoch Arden" to her. Sybil was playing chess with Lord Thorland. Tom and Lorna were playing a duet, or, rather, Tom was accompanying with the piano a solo on the violin by Lorna.. Mr. Moody, in a Shakespearian attitude, leant upon the piano, turned over the music, and leered with deep admiration at the object of his attention, the fair Lorna, who, in her playing, forgot even his presence.

" That's lovely," said Jack, as Lorna ceased playing.

" Thanks, Mr. Landale," Lorna replied.

" The last time I heard that played was in San Francisco, fifteen years ago. The player was a wizened little Italian; the scene was a rather disreputable café in Montgomery Street. There was a particularly rowdy crowd there that night, and champagne and bad whisky had made some of them more than usually nasty. They wanted the Italian to play jigs for them. He refused, and one of the drunken blackguards—a notorious gambler—called him by a particularly opprobrious name. Although he was not half his size, the Italian sprang upon the cad like a tiger-cat. Before any one could interfere, the brute drew his revolver and shot him. I picked him up, and got him to a surgeon's, but the wound was mortal. After telling me who he was, he died. He was a nobleman, a political refugee, and all the money he could save went to his daughter, who was teaching languages in New York. I forget the name now."

" Plincee Stephanie—Melican man who shootee Blob Gludgee—allee samee Bluck le Tliger man, Lesterlong, Mladam Flançois, Montgomery Stleet," said Wong, who, dressed in magnificent Chinese costume, was handing round coffee.

" How do you know that?"

" Wong allee samee time waiter along there, Mladam Flançois."

" Why on earth didn't you tell me this before?"

" Wong no talkee mluch."

" Strange what a mixture one gets in America and the Colonies !" said Lord Thorland.

" Yes, I've slept under a newspaper in Sydney docks, with the son of a duke under a bit of sacking on my right, and an unconvicted murderer under a bit of brown paper on my left," said Tom.

" Poor fellow !" murmured Lorna.

" I should like to go to Australia. They must want some good men over there," Mr. Moody exclaimed.

" You're right, Moody; they do want good men over there, but they don't want a lazy, drunken set of wastrels. The Colonies should not be made the dumping-ground for the scum of our nation. We are asking for their best blood, muscle, and sinew, and, what's more, we are getting it. If we can't send them something like it in return, we need not drench them with the refuse of our human sewers."

" Hear, hear! Jack."

" They kick at the Kanakas, and receive with open arms our moral lepers. They shout for a ' White Australia'; let it be white inside as well as out."

" Hear, hear! Jack; well said! If you talk like that, you had better go back and get elected to the Federal Parliament."

" No, no," said Lady Walgrove; " no, my boy is never

going away from me again. You'll never leave me, Jack, will you?"

"Not if God is good enough to let me stay," Jack answered, patting and stroking her hand. "I never want to leave your side again as long as I live. I have never known happiness until now—never knew what peace meant. It all seems too beautiful to last, good mother. I feel like a man in a delicious dream, who knows that he is dreaming, and can feel the waker coming to call him from his visionary heaven back to the living real hell—like poor Enoch Arden—

> "'He, therefore, turning swiftly like a thief,
> Lest the harsh shingle should grate underfoot,
> And feeling all along the garden wall,
> Lest he should swerve and tumble to the ground,
> Crept to the gate, and opened it, and closed,
> As lightly as a sick man's chamber door,
> Behind him, and came out upon the waste;
> And there he would have knelt, but that his knees
> Were feeble, so that, falling prone, he dug
> His fingers into the wet earth, and prayed,
> "Too hard to bear! Why did they take me thence?"'"

"No, no, dear boy! it is no dream. You shall never leave me again. Look in my face, look in my eyes, and tell me what you see there."

"Love at its sweetest—womanhood at its best and purest—motherhood at its grandest and noblest."

Lord Thorland and Sybil had finished their game.

"Checkmate, Lord Thorland!" Sybil exclaimed.

"Badly beaten, Miss Landale," exclaimed Thorland. Then he continued, looking at Jack, "What a dear chap your brother is! What a son! I never saw such devotion."

"He worships her—adores her," Sybil said, with just a shade of jealousy in her voice.

"And you?"

"Me? Oh! I'm a very bad second to mamma. He

is fond of me, no doubt, but it is mamma he loves. Do you know, I get quite jealous of her at times. Look! he's kissing her again! I'm going to put a stop to this. Spooning again, you two! Really! you're too public entoirely wid yer love-makin', as Bridget would say."

"Jealous, Sybil?" queried her mother, smiling.

"Yes, I am; jealous and cross as two sticks."

"Kiss your sister, Jack."

Jack looked grave, but did not move.

"I don't believe he wants to," pouted Sybil.

"Nonsense, dear!" Jack took her head between his hands and kissed her on the forehead.

"How obedient and obliging!" said Sybil, with a mock courtesy. "You kissed mamma on the lips; you peck at my forehead like a sparrow. Oh, Jack! you're not half a brother!"

"No, Sybil," he answered gravely, "but I'm trying hard to be a whole one."

"There! did you see that, mamma?" Sybil whispered to her mother. "I can't understand him! Really, at times he seems to hate me. He avoids me whenever he can. I don't like it a bit."

"Nonsense, dear! He loves you dearly."

Lorna had gone to the window with Tom. A distant report was heard, and Lorna called out—

"Oh, do come and look! The fireworks have begun at the Crystal Palace! Come, Jack! Do! do! What a lovely rocket!"

"By Jove! that is a beauty! What a height it has gone up!" said Tom.

"It will have the farther to fall down," groaned Mr. Moody. "So it is in life—

"A sharp report, some light the senses trick;
Some coloured flame——"

"And then down comes the stick," mimicked Tom. "That's all right, old man, but, you see, we've got the coloured flame, and deucedly pretty it is."

" What an insult to the moon—the chaste Diana!" exclaimed Moody.

" Well, never mind! Let's hope the moon won't see it," replied Tom.

All were on the balcony except Jack, who sank into his mother's seat by the fire in great sadness. Tom went to him, saying—

" How goes it, Jack?"

" Tom, I've a heart like lead to-night. I'm as blue as a bag of indigo."

" What about?"

" I don't know."

" Pickled salmon and pâté-de-foie-gras."

" I didn't touch either of them; I'm off my feed, Tom."

" Yes, I've noticed it. And you'll be off something else if you're not careful."

" What's that?"

" You're treating that girl shamefully."

" Which girl?"

" Sybil. You seldom speak to her or go near her. What's the trouble?"

" The trouble?"

" Yes. What is it?"

" Tom, the worst trouble possible under the circumstances," Jack whispered. " I'm wildly, passionately in love with her!"

" What?"

" It's true. It's driving me mad. Her presence in the house excites me, her touch thrills me, her kisses scorch me! I can't look at her—can't speak to her—dare not touch her! When she touches me, I shiver. I dare not meet her eyes lest she should read my secret. It's awful, Tom! There is no other word for it—it's awful."

" I never bargained for this."

" Nor I—fool that I was! As I had never cared for a woman, I—I thought I never should care, and here I am, up to my neck in a deep, absorbing passion, which has come to stay for life. I cannot leave the mother—dare not stay in the same house with the sister. The poor girl does not, of course, dream of any harm, but her innocent endearments are inordinate pain, her kisses heaven and hell combined. Tom, my sin has found me out, and in a strange way. I'm being punished cruelly."

" Sin be hanged !"

" Which is the way out of it? If I could only go away, but I can't. It would kill the dear old mother. She's a saint; I love her. I love them both. I never knew a mother's love. My coming into the world sent her out of it. My father could never bear the sight of me for it, and gave me to the care of strangers. He's gone; I am alone —not a soul in the world to care for. And these dear, good, loving people, this heavenly home, this paradise, and this horrible serpent, my passion and my sin——!"

" It's a tight corner, Jack."

Jack went to the fireplace and called, "Come here, Tom. Do you ever see faces in the fire? Look there!" he said, pointing with the tongs; " there's poor old Jack's face begging with his eyes for me to stop. And look! there's Sal, jeering, laughing, and sneering. Ugh! out with you! Out!" And he threw the tongs at the flames.

Sybil, who had come into the room, saw him, and was startled.

"Jack! what is the matter? What are you doing?" she cried.

" Beating away the bogies," he answered.

" He's got an attack of the jim-jams, Miss Landale," said Tom promptly. " He's seeing faces in the fire. He'll be seeing pink rats in his by-bye if he isn't careful. The fact is, he's too well fed and cared for. He's getting coddled; that's what's the matter. Tell him to brace up, and face things like a man. He's got his hand to the plough, and he's got to tramp the furrows. Keep him at it, Miss Landale, keep him at it." And he joined the rest of the party on the balcony.

Jack sank back into the chair. Sybil looked at him a moment as if hurt, but, relenting, sat on the arm of his chair, with her right arm over his head toying with his hair, and her left hand on his shoulder. He shuddered, but did not move.

"Now, Master Jack, I've a bone to pick with you," Sybil said, in mock severity.

"A little one, I hope? The wish-bone of a lark?"

"No, sir; the jaw-bone of a mastodon."

"Are we to pick it clean?"

"As clean as your conscience, Jack."

Jack winced.

"Had we not better call in the others to join in the feast?" he said, trying to move. But she drew him back.

"No, we will not. I don't often get you to myself, and now I've got you I'll keep you."

"But we can't manage that mastodon alone."

"Yes, we can, and we will."

"Let us begin, then."

"There! You want to be rid of me already! That's a bit of the bone we have to pick. Why do you always avoid me?"

"Do I?"

"Yes. You almost shudder when I come near you; you never kiss me unless I ask you, and only speak to me with an effort. Why is it, Jack?"

"I do not admit that it is so."

"But you must. You do not like me."

"Like you? Of course I do."

"What is it, then? Don't brothers and sisters kiss each other?"

"I never had a sister—until now," he answered softly.

"I can't stand it, Jack! It makes me wretched."

"Sybil!"

"You are never out of my thoughts. I don't believe you think of me a bit."

"Don't you?"

"No, I don't."

"You are mistaken, Sybil; I am always thinking of you. All day long I am thinking of Sybil. As I fall asleep, it is always Sybil who is in my thoughts. In my dreams it is Sybil—always Sybil, and when I wake my first thought is Sybil—how soon shall I see Sybil?—how soon shall I hear her voice?"

"Why, that's almost like a lover, Jack!"

"It is almost like a lover," he answered, in a strange, sarcastic way.

"Why are you not always like that?"

"Because I am afraid."

"Afraid of what?"

"Afraid of you," he replied.

"You need not be afraid of me," she said, and kissed his hair.

"Then, afraid of myself. Did you ever read of the breaking of a reservoir? All is safe and secure. Then comes a little break—so small that a child's hand could stay it, but the water runs on, the fissure growing larger and wider every second. Suddenly, there is a rush—a roar—the dam is burst. The flood rushes through the breach, and deals destruction and death to all that comes in contact with it."

Putting her hand over his mouth, Sybil said playfully—

"You dear, exaggerating old Jack! hold your tongue."

"Take your hand away, or I shall bite it," said Jack hoarsely. His head swam, he was on fire! He was forgetting everything but his love.

"Do, if you dare!" she exclaimed.

Jack did bite her hand, then kissed it passionately again and again. Sybil started, and left him, saying in a harsh voice—

"Jack, Jack! what have you done?" She was trembling, her hands hiding her face.

"Well—have I hurt you?" Jack asked, almost fiercely.

"Yes—no—I don't know! I—Oh, Jack!"

"Shall I kiss it again?"

"No, no!" said Sybil, putting her hands behind her back and leaning against the table.

"Now, I've offended you."

" No, not offended. But I wish you hadn't done that."

" Done what? Kissed your hand?"

" Yes—at least, like that."

" You're hard to please, miss. You complained just now that I never kissed you."

" I know—but I want—I—oh, I don't know what I want! What do you think of Lorna?" she asked anxiously.

" I think she is a very sweet girl."

" Do you think her pretty?"

" Yes."

" Very pretty?"

" Yes. Don't you?"

" She's my best friend," replied Sybil inconsequently.

" Do you consider that an answer?"

" Don't you think she'll make a very sweet, good wife?"

" I never thought of her in that way. Why should I?"

" Because mamma wishes you to do so," replied Sybil, very slowly and reluctantly.

" What?" exclaimed Jack, in astonishment.

" It is true."

" Has she told you so?"

" We've talked it over scores and scores of times."

Jack was silent for a moment, then he answered—

" I'm sorry to disappoint dear mother, but I cannot think of marriage."

" Why not?"

Jack looked at her strangely, and Sybil felt a thrill run through her whole body. Jack answered very slowly—

" Because it is impossible."

" Impossible?"

" Absolutely impossible."

Sybil looked suddenly startled and terrified, and cried out—

" Jack! Jack! you're not married already?"

" Heaven forbid!"

" You're quite sure?"

" Well, marriage is not an incident that one usually has doubts about, is it?"

Sybil, relieved, laughed, saying—

" I'm so glad!"

" I'm ' so glad,' too, if it pleases you."

" Have you ever—ever—ever been——" Sybil was blushing and hesitating.

" Ever been what?"

Breathless and gasping, Sybil continued—

" Ever been in love?"

Jack looked at her with intense longing, and answered—

" I came to this house heart-whole, loving no one."

" Have you seen any one you love, since?"

" Yes."

" Really love?"

" Really love." His breath came in gasps; he was pale and flushed alternately.

Heart-sick, and nearly breaking down, Sybil said—

" I think you might have told us, Jack."

" Do you?" quietly asked Jack.

" Who is it?"

" Do you really want to know?"

In a whisper, and trembling, Sybil replied—

" Yes."

" Mother." He paused, and, with intense yearning, continued—" You."

" No one else?"

" No one else."

Sybil flung herself into his arms, saying, " Oh, Jack! Jack!"

He forgot himself, and held her fast, but she tore herself away, confused and frightened. He was angry with himself, and went to the fireplace.

" You did give me a fright!"

" Why? Don't you wish me to get married?"

" Before you came home, I wished you to marry Lorna. Now——"

" Now ?"

" We—that is I—I mean, we want to keep you all to ourselves."

Jack was going to speak, when Lady Walgrove called—

" Sybil dear !"

" Yes, mamma ?"

" Come here, dear."

Sybil looked at Jack, as if about to speak, but did not. She went out of the room to join her mother on the balcony.

Jack watched Sybil leave the room; watched her with intense love and longing in his eyes; then he went to the fireplace, and, leaning his head on his hands against the mantelpiece, continued to stare into the fire—seeing pictures of his future, wherein he was the husband of Sybil, the father of her children; a future in which there would be no deceit, no treachery, no lying, no restraint. He was glad he had kissed her hand, for once at least, as he had longed to kiss her lips; yet he was angry with himself for doing it. What right had he to break his resolve and betray the trust imposed on him? What a coward's trick to play on this confiding, loving girl! Yet how could he refrain? What a lovely creature she was, and how he idolised her! Had she really been angry with him? What a fool—what a brute to even think of it, except with shame! Yet, in spite of his self-reproaches, there was a feeling of great exultation in his soul at the thought that he had held her for one moment with the mask off his face, the veil off his heart. For one moment, he had forgotten he was Jack Landale—he remembered only he was Jack Mowbray, and that he loved Sybil with every nerve in his body, with every instinct of his soul! Oh! how he loved her! What could he do? What could be done?

So wrapt in his visions was he, that he did not hear Lord Thorland enter the room, nor was he aware of his presence until Lord Thorland spoke, saying—

" Mr. Landale."

Jack started.

" Lord Thorland !"

" Can you spare me a moment?"

" With pleasure.   Here?"

" Yes, here will do.   A very few words will suffice. You must have noticed my preference for——" He hesitated.

Jack turned swiftly round, looking him full in the face, and, in a strained, cold voice, asked—

" For whom?"

" Your sister Sybil."

Jack shivered, and stood dumb.

" Surely you have seen——" Lord Thorland hesitated.   There was a look in Jack's eyes he did not understand.

Jack waited a moment, and then said—

" I'm afraid I'm very dense in many ways, Lord Thorland."

" I thought everybody knew.   Have they not spoken to you about it?"

" They?" repeated Jack.

" Your mother and sister."

" No, they have not."   Jack's voice was cold and resentful.

" That's strange," said Thorland meditatively.

There was another pause.   Jack, collecting all his firmness, asked—

" Have you spoken to them?"

" Yes."

" What did they say?"   Jack's voice was hard.   He had turned again to the fireplace.

" Your mother approved of my suit."

Jack breathed hard.   His heart was beating painfully, as he said—

" And my sister—Sybil?"

" Well, oddly enough, I spoke to your sister on the very day of your arrival.   She had not then seen you, and begged of me not to speak of it again until you came.

She said, I remember, that your coming might change everything."

" Might change everything! Yes."

" That is six months ago."

" And you have not spoken since?"

" No. I felt it wiser to wait."

Jack was thinking deeply. He was scarcely conscious of his own voice as he asked—

" What do you wish me to do?"

" Tell me that you look as favourably on my suit as your mother does. May I hope to——"

Jack felt inclined to laugh outright. The tension was so great. Could anything be more absurd, more horrible, than that he should be asked to give away to another man the only being he had ever loved as man loves woman? That he should have to stand, apparently, calmly by, hear this man tell him of his love for that woman and plead for an approval of his suit! Her mother had given her sanction—already she had, in thought, given her daughter to this noble gentleman—for he was that, as Jack ungrudgingly admitted to himself. Well, was it not better that Sybil should marry him, if she loved him? But, did she? He supposed she must, and yet——

He was silent so long that Lord Thorland asked—

" What is your answer, Mr. Landale?"

" Lord Thorland," Jack answered brokenly, " if—if—that is—I believe you to be a true and noble gentleman, and if—if——"

" Yes?" queried Thorland.

" If Sybil loves you, there is no man towards whom I should feel less resentment for robbing me of her."

" Thank you, thank you! I may tell your sister that?"

" Yes," replied Jack slowly, " you may tell her that."

CHAPTER XXIII

NAT MEETS A CONGENIAL SPIRIT

MR. COMSTOCK left Landale, raging with anger and resentment. It must be confessed that he had been rather summarily, if justly, ejected. He had held his post, since Sir James died, with entire freedom. There was no real control exercised over him, and he was making, by his knavery, an uncommonly good thing out of his post. He paid all the stable-bills, and there was commission from the corn-dealers, the harness-makers, the carriage-builders, the horse-dealers; little percentages from the stablemen and grooms, and many other lucrative and pleasant pickings which he fondly but delusively hoped would be his so long as he chose to honour the Landale family with his presence. From this pleasant dream, Jack had suddenly and rudely awakened him. He had not paid back all that he had stolen from Lady Walgrove, but had disappeared, thinking England too hot to hold him. He had invested some of his ill-won gains in a racing stallion of fair pedigree, and had departed with the horse, his wife, young children, and some other trifling impedimenta, for the hospitable shores of Australia. He took up his residence near Randwick racecourse, Sydney, and, in the fulness of time, met Mr. Nat Rudder.

Mr. Comstock found Nat Rudder very useful. He knew all the racing fraternity, and put him in communication with most of the trainers, breeders, and jockeys, to his great pecuniary advantage.

Jack's allowance was now arriving regularly, and Nat had removed from Paddington and taken a house at Randwick. There was a small garden in the rear, where Smudgee had a little summer-house, in which she sat, learned her lessons, and thought of Jack. She had received several letters from him, and had replied, giving him, as he desired, full accounts of herself, her studies, and her general mode of life. His letters gave her intense pleasure, and she grew brighter and more content.

She called her summer-house " Jack's Villa," and always addressed her letters from it. Scarcely a week passed in which Jack did not send her some little gift or memento. She was now as happy as she could be without seeing him, and she knew that was impossible.

Strolling down George Street, Sydney, one afternoon, Mr. and Mrs. Comstock halted opposite Talma's Photographic Studio. A simple action enough, but fraught with the gravest consequences to many of the characters concerned in this history. In a small passage leading to the stairs of the photographer's studio were exhibited many samples of his art, set in large glass frames, among them a copy of the one he had taken of Jack. This caught the eye of Mrs. Comstock.

" Comstock, come and look here," she called to her husband.

" What is it?" he asked.

" A portrait of that upstart, Landale," she answered.

" What?" shouted Mr. Comstock, hurrying to her side, and staring at the photograph. " So it is! If it isn't, I'm hanged!"

Mr. Comstock said very rude things to the portrait that he had not had the courage to say to the original. The sight of it put him in an exceedingly bad temper for the rest of the day. When, later on, he met Nat in Tattersall's bar, and had swallowed several glasses of whisky in his company, he became so impressed with the magnitude of his own wrongs that he could not refrain from pouring them into the ears of his friends.

" I'm regular upset," he said; " got a 'ump on me like a bloomin' camel."

" Picked the wrong 'un?" asked Nat.

" No fear! But—well, I've never told you 'ow I came out 'ere."

" No, you never did, 'cept you said it was on the *Oratava.*"

" I don't mean the boat—I mean what sent me 'ere. It was this way. Yer see, I managed the stables for some swells in England—real swells, mind yer—for years—the Landales——"

" The what?" asked Nat.

" The Landales, of Landale Abbey."

" Landales? Sure it wasn't Landon?"

" No, no; Landales—a big family—well-known lot. The son disappeared—came over 'ere, in fact, and went up into the bush, and——"

" What?" Nat's eyes, with anxiety and whisky, were more like those of a fish than a human being. " Go on— go on!" he urged.

" Well, he come 'ome—interfered with me, and—well, I wasn't goin' to stand any of his bloomin' nonsense, and I resigned."

" Wot was 'is name?"

" Landale—John Landale, of Landale Abbey?"

" John Landale? Sure it wasn't Landon?"

" No, no—Landale, I tell you! Well, damned if I didn't see a portrait of 'im at a photographer's in George Street to-day."

" What photographer's?"

" Talma's, in George Street."

" 'Ere, 'ave another, and come along o' me," said the now excited Nat.

The " other" was had, and they staggered along to Talma's, where Comstock pointed out Jack's portrait.

" Who d'ye say that is?" queried Nat.

" John Landale, o' Landale Abbey."

" I've got it! I've got it!" screamed Nat, in exultation.

" Got what?" asked the puzzled Mr. Comstock.

" Got the information I wanted. Got the straight tip, the ' clear griffin'! That ain't no John Landale! That's Jack Mowbray, who 'as done me—that is, done my sister an' her daughter out o' a mint o' money—'undreds an' thousands! Jack Landale! 'E—'e—" Here it occurred to Nat's befuddled brain that a man was standing by him taking in every word he uttered. It also dawned upon him that the same man had been beside him in Tattersall's bar, when Comstock first alluded to Jack. He was right. The same man had been listening; had followed him to Talma's. It was our old friend Dan Murphy, who had heard all that had passed between the two men, and had become so absorbed in their conversation, knowing as he did Jack Landale and Jack Mowbray, that he had followed them, in order to learn as much as possible concerning them. Seeing he was noticed, he moved away, but kept them in sight, and, when they returned to Tattersall's, he got to learn Comstock's name and address.

Dan was much attached to Jack, who had " done him many a good turn in the past." He shrewdly suspected that mischief was intended, but had not heard enough to know what it was. He determined to find out. He would help Jack if he could. Hanging about Nat's house, he met Sal and Smudgee. He had not known what had become of them. He knew they left Woolloogolonga for Sydney, but nothing further. Sal was not too pleased to see him. Smudgee was very glad; she liked him.

" Good mornin', Mrs. Landon, ma'am, and the same to you, Miss Smudgee," said Dan.

" My! it's Dan!" exclaimed Smudgee, shaking hands cordially with him. Sal looked somewhat disdainfully at him. She was showily dressed and in funds, while Dan was evidently in low water.

" It's a picture you're lookin', Mrs. Landon, ma'am. Be gob! you must have struck it rich!" Dan said.

" I've struck what is my own, Mr. Murphy," answered Sal grumpily.

" Divil doubt it, ma'am!"

" Won't you come in and see us sometimes, Dan?" asked Smudgee, who did not like her mother's tone. " If we hev struck it rich, we are just the same to old friends —at least, some of us is."

" I'm sure *you* are, Miss Smudgee. You're none of the changin' sort. When will I be afther comin'?"

" Whenever you like, Dan, and we'll have a chat over old times."

Smudgee wanted badly to have some one to talk to her of Jack, and she knew Dan would listen.

" It's meself will be delighted. Oi'll be wid you at tay-time; say, four this afternoon."

At the appointed time, Dan appeared, and Smudgee rose to receive him. Conducting him to " Jack's Villa," she made him very welcome, and, with the aid of whisky and soda, and some cigars, of which essentials to good fellowship there was always a plentiful supply wherever Nat and Sal were abiding, she made him very comfortable. Soon they were both engaged in enthusiastic praises of Jack, and in reminiscences of his past good deeds.

" An' it's 'im wot's keepin' us like this—'im as has given me all these lovely presents—'im as pays for everything as mother and Uncle Nat 'ave."

" What did yer call him? Yer Uncle Nat?" There was a curious look in Dan's face as he asked the question.

" 'Tain't wot I calls 'im—it's wot 'e calls 'isself."

" And how long's he been yer Uncle Nat, Smudgee?" Dan was so deeply interested, he was even forgetting his cigar, which was a particularly good one.

" Since the day father was killed at Woolloogolonga. 'E turned up that very day. 'E was 'umpin' his swag then."

" So 'e's yer Uncle Nat, is 'e? Well, and what might be his other name?"

" Rudder. Nat Rudder."

" Nat Rudder! Ah, yes—Nat Rudder. And your mother's is Mrs. John Landon. Av coorse. And where might Jack Mowbray be livin' now?"

" I don't know — wish I did," sighed Smudgee.

" Somewhere in England. At least, that's where 'e writes to me from. I sends my letters to the General Post Office, London—that's all I know."

Dan and Smudgee saw each other frequently after this. By keeping in touch with Smudgee, Dan was able to learn a great deal about Nat's doings and intentions, which knowledge he was quietly storing up for future use.

Nat and Sal were naturally greatly excited over Comstock's intelligence. They were now perfectly certain that the master of Landale Abbey was Jack Mowbray, who had fraudulently taken Landale's place and property. Comstock had told them of Tom's presence as Jack's friend and secretary, and of Wong also. There could not be a shadow of doubt now. Comstock's account of Landale Abbey, its beauty and its value, set Nat half wild with indignation at the wrong that was being done to him by Jack's usurpation. He had no vile name—and he had a copious supply in his vocabulary—that was bad enough for him.

" The thief! the swindlin' thief! The impostor! The —— fraud!" yelled Nat. " I'll hev the law on 'im! I'll jail 'im! I'll—I'll——" Gradually he worked himself up into a perfect frenzy of righteous indignation. " The thief! Ter rob us of such a property as that! The thief! Our estates—our money—our——"

" Oh! dry up about ' our' estates and ' our' money! It's no more ours than it is 'is, if it comes to that," exclaimed Sal. " And you know it!"

" Well, 'e don't know it, does 'e? Nor nobody else. For all any one knows, you're Landon's widow, and Smudgee is 'is daughter. You're 'is heiress; the property is yours, and we'll 'ave it, too! I'll go and see a lawyer now. It's a big thing, and we'll 'ave it. Bly me! what a swindler the fellow is! I'll jail 'im for life!"

" Now, look 'ere—once and for all—if yer mean any harm to Jack Mowbray, you'll count me out of it. Yer don't touch a 'air of 'is 'ead, if I know it!"

" Wot yer mean ? "

" Wot I've told yer scores of times. I'll go for the money, and the estates too for that matter, but not if it's to get Mowbray in trouble or gaol. If yer try that, I'll split on the whole thing. Now yer know it ! "

Sal meant all she said. She still cared for Jack, after her fashion ; still cherished the idea of winning him. If she could, without bringing him within the clutches of the law, get Landale Abbey, he must come to her, she thought. But callous and heartless as she was, she was sincere in her threat to tell all, if Nat attempted to harm him.

Nat went off to find a lawyer, cursing women's cranks generally, and Sal's in particular.

In Castlereagh Street there lived and practised a very shrewd and disreputable lawyer, named Raffael Moses Wolfe—a Jew, of about forty years of age. He had helped Nat in one or two very questionable transactions, and the pair knew each other perfectly. Wolfe did a little racing, a little money-lending, and many other little things just within the pale of the law. Nat knew that he was clever, cunning, and unscrupulous ; in fact, just the man he wanted. To him he went, and laid the whole case before him, concealing the fact that Sal was his wife, speaking of her as his sister.

Mr. Wolfe's ferret-like eyes glittered as he heard the story. He saw in an instant that Nat was lying in some details, but the main facts he believed. Landon was Landale—Landale Abbey was in the hands of Jack Mowbray. If Landale had married Sal, and Smudgee was their daughter, it was clear that the property was legally theirs, unless willed away by Landon. No will was in existence, therefore their claim was valid, and could not be contested. Wolfe did not trouble himself to tell Nat that he was going to learn all about him and Sal before he moved in the matter, but he did so. He traced Nat and Landon back for many years. The result of his researches was to convince him that the greatest haul he had ever made was, with some labour and scheming, to be had through Nat and Sal. He counselled absolute silence on their part. No letters were to be written, no threats made. They would sail for England by the next mail steamer, and, personally, searchingly investigate the whole case. Wolfe had no business that he would hesitate to leave for such a speculation as this. Getting a hundred pounds from Nat as earnest money, and his saloon passage paid, he made his arrangements to sail with him, Sal, and Smudgee, by the Orient liner *Oruba*, the following week.

Smudgee was in ecstasies. "England! Where Jack was! It's 'eavenly!" The same day she told Dan what was going to happen, and the quick-witted, affectionate Irishman immediately guessed the reason of their sudden departure. Indeed he had heard Nat drunkenly boasting, in Tattersall's bar, that he was going home to claim a fortune.

"My sister's the biggest heiress in England, and we're goin' 'ome to take possession of the finest estate in the 'ole country," was Nat's way of putting it.

Dan had no money to pay his passage, and no means of raising it, but he instantly made up his mind to be there as soon as Nat and Wolfe, to be, if possible, of help to Jack. He had ideas of his own on this subject, which he kept studiously to himself.

There had been a strike of ship's firemen and stokers, so he found no difficulty in getting a berth in this capacity on the *Oruba*. It was not the kind of employment he would have chosen, but it was all he could get, and he was prepared to pass the six weeks in what he called "little purgatory" for his friend's sake.

So it came to pass that when the good ship *Oruba* sailed out of Sydney harbour she carried with her Sal, Nat, Smudgee, and Wolfe as saloon passengers, and Dan as stoker. On the vessel's arrival at Marseilles the former landed and proceeded to London *viâ* Paris, while poor Dan had to endure another week of misery at the furnaces.

NAT MEETS A CONGENIAL SPIRIT

Paris and London amazed and delighted the Australians. The shops in both cities were a feast of delight to Smudgee and her mother, and, but for Nat's interference, Sal would have spent every penny they possessed. "Why, Paris beats even Sydney!" said the excited Sal.

"Pity the poor devils can't speak English," was Nat's remark.

Arrived in London, Mr. Wolfe went to reside with an uncle of his in the Minories, while Nat took rooms at the Starlington Hotel, near Leicester Square.

Determined to lose no time in prosecuting their claim, Wolfe and Nat went down to Landale to get a look at "our estate," as Nat put it. They stayed overnight at the Railway Hotel. Sal and Smudgee remained in London.

Smudgee had been keeping her keen eyes and ears open, and had gathered, from disjointed scraps of conversation, that her beloved Jack was in some danger, and her little heart was aching to see and warn him. She had tried, unavailingly, to draw from her mother some explanation of their proceedings, but Sal was too much afraid of what she might do to tell her; Smudgee had to watch and find out in her own way what she desired to know. She was much improved in many ways. Quick and observant, she had been studying and noticing things and people on the voyage to London, and much of the roughness of the bush had been removed. She was full of the "fashions," as she called them. It must be admitted that she saw them in very vivid colours. Her taste at this time was certainly a little loud. She bought the fashion books and dressmakers' periodicals, and schemed the most wonderful costumes for herself, most of which came to nothing beyond the scheming.

On the morning of Nat's return from Landale, Smudgee was engaged in studying the details of what she called a "Japanese Pegnor." She was wearing a wonderful thing in the way of a dressing-gown. It was of stiff, brocaded satin, and very much too long for her—

she tripped over it constantly. Her hair was in curling-pins. She was sitting with her hands tightly clasped to her head, her elbows on the table, poring over a paper which was lying on the table before her.

She was alone, and was reading aloud the directions for making the dress: "'9½ yards of 22-inch brocade; 1¾ yards of 22-inch satin.' Yes! Brocade—yellow, with large red flowers. Satin, green—no, blue—no, green—Yes, I'll have it green. Green soots me, with yeller and red. 'Stitch skirt seams, hem lower edge; cut down centre for placket hole. Hem both sides of opening; gather waist, stitch to waistband, regulating the fulness as holes show. Herringbone edges up to muslin.'"

Here Sal's voice was heard from the bedroom, which communicated with the sitting-room in which Smudgee was studying, calling—

"Smudgee!"

Smudgee looked towards the door, but did not move.

"Wot is it?" she asked impatiently.

"Where've yer put my blue bodice?"

"In the middle tray of the big black trunk. And I wish for the Lord's sake you'd drop calling me Smudgee! My name's Loocy." Returning to her periodical, she read on: "'Arrange hooks and eyes to fasten front invisibly. Slip stitch on the trimming band.'"

"Smudgee!" called Sal, once more.

"Wot is it now?" These interruptions were making Smudgee angry.

"Where've yer put my Venus de Medershee pink corset?"

"In the top tray of the black steamer trunk. And, look 'ere! I'm full up on Smudgee. D'ye want every servant in the hotel a-guyin' o' me? Do 'ave some sense." She went on reading. "'Mount collar over muslin or linen; stitch centre back seam, turn satin edges up to muslin; herringbone to——'"

"Smudgee!"

Smudgee clutched her hair with both hands, wildly;

her mouth worked in unuttered language. She clenched her hands tragically, but did not reply.

"Smudgee!" called her mother loudly. And Smudgee yelled back—

"Wot—his—hit?"

"Wot are yer yellin' like that for?"

"'Cos yer sendin' me horf my 'ead. 'Ere I set studyin' ter git style on me, and heligance, and wot's the use? yer distracts me—yer upsets me, and—and—I won't have no more Smudgee—leastways not from you and that new uncle you found for me. See? I won't have it! We ain't in the back-blocks now. Smudgee 'ere— Smudgee there! Why don't yer coo-ee, and have done with it?"

"Well, bring me some whisky and soda, then," pleaded Sal, in a slightly mollifying tone.

"Shan't!" rudely replied her daughter.

"I've such a sinkin' feelin'."

"Well, sink and be b-l-o-d-e—blowed!" She turned to her fashion book, and read furiously. "'Tack material and sleeve over lining, stitch seam; turn up wrist over muslin; face in with silk or sateen to match.'"

"Smudgee!" screamed Sal.

Smudgee clenched her teeth, and, under her breath, spelt out—

"D—A—double M."

"Wot d'yer say?"

Smudgee repeated the letters under her breath, "D— A—double M."

"Can't 'ear a word yer sayin'."

"P'r'aps it's as well as yer carn't," she ejaculated, and turned to her papers again.

"Do bring me the wee-est drop o' whisky and some soda."

Smudgee jumped up distractedly and went to the sideboard, tripping over her dress as she did so. She poured out the merest drain of whisky and a tumbler of syphon soda. Nodding her head jeeringly, she said—

"There! I 'ope she'll like it. There yer are!" She handed the decoction to Sal. Returning to the table, she again tripped over her dress. Giving it a tremendous kick and twist, she returned to her fashion books. But she was not to be left in peace. Once again Sal called—

"Smudgee!"

Smudgee replied, with a deep affectation of tenderness—

"Yus, dear-ie?"

"Wot yer givin' me?"

"The *wee-est* drop of whisky and some soda, my lov-ee; and it's wot yer asked for, my sweet, and if it had been any *wee-er*, it wouldn't have been none at all, my darlin'. See?" And she went on reading. "'Gather shoulder fulness into arm-hole; turn under for——'"

"Smudgee!"

"Wot—his—hit—now——"

"I can't drink this ditch-water," grumbled Sal.

"Well, do the other thing," retorted her exceedingly disrespectful daughter.

By this time Sal's patience was exhausted, and she bounced into the room. Her hair was all tousled, and she had by no means completed the process of dressing. She glared at Smudgee as she went to the sideboard and helped herself to a stiff dose of whisky and soda. Gulping the fiery mixture down, she placed her left hand on her hip, while the glass was still near her lips, and blurted out—

"Tell yer wot it is, young lady! You an' me'll come to words if I 'ave any more o' this. Pretty obedient daughter you are!"

"Yus, I think I am; but I ain't trainin' for a barmaid just at present; and if I wur, you've given me enough practice to go on with—see?"

"Wot's that?" Sal asked, as she was drinking, and looking over Smudgee's shoulder.

"That's for me—my noo Japanesy Peg-nor, if yer must know. This yer thing never did fit, an' never will," said Smudgee, kicking her dressing-gown with much contempt.

"Yer Uncle Nathan ain't come back yet?"

"No, 'e ain't. And I want to know how my dear Uncle Nathan come to be my dear Uncle Nathan. He wurn't no Uncle Nathan when he was swagging it in the back-blocks—and Uncle Nathans don't grow, or come on like bad 'abits." This was said with a meaning glance at Sal's empty whisky-glass. "They've got to be borned; and I want to know how Uncle Nathan got to be borned Uncle Nathan. See?"

"Never mind how he done it. He is your Uncle Nathan."

"Then he must be your brother, or my father's."

"He's my brother, as it 'appens."

"An' your maiden name was Berker, warn't it?"

"Yus—and wot about it?" Sal looked a little alarmed at her daughter's cross-examination. Smudgee had a most uncomfortable way of looking through people at times, and her mother shivered under her gaze.

"Wot about it?" repeated Smudgee severely. "Then I want ter know how Nathan Rudder is brother to Sarah Berker. Wot's 'e Rudder for, when you was Berker? 'As 'e bin married twice?"

"He ain't Nathan Rudder now, 'e's Nathan Berker. And don't you forget it!" blurted Sal.

"I won't. I ain't of a forgetful disposition," answered Smudgee, in a tone that added to Sal's discomfiture.

"It 'ud be better if you was of a more civil disposition, and treated yer mother with more respect."

"Oh! Would it? P'r'aps it 'ud be better if my mother did a little more to earn my respect."

"Yer gettin' worse instead o' better," continued Sal, ignoring Smudgee's remark.

"And you don't improve much," retorted Smudgee.

"You dare to talk to me like this! A bit of a chit like you! I've never 'eard a child go on as you go on.

Child! Yer more like an old woman. I don't believe you ever was a child."

"Whose fault's that? Was I ever treated like one, except by Jack? 'Ow did yer bring me up, eh? Did I ever 'ave any one to speak to except the men? Eh? If I was you, I'd let that subject alone—it's nothin' to be proud of."

How long the discussion would have lasted it is impossible to tell, but it was interrupted by the appearance of Nat, who swaggered into the room, crying—

"Ullo! you two naggin' again!"

Nat had changed in appearance. His face was shaven close, save for a heavy moustache. He was dressed in a travelling suit of large check tweed. He wore a heavy gold chain, scarf-pin, and several showy rings. He had a large cigar in his mouth, which he was chewing; it was not alight. His nose had a deeper, ruddier tinge than of yore, and he was decidedly more corpulent.

"Git yerselves straight. 'Ere's Wolfe with me."

Sal went into the bedroom, put on a gorgeously-coloured morning wrapper, and returned as Nat ushered Wolfe into the room.

"Come in, Wolfe. There's only my sister and my niece, Smudgee, 'ere."

"No, it ain't yer niece Smudgee—neither. It's Miss Loocy Landon. An' if yer'll excuse me, I'll retire ter my boo-dore. I ain't receivin' at present; and if I wur, I ain't quite dressed fur company." Here Smudgee stumbled over her dress.

Nat laughed loudly, "Ha! ha! ha!"

"Ha! ha! ha!" mimicked Smudgee. "Very funny, ain't it? But not arf so funny as the fact that you're my dear Uncle Nathan Rudder Berker—and don't you forgit it! I know yer!" And Smudgee stumbled through the door into the bedroom.

"Wot's up with her now?" growled Nat, helping himself to some whisky.

"Don't ask me!" replied Sal.

" Hev a nip?" Nat asked of Wolfe.

" No, I never drink in business hours, Mr. Berker."

The door of Smudgee's bedroom was gently opened. Nat noticed it, and snapped out sharply—

" Shut that door, Sal."

Sal closed the door, and, turning to Nat, said, " Well?"

" Well, we've been down to see the crib. It's a pallis, Sal, and the estate is a—a—Well, it's a little county."

" Did yer see Mowbray?" Sal inquired, with much interest.

" At a distance—yes. It's 'im right enough, and they've all taken 'im on as Jack Landale, and 'e's their lord and master. I tell yer, Sal, it's a wonderful place. Tell 'er wot you think the income is, Wolfe."

Wolfe answered quietly, " Anything from twenty thousand to twenty-five thousand pounds a year."

" My word!" exclaimed Sal.

" Think on it! An' all ours, if we can get our 'ands on it," said Nat.

" Well, wot are we goin' to do?"

" Tell 'er, Wolfe." Nat helped himself to more whisky, and lit his cigar.

" Well, Mrs. Landale, we're going to try to dispossess Mr. Mowbray, if we can. He is an impostor—that we can prove easily," Wolfe answered.

" Well?"

" The estate and the bulk of the income were left to Mr. John Landale, your late husband."

" Poor Jack!" snuffled Sal.

" He being dead, the next of kin is his legitimate descendant—his daughter Lucy—the young lady who has just left us."

" Me chee-ild! Me darlin' chee-ild!" whined Sal, as she sipped her whisky.

" She is his heiress, and every stick, stone, and blade of grass must come to her."

Sal was almost weeping as she exclaimed, " O Lord! My word!"

Eagerly and excitedly Nat joined in, saying—

"With me an' you as 'er ex-e-cutors and guardians, see, Sal? See? Why, we shall be regular dooks and duchesses, shan't we—eh, old girl?"

"I can't believe it's true! Me a duchess! It can't be true!"

"Bly me! Let me get my 'ands on Landale Abbey! Only let me! I'll show 'em somethin'!" bragged Nat.

"Yes; but let us settle how we are going to try to get our hands on it," quietly interposed Wolfe.

"'Ear! 'ear!" shouted Nat.

"What about it?" asked Sal.

"Mowbray is in possession, accepted as John Landale by his mother, his sister, and all who are of importance."

"Is he? Well, he ain't! See? I'm of some importance, and he ain't accepted by me—not by a lot he ain't! I 'ave got somethin' to say about that." And Sal took some more whisky.

"So have I, Mrs. Landale, and I think you'd better listen to it." Mr. Wolfe was icily calm, and his voice was cold and metallic.

"Of course you've somethin' to say. Do shut yer front winder, Sal. Don't chip in so much. Not so much chin."

"Oh! go on, go on!" retorted Sal.

"Jack Mowbray is now John Landale. Our assertion that he is Jack Mowbray is of no use without witnesses to prove it. You claim to be Mrs. Landale," Wolfe said, turning to Sal.

"Claim to be! I am."

"*Claim* to be Mrs. Landale," quietly repeated Wolfe. "But you've got to prove it."

"I've got my certificate—my marriage lines."

"That you married Jack Landon."

"Who was John Landale."

"Well?" calmly queried Wolfe.

"Look 'ere! Wot are you gettin' at? Do you believe Sal married Jack Landon?" impatiently asked Nat.

" Yes."

" And that Jack Landon was heir to Landale Abbey?"

" Yes."

" And that he died at Woolloogolonga Gully?"

" Yes."

" And that 'is heiress is our—Sal's—Smudgee—I mean Miss Loocy Landale?"

" Um."

" Wot—wot the blazes—wot—Well, wot are you gettin' at?" Nat's temper was gradually going up to boiling-point.

" Before I tell you that, suppose we discuss the terms."

" Terms! Wot terms?"

" *My* terms."

" Your terms? Well, we'll pay you handsome enough."

" What are your ideas of handsome enough?"

" Well—say a thousand quid."

" Dear me! A thousand pounds!" sneered Wolfe.

" Well—*and* expenses."

" A thousand pounds—*and* expenses!"

" Well, if it turns up all square, we might go as far as to say two thousand, mightn't us, Sal?"

" Yes, of course, if the expenses weren't too heavy."

" Just so, just so," acquiesced Nat, stroking his moustache.

" Two thousand and expenses! Um. What is your husband—that is, your husband as he calls himself—Mr. Mowbray as he is—allowing you now?" asked Wolfe, still cool and collected.

" A paltry two thousand quid a year. Why, it's contemptible!" answered Nat.

" It is contemptible," agreed Mr. Wolfe.

" Yus, ain't it? I appeals to you, as man to man—now, ain't it contemptible?"

" As man to man. it is. Twenty to twenty-five thousand pounds a year for two thousand pounds. It *is* contemptible. That's why I refused to accept your offer."

" Wot the blazes do you want, then?" Nat was much astonished and a little alarmed.

" To save time, I've drawn up a little document that I will trouble you to sign before we go any further. Will you look it over? Meantime, I'll take a cigar, if you'll let me." Handing the paper over to Nat, he went to the sideboard, and, taking a cigar, coolly lit it, and stood with his back to the fireplace, smoking.

Nat read the paper with furious amazement.

" Great Scot! What! What! 'Fifty per cent. of all moneys yielded by the said estate!' Fifty per cent.!"

" Exactly; fifty per cent.," coolly replied Wolfe.

" You take a clear 'arf of all our property?"

" A clear half of all the property brings to Mr. John Landale, his heirs, executors, and assigns," corrected Wolfe.

" A clear 'arf! D'ye 'ear that, Sal? Am I awake?"

" Is 'e horf 'is nicker?''

" Is 'e horf 'is nicker? 'E *must* be horf 'is nicker, or thinks we are!"

" To share equally with me and my child—the wife and child of Jack Landale—his property! Why? Why?" asked the surprised Sal.

" Because you are *not* the wife, and your daughter is *not* the child, of John Landale. If you are to get his property, you can only get it through me, and if I *do* get it, I'll have my share."

Had the floor opened just then, Nat and Sal could not have looked more terrified and dumbfounded than they did at Wolfe's speech. Cunning as Nat was, he had met more than his match. Wolfe had made no mention of terms until now. He had received a hundred pounds in advance and his expenses to England. Nat had thought this a remarkably generous beginning. He had estimated Wolfe's services as being well repaid at a few hundred pounds and his passage-money. He had never suspected that Wolfe knew the facts of his relationship with Sal. The knowledge that Wolfe knew everything was appalling. Still, he tried to bluster, and yelled at Wolfe, who was quietly smoking, with his back to the fire—

"Wot the 'ell do yer mean? This is Mrs. Landon, and her child is 'is. She's my sister, and I'll see her righted!"

Wolfe continued to smoke quietly.

"This lady is not Mrs. Jack Landon—her child is not his. This lady is Mrs. Nathan Rudder. You are not her brother—you are her husband, legally married to her at Polson's Matrimonial Agency, George Street, Sydney, 20th March, 1887. You were arrested and sentenced five years ago for burglary, on 20th January, 1888. Your wife met and married Jack Landon on 20th February, when he was drunk, and your daughter was born seven months after, on 16th September. You being alive at the time of her marriage with Jack Landon, it follows that the marriage was illegal, and that she committed bigamy. You have no more claim on the Landale Abbey estates than I have."

Nat was speechless; Sal was gasping like a fish out of water. It was all so unexpected, so sudden, so crushing. Wolfe smoked on coolly, his face set and impassive, his eyes glittering. Sal was the first to break the silence.

"For mercy's sake, give us a drink!" she cried to Nat.

Nat did not move. He was stunned. Wolfe turned to the electric bell button, and pressed it.

"Wot yer ringin' for?" Nat asked anxiously.

There was a knock at the door, and Wolfe quietly said, "Come in."

A waiter entered, and Wolfe turned to him, saying, "Bring those two gentlemen who are waiting in the drawing-room to me."

"Yes, sir," answered the waiter, and left the room.

"Wot two gentlemen?" faltered Nat, before whose alarmed eyes visions of policemen and detectives were passing.

"My clerk and London agent, who are to witness your signatures to that document."

"D'yer think we're goin' to sign it?"

"I *know* you are. You don't think I came from Sydney to London to look after your claim without knowing how I was to be paid for my trouble? You haven't read all that document."

"I've read quite enough for me."

"You'll find that there is a clause stipulating that, should the claim to the Landale estates fail, the said Mr. and Mrs. Rudder will pay to the said R. M. Wolfe the half of any gift or allowance in settlement of the said claim by the alleged John Landale, or any other person on his behalf."

"What!" gasped Nat. "Gimme that whisky, Sal."

"D'yer think we're goin' to sign that?" Sal asked.

"I think so. If you don't, I go down to-night to Landale Abbey, interview Mr. John Landale, and enter into negotiations with him. He will, I imagine, be disposed to pay handsomely for the information that his friend, John Landon, was never legally married to you, and that he has nothing to fear from you and your husband. It is probable that your income will be stopped, and that you will be prosecuted for bigamy."

"Sal!" gasped Nat.

"Nat!" she moaned in return.

Wolfe smoked on quietly. He held them helpless, and they knew it.

There was a knock at the door, and, at Wolfe's bidding, two obviously Jewish individuals, with shiny black clothes and still more shiny silk hats, entered. Going to the sideboard, Wolfe took up a pen, and, dipping it in the ink, said to Nat—

"These gentlemen are rather in a hurry. Sign here —Nathan Rudder, please." Nat signed. "Thanks. Mrs. John Landale, sign your name here." He handed her the pen. She signed in a dazed, helpless way. "Now, gentlemen, please." The two men signed the paper, and

Wolfe motioned them to go, carefully and coolly blotted the signatures, then wrapped the deed up and placed it in his inner coat-pocket.

"A drop of whisky, Nat, for the Lord's sake!" Sal pleaded.

Nat poured some into a glass, but, forgetting Sal, mechanically drank it himself. Sal's hand was still held out for it.

"Come on! Make haste! I feel regular faint and giddy," she continued.

"I—I—could—There! bly me! I could cry," mumbled Nat.

"The whisky!" Sal cried.

"Now, Mrs. Landale, you must take no more of that. You will please get ready to go out." Wolfe's tones were terse and authoritative.

"Weer to?" asked Nat.

"To Landale Abbey."

"What?" exclaimed Sal.

"I do not intend to give Mr. John Mowbray a moment's warning, nor time for preparation. He thinks you and your daughter are in Sydney. I shall not ask for an appointment. I have learned that he will be at home to dinner to-night. We can run down in two hours by the five o'clock train, and will be at the Abbey at 7.15. I have ordered a trap to meet us at the station. We will give Mr. John Mowbray a bit of a surprise."

"Where's the train start from?"

"Five o'clock, from Waterloo."

"Can I get ready by then?"

"I don't know whether you *can*, but you *must;* so don't waste what time you have. This is your room, I believe?" He opened the door of her bedroom.

Sal moved towards the whisky. Wolfe stopped her, saying—

"No! No more of that, if you please. We've got an hour and a quarter. I am going to take this agreement to Somerset House to get it stamped, Mr. Rudder, and I want to talk to you. Will you come with me? Now please, Mrs. Landale, hurry up. I will be here at 4.30 sharp to take you to Waterloo. Be ready!"

" Oh, I'll be ready. But wait till I come into my property! You won't boss me about like this then, if I know it!" cried the indignant Sal, as she banged the door behind her.

" Now, Mr. Rudder," said Wolfe, taking up his hat and umbrella.

" Tell me straight wot chance we've got," asked Nat anxiously.

" I'll tell you more about that after we've seen Mr. Jack Mowbray. We're on the bluff. If he's a good poker player, he may think fit to see our hand—and, Mr. Rudder, we can't afford to show it."

CHAPTER XXIV

SOME UNEXPECTED VISITORS ARRIVE AT LANDALE

LORD THORLAND'S proposal was a totally-unexpected blow to Jack. He had jealously watched Sybil, and had come to the conclusion that there was no man whom she particularly favoured. Thorland's absence, and the silence of the mother and sister, had kept from him the knowledge of that nobleman's love for Sybil. Jack could not but see that no better match could be wished for the girl. Thorland was rich, handsome, clever, popular, a thorough gentleman, and a good fellow. He would make Sybil happy, if any man could. "What right have I to object?" Jack asked himself, yet, in giving his consent to Thorland's request to pay his addresses to Sybil, he felt that he was giving away his life.

"If Sybil loves him, she will be his wife. His wife!" he repeated to himself. All the light seemed to have gone out of the world. He retired to his room—but not to sleep. For the greater part of the night he walked the floor, till, giddy and exhausted, he threw himself on the bed. Finding sleep still impossible, he went into the park, walking furiously, battling with himself, trying in vain to find some comfort in the thought that it was necessary for Sybil's happiness that she should wed Thorland. Returning to the house, he went to his room. After a cold bath and a change of clothes, he went down to breakfast. His face was drawn, his eyes bloodshot. He looked haggard and ill. Lady Walgrove and Sybil were both alarmed for him.

"My dear boy, are you unwell?" the mother asked.

"Not at all."

"Something is wrong, Jack. What is it, dear?"

"Do tell us," pleaded Sybil.

"Nothing is wrong. I—I—Well, I had rather a bad

night—nothing else. I shall be all right soon. Please do not worry about me."

"But we must worry about you when we see you looking so unlike yourself, Jack. Has anything happened to distress you? Anything that we do not know?"

"No, Sybil. I think I should like a talk with Mamsey, if you do not mind."

"Alone, Jack?"

"Yes, Sybil, alone."

"Secrets!" pouted Sybil.

"No, you shall know, but I should like to speak to her first."

"Very well, sir! If I cannot be trusted, shut me out from your confidence. But remember I am a woman, and do not try my curiosity too much." Half-jestingly, half-earnestly, Sybil said this, as she left the room. She was deeply concerned at the change in Jack's manner and appearance. She had grown accustomed to watch every expression of his face. She felt and knew that he was suffering mentally, and she longed to comfort him, to stand by his side and help him to face his trouble, whatever it might be. She never dreamed that she was the innocent cause of his distress.

"What is it, my son? Something has happened. Tell me at once—what is it?"

"Nothing but what we should be glad for, I suppose. Yet—well, it concerns Sybil."

"Yes? What is it?"

"Lord Thorland has spoken to me about her."

"Yes, dear?"

"He tells me that he loves, and wishes to marry her."

"Is that all?"

"Yes, that is all."

"And are you fretting about that?"

"Fretting! I—that is, we—are not in a hurry to part with her, are we?"

"No, but we must not think only of ourselves. We must think of her and her happiness."

" True—we must think of her and her happiness," Jack repeated in a dull, mechanical way.

" And Thorland is in every way a desirable match for her."

" Yes; it would be difficult to find a better."

" I have always thought so."

" Then you entirely approve of his suit?"

" Entirely. How could I do otherwise?"

" How could you do otherwise?" Jack seemed hardly conscious that he was speaking.

" Surely, dear, you can have no objection?"

" I? Why should I?"

" You can see no reason why she should not be his wife?"

" If she loves him, no. But does she—does she love him?"

" That I do not know. I used to think she did."

" When?"

" Before you came home."

" And after that?"

" Well, she seemed so absorbed in you, she hardly mentioned him. There has been no one but her brother in the world since he came back."

Jack's heart gave a bound, and his face for a moment was lit with a great hope, only to subside into the darkness of despair as he remembered that, however strong her feelings were, they were but those of a sister for a brother. " What did it matter, after all, whom she loved? As well Thorland as another. What is it to me?" he asked of himself.

" Will you speak to Sybil, and—and ask her if she loves him?" Jack asked, after a long pause.

" Yes, dear, if you would rather not do so yourself."

" I would rather not do so—at least, not to-day."

" Well, let the matter rest for the present. Perhaps she will speak of it herself," the mother answered.

" She will want to know what we have been saying. Tell her—that her happiness—is all the world to me—

that if she—that is, whatever her choice may be—I shall, with my whole heart, wish her joy. Tell her we think only of her—that it will be hard to part with her, of course, but her life is her own, and we are content, if she is happy." Alas! there was no contentment in Jack's soul or voice. Never in his life had he felt so hopelessly wretched.

Not wishing to meet Sybil, he sent for his horse and rode round the estate, seeking by work to distract his thoughts. He never knew exactly how that day passed. It seemed interminable, miserable, and desolate. Poor Jack! There was worse to come.

While talking to Tom in his study later in the day, Spurdy entered the room.

"What is it?" Jack asked.

"Note, sir."

"Who brought it?"

"Two men and a female, sir."

"Two men and a female?" Jack opened and read the note. As he did so, he turned deathly pale and half staggered to a seat.

"Tom! come here—quickly!" he called.

"What is it?"

Jack gave him the note. Tom read it with consternation, then asked, "What will you do?"

"You see what they say, 'If you refuse to see me, I will raise the house; I will not be sent away.' It is Sal's writing. But who are the others—the two men?" Turning to Spurdy, Jack said, "Mr. Hewley will come down and see these people. Please go and tell them so."

Spurdy bowed and left the room.

"Go down, Tom. If you cannot induce them to leave, bring them to my room. I will go to Lady Walgrove and Sybil and make some excuse to be left alone until we get rid of them."

Tom went to see Sal, and Jack rang the bell for Wong.

Wong glided into the room in his noiseless way.

"Wong, shut those windows," Jack said. Wong did so. "Trouble's coming along—to me."

"Blad tlubble?"

"Bad trouble. You remember Sal—Sal at Woolloo-golonga?"

"Allee samee Mrs. Jlack Landon?"

"Allee samee Mrs. Jack Landon. Much pull over me; may send me before judge—prison seven years. Watchee her; watchee men allee samee. Help me. Savee?"

"Wong savee wellee muchee," said Wong, drawing a deadly-looking stiletto from his sleeve. "Wong dis hab got; usee him."

"No, no! Put that away. Keep at this door. Listen. Remember allee they talkee-talkee. Savee?"

"Wong savee wellee muchee."

"Get whisky—soda—quick."

Wong left the room quickly and silently. Scarcely had he done so when Sybil came into the room.

"Can I speak to you, Jack?" she asked.

Jack was in an agony of fear lest Tom should return with Sal while Sybil was in the room. The thought that she should meet Sal was horrible to him. He replied hurriedly—

"Not just now. There is some one waiting—I mean some one I must see on business. Will you excuse me for a little while?"

"Certainly, dear. But what is the matter? You look like one who has seen a ghost."

"I can promise you I've not." He fancied he could hear Sal coming up the stairs. Hurriedly and eagerly he said, "Come along, Sybil, I will see you for a moment in the drawing-room. Come, dear, come."

His manner startled Sybil, but she did not attempt to question him further. As they left the room, Wong entered it, bringing with him a decanter of whisky, a syphon of soda, and some glasses. Setting these on the table, he went swiftly to the door and quietly closed it, drew the curtains over the window, took a small phial containing opium from an inside pocket of his dress and poured a few drops into three of the glasses, and put the others away. There was a broad smile of satisfaction on his face as he did this. Hearing footsteps, he went to the door and almost ran into the arms of Nat, who entered with Sal and Wolfe and Tom. Quickly turning his head so that neither Nat nor Sal could see his face, he left the room.

" Where 'ave I seen that bloomin' Ching-Ching afore?" queried Nat.

" Never, p'r'aps," Sal answered. " Chinamen are all alike."

Saying, " Please sit down; I'll bring Mr. Landale to you," Tom left the three conspirators to themselves.

It did not take Nat long to discover the whisky, and help himself and Sal to a copious draught of it.

" What a place! A pallis—a Crystal-Buckingham-Windsor Pallis, ain't it, Sal?" he asked, draining the glass at a gulp.

" Fancy livin' 'ere!" exclaimed Sal, following his example.

" Now, be careful! No more of that, or you'll make a mess of it," cautioned Wolfe.

" I'm all of a shiver!" exclaimed Sal.

" I got the St. Wit-us-es, I think—or the jumps."

" Shut up," whispered Wolfe, " he's here."

Jack, followed by Tom, entered the room.

" Well, what do you want?" Jack asked. He was pale, but calm and determined.

" This is our solicitor, Mr. Raffael M. Wolfe," said Nat.

" Well?"

" Had we not better be alone?" asked Wolfe, looking towards Tom.

" No, I have no secrets from my friend," replied Jack.

" All right. You know my client, I think?"

" Yes."

" Mrs. John Landon, otherwise Landale."

"Go on."

"You admit this, of course?"

"I admit nothing."

"You know I'm Mrs. Landon!" Sal was annoyed at Jack's contemptuous indifference towards her.

"Please leave this business to me," Wolfe snapped out. Nat and Sal were shifty and uneasy.

"Who are you?" Jack asked of Nat.

"I'm this lady's brother—Nathan Berker," blustered Nat.

"Haven't I seen you before?"

"Werry likely in Sydney."

"It was not in Sydney. What do you want?" Jack's manner was not pleasant. If Nat had expected him to show fear or uneasiness, he was doomed to be disappointed.

"You're a man of business, I hope, Mr. Mowbray——"

"Landale, please," Jack retorted sharply.

"Come, come! don't waste my time."

"Go on, then."

Wolfe saw that he had no coward or common man to deal with, and determined to lose no time in preliminaries. He said—

"You are not John Landale, you are John Mowbray, convicted on the 15th November, 1888, at Sydney Assizes, for being concerned in the sticking-up of the Wurramurra Bank. You were sentenced, as John Landon, to three years' imprisonment, were sent to Berrima prison, and escaped from there on the 4th January, 1889. All this time John Landon, otherwise Landale, was living with this lady as her husband—he never left her. You are an impostor. You are committing a fraud, and, in addition to completing your original sentence of three years, you will be liable for at least another seven years for this crime."

Jack heard all this without moving a muscle. He stood on the hearth, his hands behind his back, staring full into Wolfe's face. All he said was, "Go on."

" My clients have no desire to deal harshly with you, but they mean to have their rights."

" What are they?"

" Sir James Walgrove left Landale Abbey and the bulk of his fortune to this lady's husband—John Landale. He died in Woolloogolonga Gully on the 12th January last. He was buried there. The property, therefore, reverts to his heirs—his widow and his daughter Lucy, now aged fourteen."

" Go on," Jack repeated.

" On behalf of my clients, I claim the property, and demand from you a written confession of your crimes, duly signed and witnessed, and an undertaking to leave the country, never to return to it."

" What else?"

" On consideration of your doing this, and resigning the property, giving up possession peaceably and in order, we will undertake to hold our tongues regarding your Wurramurra sentence—leave that to John Landale, now deceased—and allow you what you are now allowing the woman and child you are defrauding—two thousand pounds a year."

" And per contra?"

" I go to the nearest police station, and apply for a warrant for your apprehension."

" They'd want some evidence, I fancy," said Jack quietly.

" They'll get it."

" What is it?"

" That's my business. As I have been pretty accurate in my account of the whole matter, you may credit me, I think, with knowing what I am talking about and doing."

Jack turned from Wolfe to Sal, asking, " Is this all under your direction?"

" It is." Sal's voice was low and husky.

Turning again to Wolfe, Jack asked—

" What if I tell you you have lied? That I am John

Landon—never married that woman—that I changed names and places with John Mowbray for purposes of my own which do not concern you?"

"That won't pass. John Landon was never called Mowbray."

"For the sake of argument, and without prejudice, suppose I admit the truth of what you say—Lady Walgrove has recognised me as her son, her daughter owns me as her brother."

"Lady Walgrove is a witness, I admit. Her daughter is not. She was an infant when Landale left home."

"Then the old servants?"

"They'll none of them stand cross-examination."

"How if I offer you a much larger income?"

"It will not be accepted. Nothing but your abandonment of the property and the confession I have named will suffice."

"You mean that?"

"I mean it."

Jack's face wore an ugly look as he looked straight into Wolfe's eyes, saying—

"Then do your worst, and be damned!"

"Mr. Mowbray!" exclaimed Wolfe.

"Mr. John Landale," replied Jack sternly. "I am here to save an old woman's life and her daughter's happiness, and until you have proved your case, and the police drag me out of this house, here I stay. Now, go." He rang the bell, and Wong glided in. Turning to him, Jack continued, "Wong, show these people out. If they refuse to go, I'll get you, Tom, to go to the telephone, and ask the police inspector to send some men to remove and arrest them for trespass. Now, Mr. Wolfe, you have my answer. Go."

Wolfe looked at Nat and Sal in horror. Nat was breathing heavily. His eyes were closed, his mouth wide open. Sal was muttering—

"Be hang—want—me—proper—prop——"

"What the devil's the matter?" cried Wolfe. "Here! Wake up—wake up!" And he shook Nat savagely.

Sal continued in a half-stupefied manner—

"I tell you—I'm Mrs. Jack Landon—call everybody —let 'em know—let 'em know——"

Sal's head sank upon her breast. Wong's opium had done its work upon her and Nat.

The door opened and, to Jack's horror, Sybil entered. Looking round her with amazement, she asked—

"Jack, who are these people?"

Wolfe stepped forward, saying—

"Mr. Nathan Berker and Mrs. John——"

"Say that word and, by God! I'll kill you," Jack whispered to Wolfe.

Here Tom stepped forward to Sybil, and said—

"I'm deeply ashamed to say, Miss Landale, that they are old acquaintances of mine. I have entertained them not wisely but too well. I apologise for their disgraceful condition, and will drive them to the nearest hotel."

"Please come with me, Sybil," urged Jack. "These people are intruders, and will be turned out of the house."

Taking her arm, he led the wondering girl out of the room.

CHAPTER XXV

THE REVIVAL OF NAT AND SAL

Tom Hewley had gone through many strange experiences in his brief and extremely varied career, but it is doubtful if he ever had a more puzzling task than that which he now found himself compelled to undertake, viz., the removal of the inanimate forms of Sal and Nat from Landale Abbey. Get them away he must, but how? Alternately shaking them and cursing Mr. Wolfe helped to relieve his feelings, but did not effect the removal of the slumbering ones, nor disturb the temper of the very wide-awake lawyer. Mr. Raffael Moses Wolfe had been cursed too often in his time, and by those who were much greater adepts at anathematising than Tom, to be moved at so mild a form of vituperation as that now levelled at him. Moreover, Mr. Wolfe was too much occupied with his own thoughts to trouble about Tom's abuse.

"What, in the name of Bacchus, had these two old topers, Nat and Sal, swallowed that they should be so overcome?" He did not for a moment think Jack would be such a fool as to run the risk of imprisonment by drugging these people in Landale Abbey. Yet it was impossible that a few glasses of whisky could have wrought such havoc. He smelt the decanter and the glasses. He learned nothing by that. Tom watched him with some curiosity. He, too, was unable to account for the sudden collapse of the two conspirators. He knew Sal of old. If ever there was a woman capable of "carrying her liquor well," it was Sal. Nat's features answered for him.

Growing weary of watching Wolfe's investigations, he said to that individual—

"When you've quite finished your little inquest, I shall be extremely grateful if you will assist me in conveying this cargo of alcohol"—Tom signified by a nod of the head that he was alluding to Nat and Sal—"to some more suitable storage than Landale Abbey. This is not a bonded liquor warehouse."

"You don't happen to know what *kind* of liquor my two friends contain, do you?" asked Wolfe, with much meaning in his cold tone and gleaming eyes.

"Yes, I do," replied Tom, quite divining the other's thoughts. "It is uncommonly good whisky and Schweppes' soda. Let me assist you, Mr. Wolfe." Tom took up the decanter and a glass.

"No, thanks, Mr. Hewley! I'm not taking any of that kind of forgetfulness at present. I am too much interested in watching its effect on my friends to try any experiment on myself."

"Well, then, may I beg of you to help me to remove your friends to some congenial atmosphere for the study of the uses and abuses of alcohol? This room is required for other purposes."

"My energetic and venturesome young friend, you will find that the removal of my friends will not be so easy a matter as you seem to imagine. Between them they pull down the scales at about twenty-eight stone. The lady will require the attention of at least three like me, and the gentleman of at least an equal number like yourself, to get them out of the room, much less downstairs and into my carriage. Moreover, the removal of two individuals in such a condition as that of these very estimable acquaintances of mine cannot take place without causing some considerable astonishment in the servants' hall. I presume this is not an ordinary occurrence in Landale Abbey, Mr. Hewley?"

"You may safely bet your best patent-leathers on that."

"Nor one likely to pass without remark?"

"What do *you* think?"

"That, for the present, the idea that we can shift these somnolent ones must be abandoned."

"Perhaps you will kindly make a suggestion, Mr. Wolfe?"

"With pleasure, Mr. Hewley. I'll make several, but I fear that to most of them there will be some objection."

"*Par exemple?*"

"*Par exemple*, I should like to try the effect of a bucket of water (iced, for choice) over that most estimable lady, and two buckets of the same fluid, at precisely the same temperature, over her friend. But—and here comes the objection to this suggestion—the carpet would certainly be deteriorated, and though, morally, the carpet is the property of my distinguished client, yet she is not yet in possession, and I might be sued for damages."

"You must be extremely proud of your 'distinguished clients,' Mr. Wolfe?"

"My dear Mr. Hewley, a solicitor does not take clients for the purpose of fostering pride, but for the sake of increasing his income."

"I don't think your present clients will increase your income to any overwhelming extent—do you?"

"As you start with expressing your opinion, it is a waste of time to ask mine, Mr. Hewley."

Mr. Wolfe was resting his back against an escritoire, his hands were deep in his trousers pockets, his head a little inclined to one side, while his eyes were leisurely regarding Nat and Sal. Tom was reminded of the attitude of an old raven contemplating a doubtful worm.

"Any other suggestion, Mr. Wolfe?"

"Yes. I noticed that a Mongolian servant left the room as we entered it. I would suggest that you find him, and ask for his assistance in this matter. I am of opinion that he is likely to know much more about this curious collapse of my clients than either you or I."

The hint startled Tom a little. It was just such a

thing as Wong, out of his love for Jack, might attempt. No doubt he had drugged them. Here was another serious trouble. Mischief of the most painful kind might accrue. He must see Wong alone, and, if possible, learn what he had done. Turning to Wolfe, he said quietly—

"If you will keep an eye on your friends for a few minutes, I'll find him."

"Pray do not hurry on account of my 'friends.' There is no danger of their running away just at present. You will find them here on your return, I have no doubt." Mr. Wolfe drew an easy-chair up to the fire, helped himself to a cigar, and sat down for a comfortable smoke.

Tom went in search of Wong.

Turning towards his "distinguished clients," Mr. Wolfe apostrophised them under his breath. "You drunken pigs! You swine of the beer-cellars! May all the plagues of alcohol gnaw your vitals and sodden your brains, when I have done with you! But I must keep you moderately sober until then. Pretty tools to work with, certainly!"

Mr. Wolfe rose, and, sauntering leisurely to Nat, took hold of his ear and wrung it hard enough to wake any but a drugged man to fury.

"You pig! You drunken brute! You swill-tub on two legs! Take that!" And once more the ear of the unconscious Nat was wrung.

This time, the pain penetrated even through the drug, and Nat gave a smothered groan.

"Oho! So you *can* feel that, can you?" snarled Wolfe. "Then we'll try another." And again he twisted the ear of the sleeping man.

Mr. Wolfe seldom allowed himself the luxury of losing his temper, but he often indulged his spite, if it could be done without cost to himself. His visit to Landale had not been as profitable as he had hoped. True, Jack had shown some weakness, but he was evidently not to be cowed or bullied. If driven into a corner, he was the kind of man to set his back to the wall and fight to a finish. Wolfe knew perfectly well that he was on very thin ice. As he had told his clients, he was " bluffing." Jack was a difficult man to do that with. If he had but two clever, sober assistants, he could do much, but, with these drunken fools, he could not be sure of anything.

The thought induced him once more to turn his attention to Nat's auricular organ, and again Nat groaned.

" Yes, you brute! I'll give you something to think about when you recover enough sense to think at all," he muttered.

However, even with such tools as he possessed, he was convinced he could make a very good thing of it. Meanwhile, he must get them out of Landale as quickly as possible. Mowbray might bribe them to go over to his side, in one of their drunken fits, and that would be ruin.

Tom returned with Wong. Wolfe scrutinised his face narrowly. He might as well have tried to see through the great wall of Wong's native land. His face was impenetrable.

Wolfe had met too many Chinamen to waste time in useless talk. He went straight to the point.

" What is the matter with those people?" he asked sternly, pointing to the slumbering pair.

Wong stared with placid indifference, shaking his head sadly, and said—

" Wong not know."

" Find out, then."

Wong ambled to them, looked at them, at the whisky decanter and glasses, and said—

" Too muchee whiskily hab got."

" Well, Wong," Tom joined in, " we want to get them out of the house pretty quick. Can you help us?"

Then Wong smiled, and did a very odd thing. Going to Nat, he shut that individual's wide-open mouth, took a small box from the inexhaustible sleeve, opened it, and, taking some yellow-coloured powder from it, forced it into Nat's nostrils, through which Nat inhaled noisily; then, wrenching his head free from Wong's hand, sneezed violently for some minutes, during which Wong placidly repeated the operation on Sal.

Soon, the room rang with their sneezes. Wong, watching the effect with his ample smile, said—

" Bofe pletty soon wake now plesently."

And " bofe pletty soon " did wake, if not to entire consciousness, at least to a condition in which, with a helping arm, they could walk with moderate directness downstairs to the carriage which was waiting to convey them to the station.

They were too dazed and stupid to talk. They glared about them with fishy, lack-lustre eyes, and occasionally muttered incoherently broken sentences, in which the words " whisky and soda " occurred with curious frequency. Their mouths were dry and parched, and their tongues hard and difficult to move. Decidedly, they were not creditable travelling companions, and Mr. Wolfe left them to themselves on the journey back to town, bundled them into a four-wheeler on arrival, gave the cabman their address, and, without even a word of parting, went his way to his office and wrote them a note.

The dilapidated pair, after a stiff glass or two of whisky, had thrown themselves down on their respective beds, and were once again soon in the grip of stupefied slumber.

When the note from Wolfe arrived, it was handed to Smudgee.

After seeing the waiter out of the room, Smudgee asked the chambermaid for a jug of hot water, and retired with it and the letter to her own room. Placing the letter over the hot-water jug, she quietly steamed it, opened it carefully, saying to herself, " Now, Mr. Raffael Moses Wolfe, we will see what you have got to say to my respected muvver and my beloved new Uncle Nathan Berker-Rudder."

This is what she read :—

"Sir,—We must see Mr. John Mowbray again at Landale Abbey at 3 P.M. to-morrow. I will be with you at 1 o'clock sharp, and, if it will not seriously inconvenience you, or utterly destroy your constitutions, I shall esteem it a favour if you and Mrs. Landon will keep moderately sober. Your lamentable weakness has probably ruined our chances. If you can't take a glass of whisky without deplorable results,—take *tea*. Please be ready to start immediately on my arrival, and if you can contrive to keep sober, we may redeem matters yet, and give Mr. John Mowbray a lesson he will never forget. —Yours, &c.,

"R. M. Wolfe."

Smudgee thought hard for a few moments, then, nodding her head, put the letter back in the envelope, re-sealed it, and rang the bell. "Give Mr. Mowbray a lesson he will never forgit, will yer, Raffael? Ah! We shall see wot we shall see—shan't we, Moses?" asked Smudgee of the air.

The chambermaid entered, in answer to the bell.

"'And me my 'at, Marier," said Smudgee, pointing to that article of adornment, which was lying with her mantle and gloves upon the bed.

"Yes, miss," answered the girl, bringing her the hat.

"'Ow d'ye like this 'at, Marier?" Smudgee queried a little anxiously.

"I think it most heligant, miss," readily replied the girl.

"Now, give it us straight, Marier! Is it up to date?"

"Up to date! Why, miss, it might have been made next week."

Smudgee was gratified, and said—

"You see if all Leicester Square don't copy it in a day or two."

"Shouldn't wonder, miss."

"I'm goin' on a visit to some friends in a pallis—a

pallis, Marier, understand!—an' I don't want to look as if I'd come out o' Nor's Ark."

"Lor'! Don't speak of yourself as if you was a beast, miss. You look lovely," smirked the wily Maria.

"Are you gettin' at me?" asked Smudgee, turning sharply to look at her.

"Lor, no, miss!"

"'Cos I ain't here to be got at—see? I'm goin' ter see my most pertickler friend, an' 'e ain't seen me for a year. I want to knock him—see? 'And me that 'at-pin. No, not that—the one wiv the lookin'-glass top."

Maria did as she was ordered.

"Like my stockings?" asked Smudgee, sticking out a very shapely limb for Maria's inspection.

"They're brown, ain't they, miss?" was the quite unnecessary and rather evasive question.

"Well, black's gettin' so *common*. *Everybody* wears black, so I thought I'd think o' somethin' fresh." Jamming in a hat-pin, Smudgee turned her face to the handmaiden, and inquired, "'Ow's that?"

"Well, *I* think it's lovely."

"Yes. I think Jack'll be struck."

"Jack being your brother, miss?"

"No fear!"

"Your cousin, p'r'aps?"

"No, an' 'e ain't me cousin, neither."

"Lor! miss, you ain't been an' gone an' got a young man?"

"Young man! No fear! I don't want no *boys* hangin' round me. Telephone to the orfice for them to git me a cab—a 'ansom. An' see—tell 'em to git me one wiv a 'orse in it—somethin' that can move. I ain't goin' to a funeral. *You hear me?*"

When Maria had accomplished the telephonic feat desired, Smudgee said—

"I'm goin' on a very pertickler private matter to a pallis—a pallis, understand—Marier."

" But, surely, you're not going to a pallis alone, miss?"
asked the inquisitive maid.

" Why not? Think I can't take care o' myself? You
bet! See 'ere, Marier, keep yer face shut about me goin'
to a pallis to my mamma and my dearly-beloved uncle,
or you might spoil my game."

Here the waiter knocked at the door, and Smudgee,
attired for her journey, went into the sitting-room and
placed the note from Wolfe on the table.

" 'Ansom at the door, miss," announced the waiter.

" Did yer git a 'orse?" asked Smudgee.

" Looks like a flyer, miss," replied the man.

Turning to Maria, Smudgee said—

" Tell my sainted mother *and* my dearly-beloved uncle
they're not to worry about me ; that I've gone to do some
shoppin' an' a little bit o' bisness on my own, an' that
perwided we 'as fine weather an' it don't rain cucumbers,
their obedient daughter *and* niece will be back when she
returns. And, James, keep yer eye off that whisky decanter. If you *want* to drink my 'ealth, do it open, not
wiv yer eyes shut, 'cos it's bad for yer conscience. *I*
know yer!" And Smudgee, putting on her best Princess
deportment, left the room.

The waiter thought the whisky-decanter required dust-
ing. He gave it a whisk with the napkin he carried over
his arm, and saying, " A most extraordinary young person!" he helped himself to a portion of the contents.

" ' She ain't 'arf bad when yer know 'er,
But you've got to know 'er fust.'

Well, 'ere's to 'er 'ealth, with my eyes *and* mouth
open!"

Before he could finish drinking what he had poured
out for himself, Nat and Sal came into the room, and
he hurriedly put down the glass and held the napkin
to his mouth.

Quick as he was, Nat saw him, and said—

" See 'ere, my friend, I can smell yer breath from where I stand, so put down that table-cloth. You've been at our whisky. Well, it'll come out o' yer tip—see? Now go and lose yourself."

" Yes, sir, thankee, sir," said the waiter, adding under his breath, when he got into the passage, " Mean 'ound! —that's what 'e is—a mean 'ound!"

" Where's Miss Loocy, chambermaid?" asked Sal.

" She's just gone out, ma'am, to do some shoppin', and a little bit o' business on her own. And she told me to tell you she'd be back when she got 'ome." And, with an inward chuckle, Maria followed the waiter.

" Drat that kid! Wot game's she up to now?" asked Sal of nobody in particular. " Oh, my 'ead! It's got loose marbles in it," she added, holding her temples with her hot and feverish hand.

" Oh, *your* 'ead! You should 'ave mine!" growled Nat. " Wot the blazes was that whisky made of? I didn't swaller as much as 'ud reach up to a bee's knee, but I was multi-be-argered afore I'd got the taste of it into my chest. I've drunk akee-fortis, spirits of wine, parerfin, train-oil, methylated spirits even, when I was 'ard up for whisky, but they was all sparrer's milk compared with that stuff. Oh, my 'ead!"

" 'Ow did we get out of the pallis? Did we fly? Or did they carry us out? Bless me if I can remember anythink," said Sal, helping herself to some whisky.

" Nor I. Pallis indeed! Pallis may be all right, but pallis-whisky is right orf. I've had enough of pallis-whisky to last me a lifetime. If that's the sort of stuff they 'ave on tap at our new 'ome, I'll use it to disinfect the pigs, and lay down a tap o' my own." Here Sal caught sight of Wolfe's note.

" 'Ere's a note looks like Wolfe's writin'."

" Wolfe? I shouldn't wonder. It's just come. It's wet." The envelope was wet certainly, but it had not " just come." It had been in Smudgee's hands for some time.

REVIVAL OF NAT AND SAL

" Sir,—We must see Mr. John Mowbray again at Landale Abbey at 3 P.M. to-morrow. I will be with you at 1 o'clock sharp, and, if it will not seriously inconvenience you, or utterly destroy your constitutions, I shall esteem it a favour if you and Mrs. Landon will keep moderately sober. Your lamentable weakness has probably ruined our chances. If you can't take a glass of whisky without deplorable results,—take *tea*. Please be ready to start immediately on my arrival, and if you can contrive to keep sober, we may redeem matters yet, and give Mr. John Mowbray a lesson he will never forget.—Yours, &c.,

" R. M. WOLFE."

" ' Lamentable weakness' !" repeated Nat. " I like that! That pallis-whisky would multi-be-arger a bloomin' rhinocerus !"

" ' Lamentable weakness' !" echoed Sal. " It's insult to injury. What's 'e mean by ' take tea'? Does 'e think we're kittens? Why don't 'e suggest milk while 'e's about it? I'll just drink what I like, when I like, and where I like !"

" Do, old gal. But, take it from me, bar pallis-whisky. We'll 'ave Wolfe 'ere in a minute. Are yer ready ter start ?"

" Start! I'm ready ter die, I think. Oh, my 'ead! I wish I'd never left Sydney. I never 'ad a 'ead like this in Sydney, and I've 'ad a drop or two there in my time. I believe it's this beastly climate. It's the fog that gets on yer chest, that's what it is. I'll have a drop ter keep it out, afore that sneakin' Wolfe gets 'ere. I'll ' lamentable weakness' 'im before I've done with 'im."

For several reasons, Sal disliked Mr. Wolfe. She hated his contemptuous indifference to her charms. He never once looked at her as a woman—merely regarded her as a client, and any disregard of her charms invariably caused Sal much annoyance. She hated him for having so completely got the better of Nat and herself,

325

but, in her strange, contradictory way, she hated him most because he was trying to injure Jack. True, she too was working against Mowbray, but "that was different." She meant "to do well by him in the end." Did she not intend to bestow herself upon him? But "this low-down Wolfe was working for his own bat, and did not care what happened to Jack so long as he scored." Wolfe had not done well to treat Sal so contemptuously. She was not easy to manage at any time, but, when roused to active enmity, she was dangerous. And she was not difficult to rouse if her vanity was hurt. She was in that condition known in her class as "nasty drunk," and that is something very nasty indeed.

There was a knock at the door, and, in reply to Nat's invitation to "come in," Wolfe entered. He looked at the two partners, and the whisky-decanter, and, not noticing Nat's surly "good morning," snarled out—

"You're at it again, I see!"

"Yes, I am!" Sal snapped back. "You shut yer 'ead about 'lamentable weakness.' Mind yer own business!"

"This is my business, madam, and it's hardly likely to be a profitable one, if you cannot keep sober enough to remain awake while I am endeavouring to carry it on."

"Well, I can keep sober enough and awake enough on hanythink, bar pallis-whisky," grunted Nat. "When I want to kick the pail, I'll try 'Rough on rats'; it'll be smoother than pallis-whisky, I'll bet. Now, what's the next move?"

"To see what he'll compromise at. He'll have to pay, or do his ten years. There's no time to waste. The sooner we are back at Landale, the better. Whatever we are to make out of this business must be made at once. The less delay there is, the less chance there will be of his learning the truth about you two. I need hardly point out to you that the truth is just the one thing neither of you can face with any chance of profit."

"If it comes to that," sneered Sal, "the truth wouldn't

be exactly the salvation of you. You ain't what one would call spotless, neither. In fact, my opinion of you —if you want to know——"

"I certainly do not. I have no interest whatever in your opinions or anything that concerns you—save that which affects the Landale succession. Keep your opinions to yourself, and get ready to accompany me to the Abbey, if you please." Mr. Wolfe was, if possible, more insultingly cool and polite than ever, and Sal proportionately angry.

"See here! I'm full up of this trottin' up and down the country! Accompany you, indeed! Pretty company you are! Sort o' company to land us all in quod, before you've done with us. I'm tired of it. That's my 'lamentable weakness,' I suppose! Look out as I ain't too strong for you, anyway, before we're through with this job. You won't git it all your own way. Mind that!"

Sal went to her room. It was not a pleasant look that Wolfe gave her as she passed through the door. Nor was the tone of his voice too agreeable as he said—

"A sweet woman! A perfect lady!"

"Don't judge her this mornin'," pleaded Nat. "Pallis-whisky ain't the soother ter the temper yer may think it. I don't feel altogether like a month-old lamb myself. When a party has swallered somethin' overnight that acts like carbolic acid and niter-glycerine mixed, that party is 'ardly likely ter 'ave a temper like a bloomin' cherubim in the morning."

"Pray do not apologise for the lady; I quite understand her and her playful little threats, and am perfectly prepared to meet them. Whether it is wise in her to utter them is another matter. Please hasten her preparations, if you can. We must see Mr. Mowbray again this afternoon."

CHAPTER XXVI

IN WHICH JACK'S SIN BEGINS TO FIND HIM AT HOME

WHEN Jack led Sybil from the room, after her discovery of Nat and Sal, he had no means of learning how much the girl had seen, or what she had heard of the conversation that had passed between him and them. He was far too agitated himself to ask her, at the moment. Sybil, too, was unable to control her agitation, and went to her room without a word.

"What had she heard?" Jack asked himself, again and again. That she had, even in so small a way, come in contact with them was horrible to him. Had she heard Sal say that she was Mrs. Landale? If so, what could he say or do? Deny it? Say that the woman lied? Of what use would that be, when she had her marriage certificate and the evidence of her own brother and the lawyer to prove it? Admit it? Own to the fact that she was Mrs. Landale? Was not that to convict himself of a lie in telling her but a few hours before that he was not married, that when he entered the house he had never known what it was to love? Whichever way he looked he saw nothing but shame and grief for himself and the mother and daughter whom he would gladly have died to save. He could not deny the woman's assertion, and yet to admit it was horrible. That drunken virago his wife! Entitled by his marriage with her to live under his roof, side by side with Sybil and her mother! To come in daily, hourly contact with them! No! Anything but that. Yet, how was he to prevent it? At any cost, the mother and daughter must be spared that degradation. But how? Suppose he confessed the truth—how would that help? Sal was still the widow of the son and brother, and held the power to turn Lady Walgrove and Sybil out of the house. Certainly, if they knew the truth, nothing would persuade them to stay in it an hour, with Sal as its lawful mistress. To exist on the sufferance or charity of such a creature as Sal was not possible, not even to be considered. Yet, by the terms of Sir James' will, there was little or no provision made for them. What could he do? Fight for them to the last, of course. But how? To own that he had deceived the mother, say that he was not her son, now that she had learned to love and depend upon him, was not to be thought of. On all sides, degradation, shame, and grief. How could he have been guilty of so base a fraud? There was no other word for it. As time rolled on and his memory of Landale's degradation, his piteous appeals for Jack's help grew more and more faint; as his contact with absolute rectitude and honour grew closer, so did his ideas of right and wrong become more clear. The loose moral life he had led, the careless moral standard of his fellows in the old days, had blunted, to some extent, a naturally fine instinct of honour; his new life had sharpened it, and it cut him to the very core of his heart of hearts when he thought of his sin. Yet could he not loosen himself from the coils it had wound around him?

No! he must go on to the end. He would fight these people to the finish, or compromise with them in any possible or feasible way. But would anything but absolute possession of Landale and all that it meant content the vain, selfish woman, such as he knew Sal to be? He feared not. Moreover, he knew what great factors in her actions were her temper, drink, and her jealousy. No dependence could be placed upon her word or her many moods, even when sober, but, when tipsy, she was utterly irresponsible. The outlook was dark indeed, but it was to grow darker still.

Sal's visit to Landale had a disturbing effect upon others too. Lorna had heard of Tom's avowal that she was an old friend of his. Lorna did not feel too well pleased with Master Tom, and did not hesitate to say so.

"It is not possible to express what I feel, Mr. Hewley," she said to him. "That a man for whom I felt so much—respect—could not only associate with such people, and *such* a woman—but allow them to intrude into his friend's house, and could—could——"

It was difficult for Lorna to proceed, so, womanlike, she swerved a little and asked—

"Ah! Mr. Hewley, how could you do it? How *could* you?"

Tom seemed to be weighing the amount of his sin very remorsefully as he thoughtfully replied—

"True. How could I?"

"You always struck me as being a gentlemanly fellow."

"I am *so* sorry," said Tom absently.

"Sorry!" echoed Lorna.

"That I should so fail to come up to your expectations, I mean."

"Good gracious! What were my expectations?" asked Lorna.

Tom smiled broadly, and with the most uncalled-for assurance, said—

"Me."

"You! Well, of all the——" Again it was difficult to proceed, and again Lorna fell back upon a question. "Who was the *person*, pray?"

"*Which* person?"

"The *creature!*"

"*Which* creature?"

"Good gracious, how dense you are! There was only *one* creature."

No, Tom was not dense by any means, but he was content for the time to be considered so. With a very non-understanding air, he answered—

"I thought there were three."

" There was only *one* female."

" Oh! *That* one?"

" Yes, sir, *that* one!"

" Oh! *that* one was a woman."

" Dear me!" said Lorna sarcastically. Then with her back turned to Tom, but with her eyes on a mirror in which she could watch the expression of his face, she queried—

" Known her long?"

" Oh, yes, a long time. Years, in fact."

" Yes, she looks years—many, many years! I can't say much for your taste."

" She isn't my taste."

" No? What is?"

Tom edged a little closer to Lorna, and, looking over her shoulder, watched the expression of *her* face in the mirror, as he replied—

" Some one with a young, lovely face, and a fresh, innocent heart—sweet, wholesome, honest, and loving."

" Am *I* all those pretty things?" asked Lorna.

" Yes, and a hundred other pretty things as well, that I will tell you about one of these days—if you will only let me."

" One of these days! I've no engagement between three and four, Mr. Hewley. I shall be quite disengaged at that time."

" After which, Miss Mannerly, I hope you will be engaged for the rest of your life," said the bold, bad Tom.

" Mr. Hewley, hope is a very good tonic if you feel a little run down. Take it in large doses till 3 P.M., when your physician will see you again." And Lorna, with the most provoking little smile at Tom, which made that already deeply-in-love young man fall deeper still into Cupid's toils, left him and went to her room, while Tom went on the terrace to smoke a cigar and watch her window.

As he went out of the window, Lady Walgrove entered at the door, followed by our old friend, the bush parson, Mr. Benn.

"Pray come in, Mr.—Mr.——" she said.

"Benn—Walter Benn, Lady Walgrove."

Lady Walgrove was studying the card she held in her hand, and was wondering who her visitor was. In her sweet, ladylike manner she said—

"Please sit down; I have not the honour of knowing you, Mr. Benn."

"No, Lady Walgrove, few people know me. I've lived too long away from England. Just returned from Australia—in fact, arrived only two days ago."

"Australia! Ah, my darling son——"

"Oh, yes! it was of him I came to speak," replied Benn, with such intense sympathy and sadness in his tone that Lady Walgrove wondered why he had called upon her.

"You knew him, then?"

"Yes, it was my pleasure to know him intimately for some time."

Still she wondered at the sadness of his manner. Nor could Mr. Benn understand the look of happiness that was on her face, as she said—

"Any friend of my dear son is welcome here. When and where did you meet?"

"At Woolloogolonga Gully, on the back-blocks, poor fellow!"

"Poor boy! Yes, he must have suffered terribly."

"Ah, yes! I was not with him at the time; his suffering was all over before I got there. It was a quiet resting-place under the wattle-trees. I had them planted myself, and took a snapshot of it. I thought you might like to have a copy——"

As he took out his pocket-book to find the photograph, Tom strolled into the room. As he met Mr. Benn, he stopped in dumb surprise and dread. Mr. Benn took his hand, and said—

"Mr. Hewley, I do declare! What a strange coincidence! You were there, of course. I called to give this to Lady Walgrove—a picture of the grave—you know."

It was now Mr. Benn's turn to be astonished, for Jack came into the chamber, and met his gaze, full-eyed and silently. Jack, surprised and horrified as he was for the moment, recovered himself quickly, and said, with much seeming pleasure—

"Ah, Mr. Benn! Glad to meet you again." Taking the photograph from Mr. Benn's hand, he added, "Why, a photograph of poor *Jack Mowbray's* grave! And a good one, too! Yours? Poor Mowbray! He was a good fellow. You remember, Mr. Benn, you rather liked him, I think? Sad, his death—was it not? How beautifully you read the service! And how we all sorrowed for poor *Jack Mowbray!*—the friend I've told my mother about so often. So glad you've called and met my dear mother. My sister, too—you must meet her. Where is she, by the way?"

"Mr.——" Benn was going to say "Mowbray," but Jack anticipated him, and said heartily—

"Please do not be so formal, Benn. Call me Jack. Jack Landale now, you know. It used to be Landon in the old bush days. I could not bear Landale then. Now——".

Tom attracted Lady Walgrove's attention in order to divert her for the time from observing Jack's confusion and fear. Jack took immediate advantage of this, and whispered, in an agony of entreaty, to Mr. Benn—

"You will not betray me? I can explain. For her sake, promise me you will not betray me!"

Mr. Benn was as straight as the proverbial die. Naturally, he knew nothing of the compact between Landale and Mowbray, but it was obvious that some deception was being practised upon Lady Walgrove, and he could not consent to be a party to the fraud. He answered—

"I don't know. I shall do what is right."

"It is right for you to be silent," pleaded Jack.

"Is it? I must think it over."

"At least you will be silent till you have heard my explanation? Promise me that! Do, I beg of you."

Benn liked Jack, esteemed him, believed in him. There was such real grief and horror depicted on the man's face that he was sorry for his sufferings, however guilty he might prove to be, and he answered hesitatingly—

"Yes, I'll promise that. Afterwards—well, I'll do what is right."

Jack gave a sigh of intense relief. The danger was over for the moment at least.

"Mother, take Mr. Benn and find Sybil, will you?" he said, anxious to be alone with Tom.

"Yes! come with me, please, Mr. Benn. So glad you have met my son—my dear son—again," said Lady Walgrove, giving her hand affectionately to Mr. Benn.

"Yes, Lady Walgrove, delighted," stammered the honest little man; "that is, delighted to meet you, too, delighted." And, confused and much distressed, he left the room with her.

Jack sank into a chair with a groan, saying—

"Tom, it must come. Benn will never hide the truth."

"I'm not so sure of that. He's a rattling good fellow, and when he has heard your story——"

Jack broke in hurriedly, saying—

"Then, there's Sybil. She suspects, Tom. She's changed to me since last night—*utterly* changed."

"So was Lorna at first; but she's all right now. At least she will be 'from three to four.'"

"They do not believe your yarn, Tom," said Jack, rising and ringing the bell.

"Well, it *was* thin; I must own that. I say, what was the matter with those two? Was it whisky, or——"

"I'm going to ask Wong. I fancy he's responsible for that."

In answer to the bell, Wong glided in, as imperturbable as ever. Jack scanned him narrowly as he asked—

" Did you hear those people last night say anything while I was away?"

" Allee samee 'Stralia man and Sallee woman?"

" Allee samee."

Wong nodded his head in the affirmative.

" What?"

" Sallee she say she all shivers, and she dlinks some whisky."

Here Wong smiled his particular smile.

" Yes?"

" And 'Stralia man say he got the jlumps, den he take allee samee whisky." Wong smiled once more.

" Yes?"

" Then Llandarin man heap fust shlop—lawyer feller —he say, you make a mess if more whisky you hab."

" Nothing more?"

Wong shook his head in reply.

" Man he whisky take—Sallee woman whisky take." Wong smiled again.

" That whisky was allee samee strong—eh, Wong?"

Once more Wong smiled.

" Seemed allee samee effect like opium. Why did you allee samee mixee that whisky?"

" Both go sleep—much helpee boss. Sallee woman too much talkee-talkee."

" Far too much," groaned poor Jack, remembering Sybil's appearance while Sal was screaming.

" 'Stralia man Wong lemember all 'long—Woolloo-golonga Gully time."

" What's that?" said the startled Jack.

" Hulloa!" exclaimed the equally interested Tom.

" When did you see him there?" Jack asked eagerly.

" Allee samee Tlompson's s'lecshun go burn."

" The night Jack L—that is, Mowbray—died?" Wong nodded in answer. " I remember him now! The man who beat you?"

"Wong ears hab got. Wong listen allee time he talkee-talkee to Sallee woman."

"Yes. And you had heard something he did not wish you to hear?"

Wong nodded with something that was almost akin to energy for him.

"What was that?" queried Jack.

"He muchee heap talkee. Wong not muchee hear, but he say, 'Who the blazes is that?' and Sallee woman say, 'She allee samee your daughter.'"

"Who was his daughter? Who?"

Wong was about to reply, but Sybil entered. She looked very pale and distressed. Seeing Jack, she hesitated, and said faintly—

"I beg your pardon; I did not know you were engaged."

"Pray come in," murmured Jack, in a tone scarce less faint than her own.

"I'll run away, Miss Landale," Tom said discreetly to her. Then, turning to Jack, he whispered as he left the room, "I shall be on hand if you want me."

Jack dismissed Wong.

"Wong, I'll see you again presently. Go now."

Wong went, and Jack turned with downcast eyes and beating heart to Sybil, saying—

"What is it, Sybil?"

"I am very unhappy, Jack." He feared she was about to speak of Sal, and he trembled. But she said something else—something that made his heart bound with joy. It was—"I've refused Lord Thorland, Jack."

For a moment he could not speak. All was forgotten but the great, glorious fact that she was not to marry Lord Thorland. What relief! What happiness! In as firm a tone as he could muster, he asked—

"Why?"

"I do not love him," Sybil replied simply.

"Does that make you unhappy?"

"He's a good man."

"He's a splendid fellow!" cried Jack, all the more enthusiastically now that Sybil had refused him. "But what are you unhappy about?" This was asked with deep anxiety. He dreaded her answer. It came slowly and sadly from her lips—

"You."

"Me?"

"Yes. Yesterday you told me that you had never loved."

"Yes?"

"And had never married."

"Well?"

"*Jack, I heard what that woman said.*"

Jack shook as with an ague for a moment, then, with all his nerves a-tingle with fear, he said very quietly—

"What did you hear?"

Sybil was holding on very tight to the back of a chair. She, too, was trembling, but she answered all too distinctly.

"I heard her say she was—Mrs. John Landale."

So she had heard that, after all! The horrible secret was out, so far as Sal was concerned. Jack could not speak. He felt stunned and dazed. After a moment, Sybil asked quietly—

"Have you nothing to say, Jack?"

"Nothing."

Naturally Sybil interpreted this as an avowal that Sal was his wife. Poor girl! She knew not why the thought was so horrible to her. But how horrible—how unbearable it was! Almost voiceless, she whispered—

"Then—it—is—true?"

True that Sal was his wife? No, thank God! Not quite so terrible as that, and yet he dare not say so. He could only stammer—

"She is Mrs. John Landale."

Sybil sank into a chair and buried her face in her hands. For some time there was a dead silence in the room. The clock ticked out the moments on the mantelpiece, but their hearts beat almost as audibly. When Sybil had the power to speak, she said—

" You told me you had never loved!"

" That was the truth."

" That you had never married?" She asked this with strained eyes, drawn, white lips, and tightly clasped hands.

Jack remained silent.

" Answer me, Jack!" she begged.

" I cannot," he whispered despairingly.

There was another prolonged silence, again to be broken by Sybil's quiet, sweet voice, saying—

" Then she is your—your——" Her lips could hardly pronounce the word—" your wife?"

Not a word could Jack reply; he could not deny the lie, nor could he admit the truth. He was in a hopeless knot, that could not even be cut, much less untied.

" Say something, Jack! Something to ease this awful pain!" implored the poor girl, pressing her hand on her heart. " Say something, do! Do! I don't understand why I should suffer so terribly. Other men have married the wrong woman, and, after all, it is *your* life—not *mine*. And yet—no, I feel it is *my* life too. What is it, Jack? Why do I suffer so? What is it? Tell me—tell me! In pity, tell me!"

Jack's heart ached to take her in his arms, tell her the whole truth, or to grovel at her feet and entreat forgiveness for the cruel fraud he had practised on her and the suffering he had brought her. Brokenly, he said—

" Sybil, God knows—that I—I—I would rather die than see you suffer so. But—there is nothing to be said —nothing to be done. I cannot—cannot help you. Let me go!" He moved to leave her, but she gently stayed him.

" No! No! Think a little what you are saying! You may have been led and tricked into a—marriage—of which you are now ashamed. It is a terrible mistake, but we love you, and we will try—try—to make your—your——" How could she speak the word? It seemed such a desecration. "Your—wife—welcome."

The thought was horrible to Jack. Sal welcomed by Sybil! "No—no—a thousand times—No!" he cried fervently. "God forbid! Never think of it! Never dream of it! You don't know what you are saying."

"Then teach me, Jack. Make me know—make me understand. You have made a mistake in your life, eh? A mistake—yes, dear. But I—that is—we—we can forgive that. But we must know what the error is. You have deceived us—but you are a good man."

Jack shuddered, and cursed himself for a villain.

"I! I—a good man!" he moaned.

"Yes, I feel it, I know it. There's some secret, Jack, that you are afraid to tell us. Have courage, dear. *There is no wrong that you have been guilty of that our great love cannot forgive.*"

"O God, forgive me! God forgive me!" he moaned, and, tottering to a chair, sank into it, with his arms on the table and his face hidden.

Gently Sybil went to him, and, kneeling at his feet, put her dear hands round his neck, and said with the tenderness of a mother and the yearning of a lover—

"Dear, dear Jack, you have not been with us very long, but we have loved you—mother and I—mother, all your life; I, since I can remember—while you were away from us. And now that you are with us that love has deepened, strengthened, and our whole souls are bound up in you. Jack, dear Jack, for my sake, for our dear mother's sake—*trust us.* If you have sinned, we will help you to atone. If you are suffering, we will suffer with you. *Only trust us!* Do, Jack! Do!"

"Trust you! Trust the dear mother! With all I have. With my life here and hereafter. With my soul. But not with this."

"What can it be? What wrong can you have committed that we may not know? There can be nothing that a man should keep from his mother and sister, Jack."

"Oh, stop, Sybil! For mercy sake, stop!"

"I will not, Jack! I cannot. I am urged on to this in spite of myself. The whole of me is calling for the whole of you to reveal yourself. There is a will beyond my will—a power beyond my power, forcing me, guiding me, telling me that all this wrong can be righted if you will let me help you, Jack. You must! You *shall!*"

Some strange feeling—she knew not what—held her in control. It forced her to seize Jack and hold him close to her as she said passionately—

"I *will* know! You shall not wreck our lives by this silence! You *shall* tell me!"

Then Jack lost control of himself. Her sweet face was upturned to his, her lovely form nestled close to him, her dear arms were around him. He forgot all but his love, and seized her in his arms, kissing her passionately again and again.

"Sybil!" he cried, "my dear—my darling—my love! I love—I love—I love you! I love you!" Then, with a sudden revulsion, he thrust her from him. "Ah, no! Go! Go! For God's sake, go! Leave me! Don't come near me! Don't touch me! I am a lie—one great living lie! I am a coward—a false hound—a cur! But I love you! No—don't come near me! I love you! Believe that always. Love you! Do you know what that means? You don't! You can't! How can you? Let me go away —anywhere—only away from you! I can't bear it! It is maddening me—killing me! I must go! I must! I will!" And he rushed to the door.

But Sybil rushed in front of him and blocked the way, screaming—

"Jack! Jack! Our mother—our mother! You'll kill her! You'll kill her! Stop! Pray—pray do not go!"

"God help me! God guide me! What am I to do?"

Lady Walgrove, entering the room, heard him.

"Jack!" she cried, in horror and alarm. "Dear Jack, what is the matter? Sybil dear, what is it?"

At the sound of her voice, Jack instantly controlled himself. At any price she must be spared. And he replied—

"Oh, it is nothing. Nothing."

But Lady Walgrove was not to be misled.

"Nothing?" she asked. "Nothing! You must not tell your mother that, Jack. Sybil, you have been crying. Jack, you are white and trembling. Tell me— what is it? I am frightened, Jack! What is it?"

Jack, taking her in his arms, tried to comfort her.

"There! there! Do not worry. I have been unnerved—a bit of a shock. But it mustn't trouble you, dear."

"Not trouble me? Do you know what you are saying? Can my son have a sorrow, and I, his mother, not feel it? A grief, and not share it? What is wrong? Tell me. I will know."

Petting and trying to soothe her, Jack said—

"Now, dear, you are not to be vexed and worried about my little troubles. I came home—that is, here— to make you happy, not to cause you pain. You have got to forget this, dear heart, and we shall all be happy, as we were yesterday."

The dormant strength in Sybil's nature, hitherto uncalled upon, asserted itself. She took her mother in her arms, as her mother would have held her when a child, and, facing Jack, she said firmly—

"Mother, there is a secret Jack is keeping from us, that he fears to tell us. He thinks that some wrong that he has done, while away from us, will, if we know it, separate us."

The fear of another parting from her son sent a thrill of dread through the mother's body.

"Separate us again, Sybil! Sybil!"

The girl stood erect, firm, determined, holding her

mother with a strength that she had never known before, and, with deep earnestness and conviction, she said—

"Tell him that he is mistaken, mother. Tell him that he does not know us—that he wrongs us to suppose for one moment that our love is so weak, so paltry, as to shrink from him for a fault he has committed, is sorry for, and can atone for. Tell him he is mistaken."

Like a child repeating a lesson, the mother answered—

"You are mistaken, Jack!"

"Tell him, whatever his sin is, God can forgive, and so can we."

"Whatever your sin is, Jack, we can forgive."

"That there is no sin he has committed, no wrong he has done—that can equal the sin and wrong he will be guilty of, if he leaves us again."

"Leave us again!"

The words struck on the mother's ears with a dead, dull, far-off sound, as one hears a voice in a dream. "Leave us again!" she cried. "Leave us again! Jack!" She was trembling, her eyes blazing, her fingers clutching the air.

"Jack!" Going to him, she took him in her arms. "Jack! You can't be so cruel, so callous! Think—I beg of you—think what that means! I was old—you have given me youth. I was in despair—you have given me hope. I was wretched—you have made me happy. Compared with what I feel for you now, my early love for my boy was nothing. It was poor—weak. It is now strong; it is part of me; it *is* me. Leave us again! No—no—no! I could not bear it! Oh—I should die!"

Jack knew that she spoke the truth. What could he do but yield? As long as he could, he would put off the evil hour when she must learn the whole story of the wrong he had done. Placing her gently in a chair, he knelt by her side, saying—

"There! Be comforted, poor mother. I will never leave you until you thrust me from you."

"Thank God! Thank God! Now, dear, what is all this trouble?"

"Let me forget it—at least for to-day."

"No, Jack, you are wrong," spoke Sybil firmly. "We can never be happy with a hidden danger hanging over us. What we can see and know, we can fight, and will fight with you to the end, but we will not live in the dark. I must tell mother all I know."

"Ah! don't."

"I must," said Sybil, turning to her mother. "Mother, Jack has made a mistake which he thinks is a crime. It will pain you, but you will forgive. Jack has deceived us."

"How?"

"Sybil! I implore you!" Jack cried.

"I will speak," she answered. "He has led us to believe he was not married. He is."

"Married! To whom? When?"

"That I do not know. He will not tell."

"Ah!" said the mother. "The happiness yesterday —this grief to-day! Jack, it has been told me that there was a disgraceful scene here last night; that three disreputable people were with you—two men and a woman —that the woman and one of the men were carried out of the house in drunken insensibility; that Mr. Hewley said they were his friends. Who were they? Who was that woman?"

"Jack's wife, mother."

"Jack's wife!" repeated the mother in horror.

"Yes."

"Horrible! Horrible for us all—but worst of all for you, my dear son, for it is your life that is spoiled. But not ruined, dear. If she is vile, that does not make you so. You have made a mistake—not sinned."

"That is not all," sadly answered Jack. "There is something else, there is a sin that I have committed, that I am daily, hourly committing, that I can never atone for. Will you promise me that if ever the time shall come—and it may come at any moment—when the truth shall be known to you, that you will believe that I was led into it by no base desire, no self-seeking? I did it for the best. I may have been weak—wrong—wanting in thought—but never wanting in affection—never wanting in love. Will you believe this? Promise me you will!"

Lady Walgrove, kissing him, said solemnly—

"We promise this. We will never believe evil of you. Never—never—never!"

Here Spurdy came in, with a note on a tray. Jack opened and read its contents, with a look of surprise and fear. Turning to Spurdy, he said—

"Show them up into my room."

"What is it, dear? No fresh trouble?"

"I do not know. I must leave you for a little while. I will come to you as soon as I can."

And, bowing his head, Jack left the mother and sister alone.

CHAPTER XXVII

SMUDGEE VISITS HER ANCESTRAL HALLS

WHEN Smudgee got into her hansom cab "with a horse in it," as she expressed it, she told the driver to take her to Somerset House, but that was merely to deceive the open-eared porter who held her skirt away from the mud on the wheel. As soon as she got to the Strand, she poked up the little door in the roof of the cab, and bade the driver take her to "265A Stamford Street, Blackfriars; and see here, cabby," she added, "let this racer of yours git a move on him. I'm goin' to ketch a train, not to bury me gran'mother."

"Oh, indeed! miss," said the cabby. "Werry glad, I'm sure, miss. I thought, p'r'aps, as you was goin' back to school, you wouldn't want to 'urry."

"Goin' back to school! Who are you gettin' at? I've finished at a school where they begins where sich as you leaves off. Now, suppose you takes that red nose o' yours out o' that rat-trap, and looks where yer drivin' to. If your *'orse* is a jumper, your *cab* ain't, and, as it can't leap that coal-cart, you'll hev to drive round it—see?"

"Yes, miss," said the unmoved cabby, skirting the coal-cart as a London cabman alone could do. "But don't you worry about such trifles as coal-carts. Why, that little 'oss o' mine gits over bigger things than a coal-cart. Why, miss, I've known him to git over a policeman afore now."

"Hev yer? And what was the verdict?"

"Justifiable 'omicide, miss."

"Oh! D'ye think of killin' anything to-day? 'Cos, if you do, p'r'aps you won't mind puttin' it orf until after I leave yer. *I* ain't takin' no hinquests in *mine*, this mornin'. Will yer git a move on this venerable old bag o' barrel-hoops, and let me keep my appointments, or do you expect a lady to git out and lead yer old crock?"

Here, the cabman turned too sharply round Waterloo Place, where, owing to the greasy state of the road, the horse promptly fell on his knees, and, after lifting his head a moment, apparently to see the effect it had had upon his fare, quietly lay down to await further developments.

"There you are!" said Smudgee. "Just what I expected! Why didn't your master send a driver out with this old knacker, and leave you at 'ome to attend to your gardenin'?"

"Oh, it ain't that, miss, believe me; I ain't the *gardener*. But, you see, this 'oss used to drive the Archbishop o' Canterbury, and when he 'eard your bad language, he just waited a bit to pray for you. He's a remarkably relig'us 'oss is that o' mine, miss."

"Oh, is he? Well, there's a shillin', my good man. Git some kind friends to 'elp you lift 'im orf his knees and carry him to the Salvation Army Barracks, as a shinin' example. He's a bit too good for mere cab-work. So long! My compliments to the Archbishop, when next you dine with him, and tell him it 'ud be better to confine his 'orses to mornin' and evenin' prayers. Permiskus worship in crowded thoroughfares is a bit likely to disarrange the traffic." And Smudgee, jumping lightly into another hansom, was driven off to 265A Stamford Street.

"Well," said cabby to the crowd, "she's an 'ot un, if ever there was one! And I've met a few in my time."

When Smudgee arrived at her destination in Stamford Street, she was met at the door by her old chum, Dan Murphy, who, saluting her, said—

"A bit behind, Smudgee, as the boy said when he felt the dog's teeth in the back of his pants. Wot's kep' yer?"

"Well, I got a 'orse in my cab as must 'a' been a son o' Carbine's, and, as I objected to his carrying me along

346

at a mile a minute, which was his regular figure, he just chucked up the job, and I'd to git another." Looking up at the driver, she asked, "When do you think *you* could contrive to land us at Waterloo Station?"

"Well, miss," the cabman answered, "that depends a great deal upon when we start, and whether you prefer to go straight there, or whether you'd like to see a little bit o' life fust. There's St. Paul's, and Westminster Abbey."

"Thank you, cabby, but I'm full up o' relig'us 'orses and drivers, at present, and I ain't goin' to church this mornin'. *You* don't 'appen to be a friend o' the Archbishop o' Canterbury, do yer?"

"Well, no, miss, not *now*. We ain't on wisitin' terms, just now. My old woman and his missus couldn't 'it it orf, somehow, and, as my old woman said to me——"

"I ain't dyin' to hear what your old woman said to you. She must hev said some rather nasty things to you in her time, judgin' by the worried look in your face. But if it'll ease your mind to confide in a friend, go ahead. Only, remember, it'll be in your time—not mine. Yer see, I ain't engaged yer by the hour, but by the job. Now, what is it? Waterloo Station or your old woman?"

"Well, miss, I think it's Waterloo. I think I'd better make sure of that now. My old woman is a dead cert, always."

And, with a " kim up!" to his horse, he bowled along to that station at a pace that satisfied even the rapid Smudgee.

Booking to Hayes, the two friends were soon on their way to Landale Abbey. Dan had done his best to look like (as he expressed it) " M'Ginty in his best Sunday clothes," that he might impress Jack with his prosperity. Smudgee, we know, had done her best to look like the kind of ladies Jack was now mixing with. Her true little heart was beating so strongly that she could hardly breathe at times, and yet, so excited was she at the thought of meeting Jack again, that she talked on fast and unconnectedly, all the way down. Jack was the theme, of course, and Dan needed all his innate delicacy and good nature to keep him from answering a little impatiently, when she asked him, for the twentieth time, how he thought she was looking, and what he thought " Jack would say to 'er 'at?"

" Be gob!" said the diplomatic Dan, " it's a little he'll be havin' to say to your hat. He'll be too much taken up with your swate face."

Smudgee smiled at the compliment, and looked at her face in the carriage window, the while she gave Dan a playful little kick, saying—

" Arrah! go along with yer blarney, yer soft-sawdherin' old Mickey! I'm ashamed of you!"

While travelling, they talked over the old times at Woolloogolonga Gully, what sacrifices they were willing to make for Jack, of the many kindnesses he had shown them, what a good, unselfish fellow he was. They wondered how he would meet them; whether he would be glad to see them, or whether he would have changed. Smudgee said she was sure he would not, while Dan was ready to " stake his loife on ut." Still, both were very nervous, and Smudgee terribly anxious. She was a brave, self-possessed little soul, but Jack was the god of her idolatry; she had not seen him for so long, and never among such surroundings, that she was quite white and trembling when the dignified Spurdy passed her and Dan on to a resplendent footman, who conducted them into Jack's sanctum. Never had Smudgee seen such a place. Well might her mother and Nat call it a " pallis," she thought. It never entered her unselfish, faithful mind for a moment that all this might be her own; that Jack was but an usurper, fraudulently occupying the place of the man who had stood to her in the position of a father. She had gathered up, bit by bit, the whole story, and knew that Wolfe and her parents were fighting to get the property for her, but that that could be to the detriment of Jack was not, to her, a thing to be thought of for a moment. She was here to help her friend. Her " dear knight " was in peril, and her duty was to avert the danger, if she could.

Her quick intuition, her love for Jack, and her simple honesty and sense of right made her far more of a match for her elders than many a man of experience would have been. Whether Jack would be pleased to see her concerned her far more deeply than whether she was to be mistress of this lovely place.

She started violently, then held the arm of the chair in a wild clutch as she heard Jack approaching the room. She wanted to jump up and fling her arms about him, but was not sure that was the society-way of meeting friends, and fear of being ridiculous kept her motionless, until Jack had entered and said, in a constrained tone, " Smudgee ! Murphy !"

So changed was his tone that a chill went to Smudgee's heart, and it was with a little gasp of surprise that she ejaculated—

" Jack !"

Dan was surprised, too, at Jack's reception of them. They did not know what the poor fellow had been going through that day.

" Plazed ter see yez agin, Mowbray," was Dan's greeting.

" Call me Landale, please, Dan," said Jack, in his old kind tone, and Dan hit himself a blow on the side of his head with his clenched fist as he said—

" The curse o' Crummel on me for an omethawn ! Av coorse ! Landale it is !"

Then there was a pause. Jack looked from Dan to Smudgee, and, for a moment, wondered whether they were there to injure him.

" Ain't yer glad ter see us, Jack ?" whimpered Smudgee.

Jack looked at the puckered lips and the moistening eyes, and then asked—

" Do you come as friends or enemies ?"

Smudgee was deeply hurt at the question. That she should doubt Jack was impossible. How could he ever doubt her?

" Jack, was I ever a sneak?" she queried.

Jack thought of all the hours he had passed in the Never-Never Land with the leal-hearted child, and answered cordially—

" No, Smudgee."

" Very well, then!"

Dan had felt the question too, and he asked—

" Was I iver a cur, Jack?"

" No, Dan."

" Very well, then!"

Then Jack thawed, and, with all his natural good-fellowship, echoed—

" Very well, then! I am both a sneak and a cur to doubt either of you. Shake hands."

After he had done so, Smudgee asked, rather piteously—

" Ain't yer goin' ter kiss me, Jack?"

" Yes, but you're growing into such a young lady, Smudgee, that I'm half afraid!"

" Young lady!" This, from Jack, was praise indeed. " Young lady!" Then the hat was all right, after all, and she was in the same street with his other—and more aristocratic—friends.

" Am I really, Jack? Really? Now, give it us straight! Really growing into a young lady?"

Jack temporised.

" You've improved wonderfully."

This was not too explicit, and Smudgee, longing for praise in detail, inquired—

" Wot about me 'at?"

" There's a lot about it. Flowers and feather, and birds and—— "

Smudgee's face grew set and stern, and it was with a very firm voice that she said—

" Look at me straight, Jack!"

Jack complied with her request, and looked straight at her, saying—

"There! Is that straight enough?"

Smudgee studied his face carefully, then, taking off her hat, and sticking the hatpins into it, banged it on the floor, muttering—

"Yus, quite! It's a fright—and I'm—I'm—I'm a guy!" And the dejected child flung herself into a chair and bit her lip to keep herself from crying.

"Indeed you're not. You're a very pretty little girl, but—— "

"The 'at's off—well off—right off!" And Smudgee kicked at the despised headgear.

"Looks like it, doesn't it?"

"And the rest o' me? Wot about me altogether? Am I *all* wrong?"

"You could never be that, Smudgee. Now, let's talk of something else."

"No. Let me know the worst. Am I a guy?"

"Look here, Smudgee! you're not. Is she, Dan?"

"Be gob! she's not."

"But we'll have the next eruption a little quieter as to colour, Smudgee."

"I see. I'm loud. I'm a 'ruption. That's an earthquake, ain't it?"

"It sometimes follows one."

"I've shook the earth. I've 'rupted it." This was said very sadly; then, with a little shake of her hair, Smudgee fell into her old manner, saying, "Jack, I know yer!"

"That's right, Smudgee. Now, I'll have another kiss," said Jack, advancing towards her. But Smudgee waved him off, saying—

"Not in this frock, Jack. Some 'ruptions is catchin'."

"I shall catch nothing unpleasant from you, Princess," Jack replied, again advancing towards her. But somehow, for some reason not clear even to herself, Smudgee could not let him kiss her again just then.

Jack rang the bell, and Wong entered. He looked out of the corners of his almond-shaped eyes, but gave no sign as he recognised Dan and Smudgee.

"Some wine and biscuits. And some whisky. It's my shout, Dan, and I suppose the old poison will answer the purpose." Then, turning to Wong, he added, "And, Wong, no mixee this time!"

Wong smiled, and was about to leave the room, when Smudgee, arms akimbo, barred the way, asking saucily—

"Now, look here, my bloomin' hemperer, who am I— eh?"

Wong smiled, and answered, almost with some show of feeling—

"You allee samee Smudgee."

"Yus. Me allee samee Smudgee. And why couldn't you allee samee say so when you see me fust?"

"Wong no talkee much. Wong lemember all along, allee samee."

"Shake, you bloomin', golden old griffin! Shake!" Shaking his hand, and pointing to Dan, she said, "And now, who's that?"

"He allee samee Dan Murphy."

"And phwat for couldn't yez allee samee say so when yer see me fust?" repeated Dan. "Shake!" And he shook his hand.

Wong smiled so widely that Dan exclaimed—

"Stop! Yer'll crack yer face! Be gob! Wong, but yer beauty'll niver save yer sowl."

Wong smiled as if that was of no importance, and went out.

"And now, what has happened that you are here?" asked Jack of Dan.

Dan bowed to Smudgee, saying—

"Ladies fust. Go ahead, Smudgee."

"It's all about the pallis," Smudgee began.

"The pallis?" queried Jack.

"Yus. And——" Here she was interrupted by

Wong's entrance with the refreshments. When he had placed them on the table, he smiled and again left the room.

Jack busied himself helping Dan and Smudgee, and asked Smudgee what she meant.

" Well, we're here about the pallis and Mr. John Landale."

" Go on, Smudgee."

" Now, don't hurry me, Jack, or you'll put me out, and I want ter be particular. You're 'ere as Jack Landale, ain't yer?"

" Yes."

Smudgee looked carefully round, and, lowering her voice, whispered—

" And, 'atween ourselves, you're Jack Mowbray?"

" You know I am, Smudgee."

" This pallis and everyfink belongs to Jack Landale wot's dead?"

" It belongs to Jack Landale's heiress, and she is Smudgee — otherwise Lucy Landale, John Landale's daughter."

" Does it? Well, we'll see about that. A nice kind o' duchess I should make in a place like this, wiv my taste in 'ats, I don't think! However—to proceed. Muvver and my dearly-beloved Uncle Nat was at the Alhambra a few nights ago, when who should see 'em but Dan Murphy! Now, you chip in, Dan."

Dan chipped in, as directed, with—

" ' Be gob!' I sez to mesilf, ' the very same parties as I'm wantin'!' So I keep me eye on 'em, an' followed 'em to the Starlington Hotel, an' hung about the next day, until I kem on Miss Smudgee alone, an' we had a taste of a conversation together."

" And we agreed to act in the matter o' the pallis and Jack Mowbray as pards, didn't us, Dan?"

" In order to get forwarder, I'll go backwarder. Afther yer left Woolloogolonga Gully, I went down to Sydney, an' worked on the docks, an' had me drinks at Watson's Hotel, where, wan night, Mr. Nat Rudder—otherwise Nat Berker—bein' half seas over, began blusterin' about goin' to the ould counthry to claim an estate an' fortin left by Jack Landale, that Jack Mowbray had done him out of, he said, as his sisther Sarah was Jack Landale's wife an' his niece Loocy was Jack Landale's heiress. He swore blue murther agin you, Jack, an' said he'd jail yez for seven years."

" Much obliged to him, I'm sure. Go ahead, Dan."

" He was sailing on the *Oruba* the home trip, as fust-class saloon passenger, wid his sisther Sarah, his niece Smudgee, and his solicitor Mr. Raffael M. Wolfe, Attorney, Money-Lender, of Castlereagh Street—who, by the same token, I knew to be one of the biggest blackguards in Sydney."

" Which is saying something ! I've met the individual, and I am inclined to think you are right."

" Well," Dan continued, " havin' a friendly feelin' towards yerself, Jack, an' jist shpoilin' for a look uv the ould counthry, I shipped on the same boat, as stoker, wid um. But they got off at Marseilles."

" Muvver and me wantin' to study the Parisian fashions."

" And meself had to stoke to London, an' so missed 'em intoirely until oi met 'em at the Alhambra."

" And as soon as he met me, o' course, I began braggin' about comin' into a fortin and a pallis, to him."

" ' And how'll yez do that?' sez oi to her."

" ' As Jack Landale's daughter,' sez I to him."

" ' Nat Rudder's daughter,' sez oi to her.

" ' No fear !' sez I, ' fur she's passin' Mr. Nat. Rudder off as me dearly-beloved uncle,' sez I to him."

" ' Divil an uncle he is to you,' sez oi. ' He's yer natteral born father, married to yer mother at Polson's Matrimonial Agency, George Street, Sydney, March 20, 1887,' sez oi to her."

Jack, who had been listening with a face strained with feverish anxiety, started up, crying—

"What's that? Sal was married to Nathan Rudder before she met Jack Landale?"

"She was that—two years before."

"Legally married?"

"As legal as you make 'em—in Sydney, New South Wales."

Jack was trembling with eager excitement, as he said—

"Dan, be careful what you are saying. You do not know how much hangs on this. Can you prove it?"

Dan helped himself to a stiff drink of the wine of Scotia, and smilingly asked—

"Can oi dhrink whisky?"

Jack looked relieved from a mighty incubus, as indeed he was. At least, Sal had no claim on Sybil and her mother. Thank God for that!

"How did you learn this?" he eagerly asked.

"Aisy enough. Me an' the Rev. James Polson run that same Marriage Registry betwixt us, kapin' an advertisement daily in the public press as follows." Pulling out his pocket-book, he took a cutting from a newspaper, and read, "'Polson's, 480, George Street, Sydney. Marriages celebrated, any denomination, by an ordained clergyman, with due solemnity, in strictest privacy, at Polson's, 480, George Street, Sydney, from 10 A.M. till 9 P.M., daily, Saturdays included. No notice required. Fee, 10/6. Or, marriage with guaranteed gold wedding-ring and necessary witnesses provided, £1, 1s. od. *P.S.*—No other charges whatever. All sizes of most costly wedding-rings kept in stock, if required. All cabmen convey couples desirous of being married at Polson's from wharves and railway stations free.'[1] Polson did the ceremony. I shwept the office an' did the witnessing."

"Did Sal ever recognise you?"

---

[1] This advertisement is copied verbatim from an Australian daily newspaper, the address alone being fictitious.

" Divil a recognise! She an' Nat was as full as fiddlers afore they came to the ceremony, an' were blind afore it was over."

Jack started up, and, shaking Dan warmly by the hand, said—

" Dan, old chum, you'll never know the good you've done. I shall never be able to thank or reward you. And you, Smudgee, dear girl! But, do you know what *you've* done, Smudgee? You've robbed yourself of this glorious place and all that it means."

" Not much I ain't! It was never mine to be robbed of. It's yours now, Jack, ain't it?" she asked eagerly.

" I'm afraid not, Smudgee," Jack responded sadly. " But it's not your fault, my dear little friend."

" My beloved uncle can't jail you for seven years now, can he, Jack?"

" I'm not out of the wood yet, Smudgee, but you've helped me to see heaven's own daylight through the trees. And may God bless you!"

CHAPTER XXVIII

IN WHICH MAMIE HEARS SOMETHING TO HER DISADVANTAGE

OVER an extremely artistically decorated shop—not a hundred miles from Old Bond Street—is a large brass scroll, upon which, in a free, running, ladylike hand, is written " Madame Hortense." On a bright afternoon in October there was exposed in the window of this establishment a " perfect dream " of a hat, " a vision of beauty," in the way of a toque, daintily posed on either side of a " thrill " of a matinée blouse. These three gems of madame's art were all her window contained, but these were framed in curtains and draperies of the palest spring-green tulle, fastened with Parma violets tied up with love-knots of silver cord. A mere man would barely have given a glance at the whole, and have passed on, but the ladies stayed and took in the articles in detail, with much interest. All the afternoon, there was a little knot of fair ones round the window. Among them, at one moment, were Mamie and Sal—quite unconscious that they were at the same instant admiring the toque and wondering whether the same man (Jack, of course) would admire it if worn by them and seen by him. In moving from the window, they contrived to jostle each other, and, each turning to apologise at the same moment, met face to face. Each murmured the word " Pardon," and, with that never-failing intuition that women possess, accurately " sized up the other."

Mamie felt a little shudder of repugnance pass through her, as a whiff of common, but very strong, scent from Sal's clothes met her nostrils. Sal mentally told herself that, " on the whole, she was as handsome as Mamie, and knew a lot more." Which she un-

357

doubtedly did—of some things. Mamie's mother was with her, but had not seen Sal. As they walked away, Mamie said—

"What a vulgar woman!"

"Which, honey?" asked the mother.

"The one who pushed against me."

"I didn't see her."

While the two stopped to inspect some diamonds on show a little farther down the street, Sal entered Madame Hortense's "atelier" (as she called it) to ask the price of the "vision" in toques. Madame's assistant named a figure that would have served to keep Sal and her family for a year, at least, at one time, and, in her surprise, she nearly whistled, but the atmosphere of the exquisitely pretty and refined "atelier" choked the sound on her lips. She merely ejaculated "Oh!"

"Madame thinks it a little expensive, perhaps?" suggested the assistant.

Madame had said to herself something which meant the same thing, but was not expressed in quite such ladylike language.

"You see, it is quite the latest thing we have. We have just sent one to the Duchess of Dentshire," said the assistant.

Sal wanted very much to look like a duchess, and, above all, she wished that Jack should think she did. The price, she knew, was beyond her means, at present, but if she was to be mistress of the "pallis" it was but a "flea-bite," as she mentally told herself.

"May I try it on?" she asked.

"Certainly, madame. Will you come this way?" The assistant led Sal into an inner room.

So it came to pass that, when Mamie and her mother walked back from the jeweller's to ask Madame Hortense about that particular toque, they were shown into the same room, to find the charming piece of headgear poised on Sal's handsome but decidedly-vulgar head. That particular toque was a thing of the past, so far as Mamie was concerned. Its subsequent proceedings interested her no more. Sal had robbed it of its charm to her for ever. Still, she had to get a new hat of some kind, and, as she was in the shop, she might as well see what there was to see.

Madame herself sailed majestically in, and, noting the elegance of the two ladies, mentally said, "*Les belles Américaines.*" She asked them to be seated, and requested to know what she could have "the distinguished pleasur-re of showing madame and mademoiselle."

Whatever doubt might have lingered in Sal's mind as to the advisability of buying the toque vanished when she caught sight of Mamie's expression as she saw it on her head. "Jealous!" thought Sal. Turning to the shopwoman, she said—

"I think it suits me" ("down to the ground," she was going to say, but the elegance of the "atelier" checked her), "and I'll take it."

"Thank you, madame. What name, please?" asked the attendant.

What possessed Sal to say what she did, even she might have been puzzled to explain. Was it mental telepathy, or some other occult and unexplainable cause? Who knows? Whatever it was, before she was quite aware that she had begun to speak, the words were out.

"Mrs. John Landale, of Landale Abbey," was what she said, and it was said with her eyes staring straight at poor Mamie.

Mamie was well-bred and brave out of the common, but it required a more than ordinary amount of self-control for her to prevent a cry escaping her lips. Just at that moment, Madame Hortense brought her something to look at. What, Mamie could not have told. There was a beating as of big bells in her ears, a film before her eyes, and a monotonous repetition of "Mrs. John Landale, of Landale Abbey," uttered in a coarse, common voice, dinning into her brain. What will a really brave woman not suffer mentally before she cries aloud?

What Mamie suffered then was torture. There could be no doubt about what the woman had said, for the assistant, half doubting that she had heard aright, made her repeat it.

"What name did you say, madame?"

"Mrs. John Landale, of Landale Abbey," again replied Sal, and once more did she stare full in Mamie's face. She saw very little change there. There was a tightening of the lips, a little pallor of the cheeks, but not another sign that the lady she was rudely staring at was thinking of anything else than the hat madame was holding out for her inspection.

Mrs. D'Olan had heard Sal too, and had started in a running fire of conversation with Madame Hortense in order to cover Mamie's embarrassment.

"Am I to send it there?" asked the attendant, entering Sal's name in her book.

"No," replied Sal, with something as near a blush as her brazen cheeks could show. "I am staying in town just now. Send it to the Starlington Hotel, Leicester Square."

"Will madame pay for it now?" asked the somewhat suspicious shopwoman.

"No," answered Sal sharply. "I'll pay for it when I git it. Let me 'ave it by four this afternoon, please. Not a minute later, or I shall be hout." And, with a curt "Good day," the death-dealer to Mamie's peace of mind sailed out of the shop.

Poor Mamie had now no interest to bestow on anything Madame Hortense had to show or say, and, asking her mother to speak for her, she walked to the street door to breathe the outer air and hide her quivering lips from the sharp eyes of that lady.

When her mother joined her, she murmured—

"Let us go home." And, calling a cab, they were driven to their hotel.

Mrs. D'Olan knew her daughter too well to pester her with any remarks on what they had heard until they were secure from observation in the privacy of their own rooms. Then, taking Mamie in her arms, she said—

"Honey, you don't believe that creature?"

"I don't know what I believe," whispered Mamie. "I am too stunned to think."

"She is some swindler, using the name for bad purposes. She cannot be Mrs. Landale. He would surely never have married such a creature as that."

"It is hard to say whom men will not marry. They do such strange things," answered Mamie, sadly and wearily.

"But he never spoke of being married, and Sybil said he was single."

"There was a reason for not speaking of his marriage, if that woman is his wife."

"I don't believe it. She is a bad, low-down person that Jack would never dream of marrying if he were in his sober senses."

"Perhaps he was not when he married her."

"Well, honey, I can't and won't believe that that man could be such a humbug as to pass for single if he were married. He is too straight. There's something wrong somewhere, and I don't think it's in Jack's locality. Anyway, I'm not going to believe it because that woman said it."

"Nor I. I'm going to learn the truth from other lips than hers, and learn it right away."

Going to the writing-desk, Mamie wrote a telegram to Lady Walgrove, saying that she would much like to run down to Landale next day, and asking if it would be convenient for her to come.

To her deep regret and consternation, she received an answer from Sybil saying that "neither her mother nor herself could receive any one at present, as they were not very well, but they hoped to be able to see her later." A mere ordinary indisposition, Mamie knew, would not prevent Sybil from receiving her. Was there trouble at Landale, and was this woman the cause?

THE NEVER-NEVER LAND

With the business-like faculty of her country-people, Mamie sent for a private detective and commissioned him to find out all he could about Mrs. John Landale, of Landale Abbey, at present stopping at the Starlington Hotel, Leicester Square.

In the course of a few hours, she learned that Mrs. John Landale was staying at that hotel with her brother and daughter, and that she had but lately arrived from Australia. There was but one John Landale, of Landale Abbey, and that was Jack. Sybil had said again and again that she had no near relations save her mother and brother. If this woman *was* Mrs. John Landale, of Landale Abbey, she was Jack's wife. Of that there could be no doubt. He was married to her, doubtless, in his wild days abroad, was ashamed of the union, and was hiding it from the mother and sister. Probably this woman had come to England to assert her rights, had been to Landale, or had written to Lady Walgrove, and that lady, in her distress and grief, was unable to see any one. Hence her refusal.

Mamie had gauged the situation fairly well. That she was not quite right in her conclusions was Jack's fault, not hers. She could not surmise or suspect that Jack was an impostor, and was not John Landale at all. Here Mamie's strong will and common sense came to her aid. If Jack was married, he was not a straight man, nor was he free, and certainly Mamie Doolan (as she called herself, at times) was not going to fight for a married man. Her love might kill, but it should never degrade her. If he belonged to this woman, or any other, he was dead, so far as she was concerned. Meantime, she must wait and watch. Black as circumstances made his case look, there might be some error, and he might be innocent. She could not believe he was so false to his mother and sister. Of course she had no claim on him. He had never pretended anything more than friendship for her, and, if he chose to keep secret a disgraceful or unfortunate marriage, he could do so without much blame.

MAMIE HEARS SOMETHING

So Mamie reasoned, pro and con, over and over again. Always with a bias and a kindly feeling towards Jack in her thoughts, but in her heart, for the first time, was the deep conviction that never could she be his wife. She had feared it after the parting at Queenstown; she knew it now. Her strict sense of right and wrong helped her in this struggle. He had not approached her; she could not make another advance, even if he were free. If, as now seemed almost sure, he was married, she must get the better of her love. She was of too true a nature, too constant to forget, but at least she could and would conquer her passion for him. She dearly loved her parents, and knew how they would grieve if they thought her unhappy. For their sakes, she must fight with herself, and seem happy, as of old. If, when alone, she shed some bitter tears, no one saw them—no one knew. Even her mother was deceived, and told herself that "Mamie had not cared so very much for Jack, after all."

So Mamie bore her disappointment in silence; she was kind and gentle as of yore, and, if possible, more beautiful and attractive. She had admirers by the score, but no man could say she showed special favour to him. That time was yet to come. There was happiness in store, although she knew it not.

Meanwhile, she suffered and endured.

CHAPTER XXIX

IN WHICH JACK GETS HIS BACK TO THE WALL

ONCE more, Mr. Wolfe, Sal, and Nat were beneath the roof of the mansion they were claiming. The exhortation of Mr. Wolfe had produced the desired result, and the two delinquents were most uncomfortably sober. It had cost them many a bitter effort to deny their empty stomachs "just one" before they started, but Wolfe was inexorable. Not a drop would he permit, either then or on the road. The most unusual abstinence, her dislike of Wolfe, a sense of coming disaster, and that "awful sinking feeling" made Sal's temper anything but seraphic. Her manner to Mr. Wolfe was not "quite too charming." His remark about her "lamentable weakness" rankled sorely, and not even the success of the "toque" served to pacify her.

She was in one of the moods which made her dangerous—a mood which made her utterly reckless, selfish, morose, and spiteful. She felt the want of her usual stimulants badly, and hated Wolfe for the restraint he had put upon her more and more every time she thought of it.

She was anxious for, yet dreaded, the coming meeting with Jack. He, on the contrary, knowing that those he loved were, at least, safe from those whom yesterday he had so feared, was in brighter spirits than he had been for days. Wolfe, quick to read character and expression, instantly saw that Jack's manner had changed, that he looked more secure and hopeful, and wondered what was the cause. Had he learned anything since their last visit? If so, what, and how?

Jack barely acknowledged the presence of the three

confederates on entering the room where they were awaiting his coming, but, facing them squarely, said—

" Please come to business. I've no time to waste, and Landale Abbey will be the sweeter and better for the absence of all of you."

Not a pleasant beginning, nor a hopeful one, thought Mr. Wolfe, but he replied coolly—

" Bounce and impertinence will do you no good, Mr. Mowbray. Our position is too strong for either to shake us."

" If you are so sure of your position, why are you here to bargain with me?" asked Jack.

" Because we are willing to compromise in the matter, privately. We desire to save a public exposure, which will be most distasteful to you and to us."

Jack looked at them all, with the utmost contempt, for several seconds, before he said, with icy coldness—

" Yes, it would, no doubt, be distasteful to persons of such exquisite sensibility as the convicted thief, Nat Rudder—I beg his pardon, Nat Berker—and his spotless and pure-minded sister, and to Mr. Raffael M. Wolfe, the money-lender and swindling blackmailing attorney of Castlereagh Street, Sydney!"

" Decidedly, Mr. Mowbray has something up his sleeve," reflected Mr. Wolfe, " and, obviously, he does not mean to waste much time in coming to business."

The window leading on to the terrace was open. Lady Walgrove and Sybil were about to enter, when they saw who occupied the room. Lady Walgrove turned to leave it, but Sybil firmly held her mother's arm, and whispered for her to remain. She did so, and, unseen and unnoticed, they were witnesses to all that occurred between Jack and his opponents.

" You are impertinent, Mr. Mowbray," retorted Mr. Wolfe.

" Hold your tongue, you ruffian, until I've done!" was Jack's reply. " You know the law, and are aware that what you have been doing with these two persons is conspiracy, punishable with long imprisonment. You came here, knowing that you had no legal claim to this property, hoping to work on my fears, and, by so doing, to rob two women who had never harmed either of you, but whose brother and son you, you wretched woman, had ruined. You cared nothing for the agony you might cause them, or the pain you were inflicting on me. Money has been your aim, and to get that you are prepared to wreck two noble lives. You," he went on, turning to Nat and Sal, "were more than handsomely provided for. I allowed you two thousand a year. From henceforth, you will never get a cent from this estate, nor be allowed to set foot on it again. Last night you declined an increase on the two thousand a year. To-day I strip you of everything, and send you back to the gutters you came from."

"Bly me!" tremblingly ejaculated Nat.

"My word!" gasped Sal.

"You'll do nothing of the kind," said Mr. Wolfe. "You are an impostor, and you know it. This lady is Mrs. John Landale, widow of the late legatee, and the owner of this property."

"This woman is nothing of the kind," retorted Jack. "She is Mrs. Nathan Rudder, the wife of your fellow-scoundrel and conspirator, married, as you know, to him at Polson's Matrimonial Agency Office, George Street, Sydney, two years before she ever met with her dupe, poor John Landale." Here, the two women, who were listening, clutched tightly each other's arms. "She is a bigamist, and you both know it. You have no claim on this estate, and, thank God, no claim on the noble women whose property it is, and will be."

"Bluff! All bluff! You've no proofs—no witnesses," blustered the attorney. His confidence and coolness were leaving him.

Jack rang the bell, and Wong entered, showing in Dan and Smudgee.

"Have I not witnesses?" asked Jack. "Dan, who are these people?" he continued, pointing to the trio.

Sal and Nat were shivering with fright, and were nearly collapsing when Dan answered—

"They are Mr. and Mrs. Nathan Rudder, married by James Polson, in his office, George Street, Sydney, March 20th, 1887, in my presence, and 'twas meself witnessed the certificates and the entry."

"Why, I never saw you before!" gulped the astonished Nat.

"No, for you was blind drunk, and so was yer lady, and neither could see nothing."

"This will have to be proved," Wolfe said.

And now came one of Sal's unexpected mental somersaults, which, had Mr. Wolfe been a cleverer man than he was, he would never have risked.

"Oh! shut yer mouth," she shouted. "We're done. The game is up. Proved, indeed! There's proof enough in Sydney to jail the lot of us—yus, you included! A pretty mess we're in, thanks to you and your 'lamentable weakness,' Mr. Raffael Moses Wolfe!"

"Don't chuck up the sponge, Sal," whispered Nat.

"Yus, I shall. *I* know when I've had enough, if other fools don't."

Wolfe was livid with rage. Advancing on her with clenched teeth, he spluttered out—

"You contemptible, drunken slut!"

Mr. Wolfe had better have remained at a safer distance, for, quick as thought, saying, "Wot's that?" Sal sent the whole force of her muscular arm in a sounding slap on his face, and then, arms akimbo, asked, "'Ow's that for 'lamentable weakness,' eh?"

He moved towards her, but hesitated as she said—

"Now, come on and get another!"

"Brayvo, muvver!" applauded Smudgee, coming forward.

"Wot on earth are *you* doin' 'ere?" asked the surprised Sal.

"Lookin' after the family estate," coolly replied her daughter, "an', as I don't 'appen to 'ave a double-barrel microscope to examine it with, up to the present, 'ard as I've looked, I've seen nothing. Muvver, and my dearly-beloved uncle, it 'urts me to say it, but you're bushed—you're done."

"So you 'ad a 'and in this, my girl, 'ad you?" snarled Nat venomously. "You come along 'ome. I've somethin' to say to yer that ye'll hev to listen to."

Jack interposed, saying—

"She shall not go with you, unless she wishes. Smudgee, will you let me take care of you? Or will you go with them?"

"It won't break my 'eart if I never sees my dearly-beloved uncle again, but my muvver is my muvver, an' I ain't goin' back on her, now or never."

Sal sniffed vigorously, with real or assumed emotion, as Jack said to her—

"If I provide for her and her education, you won't object, I suppose?"

"No. She ain't a bad daughter, if she is a queer un."

Here Wolfe caught sight of the agonised mother and daughter, and he played his last card.

"Ah! I've not done with you yet, Mr. Mowbray. Lady Walgrove and Miss Landale, I presume?" he asked, turning to those two ladies, who made no reply.

Jack, horrified, turned, saw that they were there, and had heard everything.

"Hold your tongue, you scoundrel!" he said sternly. But Lady Walgrove said, quietly and firmly—

"No, let him finish. Go on, sir."

"Lady Walgrove, this man is an impostor," snarled Wolfe. "Your son is dead. Died, and is buried, at Woolloogolonga Gully, in Australia. This is John Mowbray, a man who resembled him, and who has taken advantage of that resemblance to deceive and defraud you."

Lady Walgrove heard this terrible accusation against the man she believed to be her son, and whom she loved as such, with great but varied and confused emotions.

"Not her son!" Jack, her boy, the child she had lost for so long, was dead, and this man, whom she had learned to love as her child, an impostor! No, this stranger was lying. Yet, why did not Jack speak? Why did he not tell this man that it was false? This honest, unselfish, noble, manly fellow a fraud, an impostor! Could she be so deceived?

Tom had entered, and had listened to Wolfe's accusation. Finding that Jack did not speak, he did.

"Lady Walgrove," he cried, "that is partly true and partly false. Your son, when dying, begged of Jack to take his place, to save your life, he said——"

Sybil moved towards Wolfe. On her the revelation had a complex effect, too. She quietly interposed, saying—

"Let that man go on. Let us know all the truth."

Wolfe did not hesitate. His game was up; his cause lost, but at least he would make the three victors suffer.

"He is a convicted thief," he said. "He was sentenced to three years for robbery at Sydney Assizes, in November, 1888."

Tom flushed with indignation at Wolfe's heartlessness, and, full of pity for his friends, said, with such sincerity that his words rang with truth and conviction—

"Lady Walgrove—Miss Landale—I'm sorry to pain you, but you ask for the truth. I am able to give it to you. Your son, Lady Walgrove, is dead—died in Mowbray's arms. He, not Mowbray, was dragged into the robbery, when intoxicated, by the ruffians who planned it. He was not conscious of what he was doing. Mowbray had nothing whatever to do with it—was not even near the place when it was committed. His likeness to your son led to his arrest. Mowbray was alone in the world—your son had a wife and child. To save your son he let them believe he was Landale, and suffered for him. He can clear himself of the charge at any moment, for there were a score of witnesses to prove he was a hundred miles away when the robbery was committed. I've been his intimate friend for many years, and never knew him to do a wrong act, or even an unkindly one, in all that time. If he is not your son, he is a man to be proud of, for, in spite of his deception upon you, a straighter, better, kinder fellow never lived."

Why did Sybil feel such a strange rush and glow of pride and pleasure as she listened to Tom's words? It is certain that she had not felt such happiness for many weeks as she did at this moment.

" Has this man anything more to tell?" she asked.

" Nothing, Miss Landale," replied Jack. " Wong, see these people out of the house."

CHAPTER XXX

IN WHICH SMUDGEE PLEADS FOR HER "KNIGHT"

NAT, Sal, and Wolfe left Landale Abbey in a very dejected and sulky condition. Their apparently well-laid schemes had gone wofully "agley." Their chickens had been prematurely counted, the hatching process had found them all badly addled; there was not a solitary weakling alive to reward them for the long days of incubation. Not only had they failed to secure the "Pallis" (Landale Abbey), but they had lost the allowance Jack had apportioned them. They were penniless and without resources once more. And in London, too, of all places.

Nat was too crushed to talk, Wolfe too furious. Sal's surrender he could not understand. The slap she had given his face rankled less than the quietus she had administered to his schemes. What was the cause? He could not fathom it. The least depressed at the unexpected collapse of their hopes was Sal. Oddly enough, that strange mixture of moods and instincts felt a certain satisfaction in Wolfe's discomfiture, although it had ruined herself. Jack's manly fight, although against herself and her interests, had heightened the feeling which passed for love in her breast, and never had she liked him so well as now. The thought that she had lost him hurt her far more than the loss of the property. Womanlike, she was angry, not with herself for her share in the attempted swindle, but with her accomplices, Nat and Wolfe. The former she hated now with a dull, negative hate. Wolfe she loathed with a liveliness that was unusual to her indolent nature. If it were ever in her power to do Wolfe an evil turn, she would certainly avail herself of the opportunity to the full. Wolfe, on his side, would cheerfully have strangled her could he have done so with impunity. He contented himself with sending in, immediately on his return to London, an enormous bill of costs to Nat. Quick as he was in the delivery of his account, he was too slow, for the slippery Nat had, with Sal, left the hotel with their bill unpaid an hour before Wolfe's messenger arrived, and the manager of the Starlington Hotel knew them no more.

After her mother and father had left the room, at Landale Abbey, Smudgee looked long and earnestly at Lady Walgrove and Sybil, and from them to Jack's pale face and deeply-humiliated attitude. She had never seen her "knight" ashamed before. Her heart ached at the sight. She did not understand all his crime. Indeed, she was not sure that he had been guilty of a crime at all. She had listened to Tom's defence of Jack, and was content with it. At first, she was fiercely resentful of the cause of Jack's humiliation, which she unjustly attributed, in a roundabout way, to Landale, Lady Walgrove, and Sybil. Why had Landale asked him to take his place? Why did these two strangers come between her and her knight? Why should he stand abashed and degraded in their presence? But her quickly divining spirit saw the love for Jack pent up beyond the sorrow at the discovery of his deception, and her natural sympathy with all suffering prompted her to make an effort to soothe in some little way their grief and bitter disappointment. Stepping forward a little, she said, in a low, tear-broken voice—

" Please, ladies, I know Jack done wrong this time, but 'e's never done wrong before. Don't yer send 'im away. 'E's the best man as ever lived. 'E worked for me farver—I mean, Mr. Landale—when 'e was too drunk to work for hisself, nursed him when 'e was sick, an' kept him as sober as 'e could, when 'e got better. There never was a day as Mr. Landale didn't say as 'e was 'is guardian angel. An' so 'e was."

" Hush, Smudgee !" whispered Jack.

"Yus, it allers is 'ush, 'ush, when any one tells the truth about yer! Never lettin' people know the good yer does. Never yellin' out, as others do, at your own hurts. I don't care wot yer done about this blessed property— you're a true knight, after all, and you couldn't do a real wrong thing, if you tried. I carn't say any more, 'cos I'm chokin', I think—but—I—I—I know yer!" And, breaking down utterly, she left the room, followed by Dan and Tom.

For a few minutes there was silence in the room. Lady Walgrove was in a chair, with Sybil at her feet. Presently Jack said, softly—

"Lady Walgrove—Miss Landale—I cannot excuse myself. There is no excuse to make. You promised me, when the truth was known, to believe that I loved you through it all. Do you believe it?"

Lady Walgrove looked up at his worn, sad face with infinite pity, and said—

"I do believe you loved us."

"Thank you," Jack sighed with gratitude, and turned to Sybil, asking—

"What do you say, Miss Landale?"

Sybil could say nothing. Her feelings were too complex for speech. The thought that Jack was not married gave her unspeakable pleasure. His abject humiliation brought her intense pain. She had so gloried in his strength, she was abased by his shame. Did she feel anger at his deception? She felt that she should do so, and yet she could not find the resentment that should have come so naturally. She had been basely deceived. This man had taken the place of her brother. He was an impostor. She had no brother. Why, then, did she not hate the man who had usurped his place? Then the thought of her abandonment to her supposed sisterly love, and the memory of the kisses and embraces she had bestowed upon Jack came upon her with a rush that sent her blood whirling to her face and breast with a force that she could almost hear.

She could not speak. Jack waited with eyes downcast for the words that would not come. At last the suspense became intolerable. He felt that, to spare the mother and daughter more pain, he must leave them. In a choking voice, he said pitifully—

" I promised you that I would never leave you until you bade me. I am going to my room. I shall be ready to go from this house in an hour. A word sent to me will be enough. I do not ask you to forgive me—I dare not hope that you will. I ask that you will believe that I had no thought to rob you, or swindle you out of a penny. Your banker will tell you that you are richer than you were by my coming. Believe this. More I will not venture to plead for. Farewell."

Before they could speak, he had left them.

CHAPTER XXXI

IN WHICH JOHN MOWBRAY MAKES HIS REAPPEARANCE

DAZED as he was with the succession of heavy blows that had been showered upon him in the past few days, Jack was, for a time, unable to form any plan of action for the future. That he must leave Landale, he knew. To remain was impossible. Beyond, and below the grief this knowledge brought him, was a feeling of intense relief that the mask had been removed, the veil lifted, and all necessity for further lying and deception at an end. He was free once more. Free to work out some redemption for the past, with no motive for sinning anew in the future. For the mother and daughter he had the profoundest pity; for himself the most supreme contempt. Argue as he might, he could not bring himself to believe that his usurpation of his dead friend's place was as excusable as Landale had said it was.

As his brain gradually cleared, he decided that the first thing to do was to tell all those who had trusted him the truth. Locking himself in his room, he began to write, first of all, to the two women whom he had so grievously wronged. It was a hard, bitter task to debase himself before those whom he so loved and reverenced, but it must be done, and that unsparingly.

"I must ask you," he wrote to Lady Walgrove, "to give me back my promise not to leave you. Now that you know the truth, to stay is impossible. I ask no mercy—expect none. It is true that your son did beg of me to take his place, even before he knew that he was near death. He implored me, for your sake and for that of your daughter, to do so. He was, in his own eyes, unfit to meet you. His marriage and his manner of living had so degraded him in his own esteem that he felt he dared not face you. I think he was wrong, and had he lived I believe that I should have prevailed upon him to think with me. Would to God he had not died! Then came his accident, and his last request—almost command—that I should come to you. Should I have let him die with his wish ungratified? I think so now. I did not think so then. The easy, reckless life we had led, the loose code of morals of those we associated with, had blunted the senses. It seemed that I was 'to do a great right by doing a little wrong'; that, by the right I was doing in comforting you, I should more than wipe out the wrong of the deception I was practising. I saw, from the moment I met you and your daughter, that this was all sophistry, a mere juggling with the truth. It was then too late to draw back. Nor was my desire to serve my dying friend the only incentive that prevailed with me. Your letters aroused in me an almost unconquerable longing to go to you; to call you mother and Sybil sister; to know, for once, what a home was like; to have some one to care and work for; to have some one to care for me. Had I come to you as his friend, I might still have served you, honestly, proudly. I have never, as I told you, robbed you of a penny of your money. I have taken only the wages of a servant. But I have done worse than that. I have stolen your love. It has been a daily, hourly theft. Mean, thoughtless, heartless. I longed for it as a blessing. It was a torture. Every caress was a stab, every endearment a blow. If at times I forgot—and there were moments when I at least half-persuaded myself that I had forgotten—the reawakening of memory was a redoubling of my pain. The more you both grew to love me, the more I suffered. I loved you both. How much you will never know. I shall love you always. You are the only mother I have ever known. 'Mother.' Do you know how sweet the word can be to such a man as I am? To your daughter I owe more agony still, for (forgive me this) I love her with all the strength of my body and soul. I would give the world for her good opinion of me. She must despise me. I will not pain you by dwelling further on the wrong I have done her. I will not excuse myself. I will only ask you to let me go out of your lives, and regain elsewhere some of the respect I have forfeited. I will, if you wish, put all the accounts into an auditor's hands. Hewley can stay and manage for you until you can engage another steward. He is honest (save in his complicity in my fraud), and you may trust him fully. If, on the other hand, you think it better to rid your house of us both, he will leave with me. Send me permission to go.

"JOHN MOWBRAY."

Reading this letter over before he sent it to Lady Walgrove, he felt that he had spoken all too lightly of his crime, but he could not rewrite it. He added a postscript, saying, "I dare not write to your daughter. Let this letter be for both. I feel that, in spite of all my desire not to excuse myself, I seem to be doing so. I have tried not to palliate my fault, but fear I have not succeeded."

This letter he sent at once to Lady Walgrove, then packed the few things that he could honestly consider his own, and went to find Tom, and arrange for his departure.

CHAPTER XXXII

IN WHICH JACK IS JUDGED

WHEN Jack's letter was brought to Lady Walgrove, she opened it with trembling fingers, but for a time could not summon up courage to read it. Sybil knelt by her mother's side and waited.

When at last her mother began to read, her voice failed her. Sybil quietly read the letter for her.

For some minutes after the reading was over they were silent. Sybil was trembling from the rush of her conflicting emotions. Her love of truth was a part of herself. She could not even think a lie, could not understand others lying. That Jack had done so shocked her horribly. She had never suspected him of an untruth since she had known him. Indeed he had never told her one, save on the subject of his identity. Yet, grieved as she was, a strange feeling of rest and calm gradually came upon her. She was a woman, and she loved this man as a woman loves the man she wants to marry. She knew it now. And he loved her. Can anything excel the infinite mercy of a loving woman? Gradually his faults receded, and his fine, noble qualities became stronger and clearer to her. Scores of little proofs of his love and devotion rose before her mind, hiding and thrusting back his offence against her, until at last she began to excuse and pity him. She loved him, and he loved her. What mattered the rest? His crime had injured no one but herself and her mother. Not even them.

She turned to her mother, and, holding her tightly to her, said—

"What are we to do, mother?"

In both their hearts was the same thought. "He must not leave us." Each was afraid to utter that thought.

"I don't know, dear. It is all so strange; such a shock."

"He says he must leave us."

"Yes."

"It is right, I suppose?"

"I don't know."

Again there was silence, each trying to find courage to own the truth, that to part with him would be unbearable.

"What are we to do, Sybil?"

"What do you wish, mother dear?"

"What can I wish? He has been so good to me, made me so happy—happier than I have been since your father died—that it does not seem possible that I can bear parting with him. But, my child, it is not only I who have to be considered. What of you? You see what he says. He loves you. What have you to say? What are your feelings towards him?"

Sybil hid her blushing face on her mother's breast.

"How can I tell you, mother? I have looked upon my regard for him as the love of a sister for a brother, yet at times I—I—could not understand—why I—that is, could not understand myself. It troubled me terribly. I could not tell you, but my jealousy of others in regard to him, the horrible pain when I thought that he had deceived us about his marriage—nothing that I feel now can compare with that agony. Mother, what is the use of trying to explain? I love him; love him as I could never love any other man in the world."

Lady Walgrove silently stroked the beautiful head that was nestling on her bosom. Was she shocked or grieved? Neither. She was glad. Jack's crime was great, so had been his punishment. Surely if ever sin was committed under extenuating circumstances, this was. All her charity, all the "mother" in her went out towards Jack. Had he been selfish in taking the place of her son, was she not selfish in wanting him to keep it? And she did want him to do so.

"Darling," she said softly, as if half ashamed of the question she had to ask, "could he not still be my son?"

"Mother!"

"After all, is his sin so great? He has never wronged us, save in gaining our love. Well, is that so great a crime? Has he not brought us happiness? Why am I grieving now? Not for the wrong he has done, but for the knowledge that he is not what we believed, and that he may go from us. Could I have loved him more if he had been my son? I answer, No. Can I forgive him? I have already done so. I have seen his agony during the past few days. I recall now a thousand things which were done to save me pain, not one can I remember that grieved me. If tender care, watchfulness, consideration, respect are what a mother longs for in a son, have I not had all these, and with them the most unselfish devotion and love? After all that we know of him, to suspect him of a desire to defraud us would be absurd. Our property, our people, ourselves are the richer and happier for his coming. If he goes, it will never be with my consent. My child, what have you to say?"

"Mother, I love him," was the simple answer.

What more was needed?

"Let us go to him, Sybil?"

Hand in hand, they went to Jack's room.

Jack had not expected them, and was startled at their appearance. They were shocked at the change in him. He seemed years older; his face was lined and drawn, his eyes looked tired, as though worn weary from many sleepless vigils. But what pained them most was the entire change in his manner. He looked so humiliated, so contrite, that the two women could scarce keep back their tears. All the strong sense of masterdom, so characteristic of Jack, was gone, and, at the sight of the alteration in the man they loved, the two innocent souls began inwardly to reproach themselves as the cause.

Jack, in his turn, saw the two pale, distressed faces that he worshipped, noted the sorrow written in them, and cursed himself for the fault that had brought them such pain.

Lady Walgrove was the first to speak.

"We have come to you in answer to your letter, Jack," she said.

"Jack!" At the sound of the old name Jack started and looked eagerly at Lady Walgrove, and from her his eyes turned to Sybil. What was he to say?

"Yes, Lady Walgrove?" he asked, in a questioning tone.

Lady Walgrove shivered as she heard her name pronounced. Was it never to be "mother" any more?

In a hurt tone she said—

"Lady Walgrove, Jack! Is that what you are going to call me?"

Jack stared at her in astonishment. No reproach! No resentment! Only tenderness and love.

"What else can I call you now?"

"Am I never to hear you call me mother again?"

"Can you dream of it? Now you know of my deceit, my crime."

"I do not wish to belittle the fault, Jack, but I must not be harsh in judging it. That your account of how you were impelled to commit it is true I do not doubt. Nor can I for a moment question your statement that you have never wronged me in any other way. From the time I first saw you and accepted you as my son, I inwardly wondered to find you so different—so much better, kinder, more tender than I had dared to hope for. My son, I could not fail to see, had been callous, indeed cruel. Month after month, year after year went by without a word from him. For years I did not know whether he was alive or dead. When, at times, we had a few hurried lines from him, they gave but little information, seldom an address to enable us to reply to them. My longing for him was killing me, and yet I almost dreaded his return. You came. I was amazed, delighted, happy. Where I expected selfishness, I found absolute self-sacrifice; where I looked for coldness or indifference, I found devotion and love. Can you wonder, now that I know the truth, that the regret for your fault is drowned in the sorrow of the thought that I must lose you? Think of that wretched woman who was associated with him. Had he returned, I must have had to receive her as my daughter—as Sybil's sister. Think of it. But it is not only this that you have saved us from. You have saved me from death. Had you not come to us when you did, I should have died. Will you leave us now? Will you undo all the good you have done?"

Jack, listening with deep emotion to Lady Walgrove, had strained his ears to catch some word of real justification for his crime, but could find none. The more nobly these women behaved to him, the greater seemed his sin against them.

"Lady Walgrove, if anything were needed to convince me that I cannot stay it would be your generous forgiveness. The greater your kindness, the more hideous my crime seems to me. To meet you daily, hourly, as I have done, now that you know me for what I am, is not possible. I must go."

"Jack!" cried Sybil. "You will not!"

"Do not make my task harder than it is. I must go. Let it be as though we had never met. I am young yet; the world is still before me. I can, and will, redeem myself. When I have done that, when I feel that I can look you straight in the eyes again and honestly say the debt is paid, my honour is solvent once more, then I will ask you to let me come to you as a friend. Until then, I beg of you to let me go. It must be so."

Vainly they pleaded. In the end, feeling the hopelessness of further entreaties, they gave him back his promise, and he went from Landale alone.

CHAPTER XXXIII

UNDER THE SHADOW OF TABLE MOUNTAIN

Two years had passed since Jack left Landale. After putting the affairs of the estate in order, he volunteered for the war in South Africa, and was sent at once to the front. His fine horsemanship and skill with the rifle, his long experience of bush and camp life in Australia and America, made him invaluable as a scout, and his devotion and bravery won him a commission within a year.

After the signing of peace, his regiment was disbanded at Johannesburg.

During one of his scouting expeditions in the Transvaal he had encamped on a deserted farm, the homestead of which had been burned. All that was left were the walls of the house and the Dutch brick oven. His old mining experience came in handy. Prospecting about the place, more from habit than design, he found signs of gold. Keeping his discovery to himself, he mentally marked the spot, and when he was discharged returned to it. Finding that the owner had been killed at the front, and that the farm was in the hands of an agent, he bought it, paying down a third of the value and leaving the rest on mortgage. Returning to Johannesburg, he endeavoured in vain to form a company to exploit his property. The forced inactivity of the mining market made men fight shy of new speculations just then.

From Johannesburg he went to Kimberley, and hung about offices, interviewing capitalists and seeking help for his schemes. Whether the worry of his quest and his absence from Sybil preyed upon him, or the change from the free, open life on the veldt to the fever-tainted atmosphere of the towns affected him, it is hard to say —probably it was a combination of all three things— but, like thousands of others, he weathered all the hardships of the war to be bowled over in the comparative luxury of peace. In a few weeks the dreaded Kimberley fever had him in its grip. Disdaining to give in, and thinking that the illness, whatever it was, would pass off, he travelled down to Cape Town. On arriving there, he drove out to Sea Point, thinking that the sea air would soon put him right again. Getting a room at the Queen's Hotel, or, rather, its annex, a bungalow standing in the hotel gardens, he sent for a doctor.

He had promised Lady Walgrove to keep her always advised of his whereabouts, and to notify her if wounded or ill. He cabled her his address and promptly lapsed into insensibility. Week after week he battled with the fever, and more than once it seemed to the watchers that he must succumb. The doctor telegraphed to Lady Walgrove the serious nature of his case, and, without an hour's hesitation, the devoted mother and daughter decided to sail at once for Africa.

As the poor fellow tossed in his delirium from side to side, he raved incessantly of Sybil. His delusions took on strange forms. At one time he was back on the mighty sierras of Nevada and California. He saw again the giant pines, the heaven-capped peaks, the rushing torrents, but he was not alone. Sybil was with him. Once more he was in the drought-parched bush of the Never-Never Land. Sybil was there. Then back to Landale. There, too, her dear presence walked side by side with him. Stranger than these visions of scenes well known were those of places he had never visited. In sunny Seville's streets he moved, with Sybil, seeing all its gay life and brilliant colouring in his vision, as he afterwards saw it in reality. In Venice he floated with her through its silent waterways and strolled through its picture-galleries, seeing such glories of form and colour as no artist ever limned on canvas. He was conscious of no pain, save a strange difficulty in moving from place to place in his dream journeys, but, compared to the joy of being with Sybil, that was as nothing.

Meantime the liner, *Walmer Castle*, with the woman he loved on board, had come to anchor in Table Bay. The mountain had on its " table-cloth," as it is called —a curiously flat cloud of mist which at times covers its summit. On this particular evening it was remarkably clear-cut and distinct. The setting sun lit it up with most exquisite shades in pink and gold.

Directing Sybil's attention to it, Lady Walgrove whispered—

"An omen, dear. The Cape is all rose-coloured. We shall find him better."

Since leaving Madeira, they had not touched at a port, and had received no news. Their anxiety was naturally intense.

The doctor had come to meet them, and, leaving the baggage to the care of the servants, they drove at once to the cottage where Jack was lying. As they walked up the garden surrounding the house, the sound of his voice came to them through the open window.

" Sybil! Sybil! Come—come—quick! quick!" he was saying.

She thought he was really conscious of her presence, and was imploring her to hasten. Perhaps some other sense was aware of her approach, but the normal ones were, for the time, dead.

Sybil needed no spur to urge her on. In a moment she was at the door of the room, and, with a caution from the doctor and nurse to be on her guard, she entered.

What a thrill ran through her heart as she saw once again the man she so faithfully loved! So changed was he, so weak, so helpless. The tears fell silently down her cheeks as she looked at him. He was scarcely recognisable. The hollow cheeks, pallid with weakness, the sunken eyes, telling of weeks of suffering, and the beard, which had been allowed to grow, completely blotted out the handsome, healthy Jack of the past, leaving barely a shadow of what he had been to meet the eyes of the women who had travelled so many thousands of miles to see him.

"Sybil! Sybil!" he muttered.

The doctor motioned her to go to him. She went, and, placing first her hand on his fevered forehead, she kissed both of the closed eyes. All muttering and tossing ceased instantly. For a few moments he was perfectly still. Then his eyes slowly opened, and turned wonderingly towards Sybil. He gave a deep sigh, as of great thankfulness, and, holding feebly Sybil's cool, soft hand, he sank, without a word, into a peaceful slumber.

The doctor whispered—

"Miss Landale, you have done more than I could have done; you have saved his life. The crisis is passed. He will live."

When Jack awoke, it was to full consciousness. The fever had left him, and, although weak in body, his mind was perfectly clear. He looked round the room, and, seeing no one but his nurse, could not but think the momentary glimpse he had caught of Sybil had been a vision. Afraid to ask, he remained silent, puzzling his brain in endeavouring to separate delirium from fact. He had so often seen her in his dreams, and so clearly, that he began to fear that this appearance of his loved one was, like the others, the product of his imagination. And yet, there was an indefinable difference in his feelings that he could not account for. Was it possible that she had indeed come? He must know.

He called the nurse to him, and, not having the courage to put the direct question, he asked—

"What day is it?"

"Thursday," she answered.

"How long have I been ill?"

"Oh, not so very long," replied the nurse discreetly.

"What has been the matter with me?"

" You must ask the doctor about that. Whatever it is, you are all right now. Do you fancy anything?"

" To eat, do you mean?"

" Yes."

" I feel that I should like something. I leave it to you."

" Very well. I'll go up to the hotel and order you a nice little lunch. But first let me make you a little more presentable. You are not fit to receive visitors, with that tousled head and beard."

" Beard! Visitors! What do you mean?"

" What is this?" asked the nurse, combing gently at a four weeks' growth on his chin.

" What visitors? Tell me quickly, nurse, there's a good soul! Who has called? When? Are they here now?"

" Now, if you're going to get excited, I shall tell you nothing. I don't know that I ought to tell you, anyway."

" I'll be quite calm and quiet, if you will only tell me who it is. Who is it?"

" Who would you like it to be, out of all the world?"

" Ah! That's not possible."

" Everything is possible, nowadays, with cablegrams and fast steamers——"

" Is it—is it——"

For answer, the nurse went from the room, and Sybil entered it. In a moment her arms were round his neck, and the poor, weakened fellow was resting his face on her breast—where, perhaps, it would be as well to leave him, for the present, at least.

It need scarcely be said that Master Jack had a fairly good time of it during his rapid convalescence. In a few days he was helped to totter out on to the verandah, to sit in the delicious, fresh air and be petted by his friends to his heart's content. He was too weak to resist or argue, and they had it all their own way with him. The verandah faced the sea, which beat up within a few yards of the garden wall. The long rollers came sweeping in, hurling themselves against the rocks. The white spray shot high into the air, glittering in the sun like myriads of diamonds. Wonderfully near to the shore for such monsters, whales were lazily blowing, as they crossed the Bay. The sea was, under the blue sky, a deep sapphire. Bees were humming among the flowers, doves were cooing to each other among the trees. Jack and Sybil were alone.

Little had been said about the past. Jack had been too feeble to approach what must be an agitating subject. He was stronger now, and, like most men of his generous nature, he could not be content with letting any fault of his pass over lightly.

"I want to speak to you of——" he began. But he was not allowed to proceed. Sybil had been expecting this "harking back" upon his fault for days, and had quite made up her mind how to face it. She interrupted him, saying—

"Now, Jack—*dear* Jack—if you are going to rake up that wretched old bogey, that I have laid to rest for ever, I am not going to stand by and see him resuscitated. He's dead; let him rest. You still love me, I suppose?"

She "supposed"! It was not a matter for supposition for any one who could see the poor fellow's face.

"You *suppose!* Oh, *Sybil!*" was his feeble retort.

"Well, then, I know. Oh, JACK! And all this self-condemnation has got to stop. It's not a nice compliment to my discrimination or taste to be calling my future husband bad names continually."

"Your—*what?*" gasped Jack.

"My husband. You surely don't mean to say that you refuse me!"

Jack had nothing to say. He was very weak, you see. But if he could not speak, he found a use for his lips which Sybil endured as best she could. As the doves took no notice of Master Jack's misbehaviour, as the bees continued to hum, and the whales to blow, as if nothing out of the common had happened, and there was no one else at hand to object, I really do not think that it is for me to interfere. I have no doubt Sybil will be able to explain the matter to her mother, and, after all, it is more their affair than mine. Of course it was all very wrong, improper, and that sort of thing, but it is no use throwing stones, with so many glass-houses in the immediate neighbourhood. It is but mere justice to recall the fact that he was feeble, and had not yet recovered from his very serious illness. One cannot judge a man harshly while he is in *that* state.

CHAPTER XXXIV

WHICH ENDS THIS "STRANGE, EVENTFUL HISTORY"

WHEN Jack left Landale, Lady Walgrove, acting on his advice, retained Tom as his substitute *pro tem*. Tom "knew a thing or two." One of the things with which he had become acquainted was the fact that it is well to be early if you want a fair chance at the early worm. Tom looked a long way ahead, and, in looking, descried certain possibilities which it was well to be prepared for. Knowing that Jack was off to Africa, he let it percolate, gradually, through Landale that Mr. John Landale had been suddenly called to Australia to look after some property there; that he had gone up country into the bush, and that meanwhile all letters must be addressed to Mr. T. Hewley, as no letters would be forwarded. Having thus got Mr. John Landale into the Never-Never Land (from which place, as the reader knows, he had never stirred), Tom left him there, to await the second killing, which he foresaw must, eventually, be necessary. When he saw Lady Walgrove and Sybil off to Africa he conjectured, not without reasonable grounds, that this second departure of Landale was not likely to be long delayed. His surmise was confirmed by a cablegram, concocted on the verandah shortly after the occurrence of the incidents recorded in the last chapter. Sybil had evidently explained to her mother's satisfaction Master Jack's misbehaviour, or else it would not have been possible for Lady Walgrove to be pouring out tea for an interesting invalid who was delighting her heart by calling her "Mother."

There had been a long consultation as to the wording of a cablegram to Tom, the outcome of which was the following:—"Delighted to tell you that I am engaged to marry Miss Sybil Landale. Use this information as you may think advisable.—JOHN MOWBRAY."

"Umce," quoth Tom to himself, when he received the message, "Mr. John Landale's death-warrant. But, as his untimely end, coming just now, might delay John Mowbray's wedding with his sister, I think I must respite him for a few weeks."

Tom cabled back: "Congratulations. Am writing." In the fulness of time, Jack received the following letter from him :—

"DEAR MR. MOWBRAY,—It gives me much pleasure to repeat my congratulations on your coming marriage. I conclude, as a matter of course, that you have not only Lady Walgrove's consent to the match, but also that of her son, who left, two years ago, for Australia, which country must possess a strange fascination for him, or he would never give up this beautiful Landale for so long. I have heard a rumour that he has lately met with some accident; it is but a rumour, but there may be truth in it. If he were to die just now, it would be very unfortunate, as it would, naturally, delay his sister's wedding. I hope *that* is an accomplished fact by this time, or, rather, that it will be by the time this reaches you. By the way, did I ever tell you what a strange resemblance you bear to Mr. Landale? I have told everybody here of it, and they are quite prepared to see an extraordinary likeness, when they are able to compare the two faces. It will, no doubt, be some time before you return, as you will be sure to wish to give your wife and her mother a trip around the world, more or less, before coming to Landale. Taking into consideration the long time Mr. Landale has already been absent, it is not at all sure that he will be so well remembered that the likeness between you will attract so much notice as I think it will. It is very marked, however, and may strike others as it does me. I hope to hear of your marriage within the next three weeks.

Please convey my respectful congratulations to Lady Walgrove and Miss Landale, and, believe me, truly yours,

"T. HEWLEY."

The result of this exceedingly sophisticated epistle was a marriage quietly performed at Cape Town, in which Miss Sybil Landale became Mrs. John Mowbray. The news of this interesting ceremony was at once cabled to Tom, and a week or two afterwards that astute gentleman let it get abroad that the news had been received of the sudden death of Mr. John Landale, in the bush of the Never-Never Land, and, a little later, of the departure of Lady Walgrove and Mr. and Mrs. John Mowbray to visit his grave and wind up his Australian affairs.

The latter operation did not take long, as the reader will surmise. Still, it was a full year before the party returned to their home at Landale, and, by that time— dear old Bruds having left for another world—there was no one to say more than that "Muster Mowbray did certain sure favour Muster Landale—'cept Muster Mowbray wur older and more jolly like."

"And more jolly like" Jack was indeed, for he had been forgiven freely, his South African property was yielding him an immense income, he was perfectly independent of his wife's property, which he managed quite as well as did the late John Landale. The burden of his sin had fallen from his shoulders, and he was as happy as a man could hope to be.

Perhaps it is not quite true to say there was no one to discover that Jack Mowbray had once passed as John Landale. There were two who knew it. They were Smudgee and Mamie D'Olan—Mamie D'Olan no longer, for Mamie is now the mistress of one of the stateliest homes of England, wearing a coronet with queenly grace and distinction—happy, honored, and beloved.

And Smudgee? Ah! dear little Smudgee! Her story has yet to be told.

OLIVE LATHAM

By E. L. VOYNICH

Author of "Jack Raymond" and "The Gadfly."   Cloth, $1.50

·"The author's knowledge of this matter has been painfully personal. Her husband, a Polish political refugee, at the age of twenty-two, was arrested and thrown into a vile Russian prison without trial, and spent five years of his life thereafter in Siberian exile, escaping in 1890 and fleeing to England. Throughout 'Olive Latham' you get the impression that it is a veritable record of what one woman went through for love. . . . This painful, poignant, powerfully-written story permits one full insight into the cruel workings of Russian justice and its effects upon the nature of a well-poised Englishwoman. Olive comes out of the Russian hell alive, and lives to know what happiness is again, but the horror of those days in St. Petersburg, the remembrance of the inhumanity which killed her lover never leaves her. . . . It rings true. It is a grewsome study of Russian treatment of political offenders. Its theme is not objectionable—a criticism which has been brought against other books of Mrs. Voynich's."—*Chicago Record-Herald.*

"So vividly are the coming events made to cast their shadows before, that long before the half-way point is reached the reader knows that Volodya's doom is near at hand, and that the chief interest of the story lies not with him, but with the girl, and more specifically with the curious mental disorders which her long ordeal brings upon her. It is seldom that an author has succeeded in depicting with such grim horror the sufferings of a mind that feels itself slipping over the brink of sanity, and clutches desperately at shadows in the effort to drag itself back."—*New York Globe.*

J. B. LIPPINCOTT COMPANY, PHILADELPHIA.

HEART OF LYNN
By MARY STEWART CUTTING
Illustrated. Cloth, $1.25.

"The tale, sad and merry, of a family fallen upon hard times, of their struggles, and the final happy ending to all their woes. The different girl characters are admirably done, the two boys are manly, wholesome fellows, and the whole story tells itself naturally, with just enough of romance, and mystery, and fun."—*Chicago Tribune*.

"Mrs. Cutting's 'Heart of Lynn' is a sunshiny domestic story of the Alcott variety. There is a bevy of sweet and lovable girls ; the family has to build its fortune amid discouragements and trials ; their ingenious ways and means and their courage amid trials and temptations make a pleasing story—pleasing because of its unpretentious and heartsome qualities."—*Pittsburgh Gazette*.

"Lynn was the brave, unselfish, hopeful daughter in a family struggling with reduced circumstances. Her efforts to become a wage-earner brought her into some amusing situations. Her 'merry heart,' however, carried her the full 'mile,' and we leave her dreaming of a happy future quite within her grasp."—*New York Outlook*.

"A sweeter, more wholesome little tale than Mrs. Cutting's latest novel has not appeared recently. It has the same quality of intense humanity that distinguished the 'Little Stories of Married Life.' Makes valuable reading for girls, whether they are in the industrial struggle or not."—*The New York Evening Post*.

" 'The Heart of Lynn' is as sweet and as healthful a book as any published for a long time."—*Philadelphia Public Ledger*.

"The style is charming in its pure simplicity, the characters lifelike and the conversation and incidents natural."—*Baltimore Sun*.

"An entertaining and well written story, light and charming."—*New York Sunday Sun*.

J. B. LIPPINCOTT COMPANY, PHILADELPHIA.

FATE THE FIDDLER

By HERBERT C. MACILWAINE.

12mo.   Cloth, ornamental, $1.50.

" The book is remarkably attractive."—*Journal*, Detroit.

" In a remote district of the great inland-continent of Australia two young men started their cattle ranch, and their successes and failures alike form the warp and woof of the tale, which gives a fair idea of the processes by which that country, in like manner with our own great West, has been brought under the orderly hand of modern civilization.   All this is interesting, but the chief interest lies in the virility of the story, depicting a life untrammeled by the world's conventions." —*Post*, Washington.

" The story suggests the Manx stories of Hall Caine, but Caine has never produced work that equals MacIlwaine's in strength of description.   ' Fate the Fiddler' may well be classed among the really great works of fiction of the age."—*Times*, Denver.

" Of course there is a love story, but it is subordinate to the stirring life of the frontiersmen amid scenes of peculiar wildness and beauty. The situations are thrilling and the descriptions powerful."—*Evening Wisconsin*, Milwaukee.

" This book has been called pre-eminently ' a man's book' on account of its rugged strength and its lack of any soft sentimentality. Man's book or not, it is intensely interesting to readers of either sex. . . . Mr. MacIlwaine is an entertaining and clever writer.   His descriptions are fine, his knowledge of men deep, and his skill in depicting the settler's life in Australia well worthy of note."—*The Worcester Spy*.

" Under Mr. MacIlwaine's pen the narrative palpitates with life— the huge life of unbounded horizon, a thousand square miles of untouched territory, of elemental conditions, of unbridled freedom, save only as one is tied to the work for the sake of his best prospects. Some such life has been in our own great West, but no Mr. MacIlwaine has yet done justice to its spirit, though of studies of isolated characters and phases we have many from skilled pens."—*Times*, Kansas City.

J. B. LIPPINCOTT COMPANY, PHILADELPHIA

Lightning Source UK Ltd.
Milton Keynes UK
UKHW030630120521
383587UK00007B/362